THE MODERN HISTORY
OF ART THERAPY
IN THE UNITED STATES

THE MODERN HISTORY OF ART THERAPY IN THE UNITED STATES

By

MAXINE BOROWSKY JUNGE

With a Foreword by

Myra Levick

CHARLES C THOMAS • PUBLISHER, LTD.
Springfield • Illinois • U.S.A.

Published and Distributed Throughout the World by

CHARLES C THOMAS • PUBLISHER, LTD.
2600 South First Street
Springfield, Illinois 62794-9265

© 2010 by CHARLES C THOMAS • PUBLISHER, LTD.

ISBN 978-0-398-07940-6 (hard)
ISBN 978-0-398-07941-3 (paper)

Library of Congress Catalog Card Number: 2010008255

With THOMAS BOOKS *careful attention is given to all details of manufacturing
and design. It is the Publisher's desire to present books that are satisfactory as to their
physical qualities and artistic possibilities and appropriate for their particular use.*
THOMAS BOOKS *will be true to those laws of quality that assure a good name
and good will.*

Printed in the United States of America
MM-R-3

Library of Congress Cataloging in Publication Data

Junge, Maxine Borowsky
 The modern history of art therapy in the United States / by Maxine
Borowsky Junge; with a foreword by Myra Levick.
  p. cm.
 Includes biographical references and indexes.
 ISBN 978-0-398-07940-6 (hard)–ISBN 978-0-398-07941-3 (pbk.)
 1. Art therapy–United States–History. I. Title.
 [DNLM: 1. Art Therapy–history–United States. 2. History, 20th Century–
United States. WM 11 AA1 J95m 2010]

RC489.A7J857 2010
616.89'1656–dc22   2010008255

*For all art therapists everywhere who have struggled
to make art therapy a profession.*

FOREWORD

In the first sentence of this book in the Preface, Maxine Borowsky Junge describes this work as "in some ways my legacy to the art therapy profession." Having now read this singular book defining Dr. Junge's viewpoint of our history, it is that, and much more.

In 1994, Dr. Junge gave us *A History of Art Therapy in the United States,* a work I have valued these many years. Now, this most respected colleague provides us not only with a "Modern" history of our profession, but a history of our society in which art therapy evolved and grew. As someone well versed in systems theory, Junge has integrated our profession of art therapy with the world around at different stages of our development. She describes, questions and challenges us to think about and recognize how societal and cultural changes, beginning early in the twentieth century, into this century, have impacted the unfolding and definition of art therapy.

Part I describes the "Early Days." Junge reminds us of prehistoric influences; the work of Prinzhorn (1922); the early provocative writings of Margaret Naumburg in 1940 and Edith Kramer in 1958. During this period the first seeds of a relationship between art and psychiatry were sown, not to be harvested until much later. While the 1960s brought a small number of artists into psychiatric wards in hospitals to work with mentally ill people, dichotomies were rampant–the "label" of patient versus client, art and aesthetics versus diagnosis and treatment, psychological testing versus art therapy images. It also was a time of innovative educational models, such as the Montessori method.

In Chapter 2 of this section, Dr. Junge blends the 40s, 50s and 60s into an intricate and intriguing mix of a country recovering from a depression and finding a new approach to treating mental illness–artists working with patients in state hospitals and psychiatric wards. At the same time John Dewey's ideas were changing our education system and asking teachers to look at the whole child. Sigmund Freud and psychoanalysis provided a fertile ground for psychiatrists and artists to examine the art work of patients for clues to the unconscious mind. Dr. Junge's connections are amazing. I cannot help but wonder how many of us would have been invited to join the caregivers in mental health if it had not been for the earlier WPA Arts Project.

The next three chapters of the book, meticulously review the lives and work of those early artists who had never heard of art therapy–Florence Cane, Margaret Naumburg and Edith Kramer and their impact on shaping the field of art therapy.

In Chapters 6, 7 and 8, Dr. Junge takes a look at the geographical sites that nurtured art therapy: Menninger Foundation in Kansas where Mary Huntoon and Don Jones opened the door to artists; Washington, D.C. where Elinor Ulman began to publish an art therapy journal; the National Institute of Mental Health in Bethesda, MD, which invited Hanna Kwiatkowska to do art work with schizophrenic patients and their families. Community Mental Health Centers were being opened up all over the country to treat patients released from state hospitals and were hiring artists. My first office in 1967 at Hahnemann Medical College and Hospital in Philadelphia was in such a center.

While some of the problems and influences in other countries may have been different than those in the United States, Dr. Junge reminds us, in Chapter 10, that in Canada and England, art therapy was evolving in a parallel manner to the United States. In later years these movements would enrich art therapy in collaborative interactions between art therapists in these three countries.

As one of the first educators in this new field in the late 60s, I personally became passionate about the development of an art therapy organization to establish an identity and standards for myself, my colleagues and particularly for all of our students. I sincerely appreciate the comprehensive and compassionate chapter describing this intense and bumpy road to the establishment of the American Art Therapy Association.

In the next chapters, Dr. Junge gives us images and insights into the lives, beliefs and practices of our pioneer art therapists: including Robert Ault, Harriet Wadeson, Helen Landagarten, Janie Rhyne, Judith Rubin and many others whose influence and contributions are inherent in our profession.

Obviously, the face of art therapy has changed in the 15 years since Dr. Junge wrote her first rendition of art therapy's history. In this new work she moves into the past two decades. Her sensitivity to the environment and awareness of the impact on art therapy's growth as a profession is intrinsically woven into the tapestry of these years.

Ever the teacher, she concludes many chapters, throughout the book, with a summary of dates and events to remember, study questions and ends the book with a relevant assignment. Her discussions raise questions that hopefully our future students and colleagues will explore and work to answer.

In a personal conversation with Dr. Junge, prior to writing this Foreword, and knowing my commitment as a founder of the American Art Therapy Association, she asked that I try to realize that art therapy is much more than our national organization. I know she is right. The American Art Therapy Association may represent us and set standards for us, but how we identify ourselves and practice our profession in our society is the true essence of art therapy.

Dr. Junge has skillfully interwoven the images of our pioneers, the evolution of our profession and snapshots of American society in which each of us has lived. She is an art psychotherapist who has integrated and reflects the juxtapositions of society: How culture has impacted art therapy's development and influenced the past and present of our pioneers and peers. She has not only given us an incredible history, but a task: Through *The Modern History of Art Therapy in the United States,* she asks that we understand where we have been and what we are so that it will lead us into the future.

MYRA LEVICK, PH.D, ATR-BC, HLM

PREFACE

The Modern History of Art Therapy in the United States in some ways is my legacy to the art therapy profession. Over the years, art therapy pioneers gave their careers and, in many ways, their lives to art therapy. Their contributions created a fascinating and innovative profession.

In this book, the reader will find the formal and informal beginnings of the art therapy profession and its intrepid pioneers. For each decade, there is a chapter describing the essential occurrences of the times. It is my intention with these to provide the historical context–to show the ground–in which the field developed. Sometimes, this context propelled art therapy forward; sometimes it provided challenges art therapy needed to overcome. Important movements and milestones are highlighted including dilemmas and crucial events of the decades of art therapy's evolution along with many sections relevant to the questions and concerns of art therapists now.

I had some help with this book: There is a chapter describing and evaluating art therapy assessments by Frances Kaplan, an interview with Canadian art therapist, Kay Collis by Michelle Winkel and a personal story of her journey to a state license by New Yorker Ellen Greene Stewart. My central goal is to bring art therapy's history alive for others, as it is for me, and to make it useful to the art therapists of today. Most chapters conclude with a chronology of important events, dates and study questions intended to encourage the reader's critical eye. At the end of the book with "The Last Study Question" readers are challenged to create their own complete art therapy chronology choosing which important events and dates to include. There is an extensive Reference list and a Subject Index and Name Index at the end of the book.

However, this *is* a history and as such, I look *back*. To draw on, I have my own long experience and career as an art therapist in which I have been a passionate and sometimes critical observer, but one who has tried to make conscious sense of the ebbs and flows of the profession. I consider myself lucky to have discovered and been a part of the development of art therapy. But like all inherently conflictual love affairs, I have sometimes observed art therapy matters with astonishment, dismay and consternation. This book, then, is written by an apparent "insider" who embraces her outsider status because I have discovered that the view from there is more clear.

I come from a storytelling family and my family traditions are important to me. As a scholar, I am influenced by the Feminist Movement. In that spirit, I frankly acknowledge that histories are never objective nor are they "truth." All history is slanted subjectively through the storyteller's choices and often reflects the particular interests of the writer. For example, the focus on men in most written histories previously manifested the prevailing and driving cultural power and sexism of the United States—*what was looked at was what was seen.* In any history-telling, "the way it went," is obviously a *creative act* reflecting in part the author's storytelling abilities: I acknowledge the "truth" of that statement with *The Modern History of Art Therapy in the United States.*

It may seem strange to some that this book is my second history of art therapy in the United States. My first—*A History of Art Therapy in the United States* (with Paige Pateracki Asawa,) after nine years of research and writing was published by the American Art Therapy Association in 1994 for their 25th anniversary. It was my first published book. *The Modern History of Art Therapy in the United States* is my fifth book and it is a whole new work, informed by an additional fifteen years of development—art therapy's and mine—and my continued passion for the field.

Although these two histories may appear to provide bookends to my career as an art therapist, it was no accident that I, a Californian, would write that first history. I believed then (as I believe now) that those who "hold the pen" control the power and I knew that most of those then considered pioneers in the art therapy profession were from the east coast; I argued with that perspective on long walks where I often do some of my best thinking. And it made me angry. Writer Clancy Sigal said "I am hopelessly addicted to things that work." Me too and I knew that slanting the history toward the East didn't work and was a partial and false telling of the story. More importantly, I thought it a disservice to art therapy and its history which I found to be more complicated and mysterious, more extraordinary and compelling.

Perhaps I was driven to write that first history because I was a Californian—an "outlier." As a Californian, I never considered myself part of any eastern "establishment" and I hated flagrant discrimination and obvious political maneuverings of any kind. I knew there was much more to the story in other parts of America that might not have made it into print and therefore remained private and remarkably invisible. In my nine years of researching that first book, I talked to many art therapists from all parts of the country who had been working in the trenches for years and who told me their stories.

The first history began as a paper at Fielding Graduate University where I was pursuing my doctorate; it grew and grew and broke its bonds as a paper, until it finally became a book. Sources were the Mary Huntoon Collection Archives at the University of Kansas, the Archives of the American Art Therapy Association which were then at the Menninger Foundation in Topeka, Kansas, oral histories of art therapy pioneers produced by the Department of History at the University of Louisville, discussions and information from numerous art therapists across the country and information from journal articles and books on art therapy.

In addition to those original sources, for this new history I am lucky to have in-depth life stories of many pioneering art therapists published in *Architects of Art Therapy, Memoirs and Life Stories* and a number of current stories and opinions by art therapists who have contributed wonderful information to this volume. The reader will find a number of "Personal communication" citations in the history. These are all direct quotes from the many art therapists who have honored me with their thoughts and stories.

Along with Paige Asawa, Robert Ault and Linda Gantt must be mentioned as being extraordinarily instrumental in completing that first history volume. Bob offered loving encouragement and, with his wife Marilynn, fed me, housed me in Topeka and drove me around as I scouted the American Art Therapy Archives and Mary Huntoon's papers at the University of Kansas. I think Bob was miffed that Menningers' and what happened there for art therapy was not usually mentioned as history. I spent a long weekend in the snowy wilds of West Virginia at Linda Gantt's house. With the warmth inside, we worked together as we watched the starkly beautiful winter landscape outside through the windows of her library. I have never forgotten that lovely space, nor Linda's helpful presence and important historical additions. She wouldn't let me quit.

I titled the first book *A History of Art Therapy in the United States*[1] because it was my hope and expectation that others would write an art therapy history emphasizing what they felt was most essential for fledgling (and sometimes, not so fledgling) art therapists to learn about their profession. I imagined it might be quite different than mine. But many of the first art therapists were so busy inventing themselves as art therapists and creating history that they didn't have time, nor interest to write about it; second and third generation art therapists were usually busy being clinicians. Nevertheless, I was always fascinated by the courage and daring deeds of my "ancestors" many of whom I knew. It seemed to me they had taken their obsession with art and with people and, almost out of whole cloth, had created an important mental health profession. Another concept which drove me to write was the idea

---

1. Its first working title was *An inclusive history of art therapy in the United States.*

that in order to further establish art therapy as a legitimate, evolving discipline, it needed to have a documented written history as its bedrock and back story.

To my surprise, in the 15 years since the first history's publication, no other history in book form has been written and *A History of Art Therapy in the United States* remains, to date, the *only* history of the profession as a separate book. I have been honored through the years that many art therapy training programs nationwide have used the book to educate their students.

But the 1994 *A History of Art Therapy in the United States* was published a long time ago and many things have happened since in the life and evolution of art therapy. In addition, the 1994 history was pretty much limited to the "formal" version of art therapy and the formation of the American Art Therapy Association, so important in the development of the profession. Long ago I wanted to bring the original book up to date, but my relationship with the publisher, as is often the case, was not a happy one.

Inclusion has always been a problem in art therapy's history. Even as I worked on that first one, I knew there were many art therapists whose names and accomplishments for whatever reasons hadn't made it into the Archives, conference presentations or publications. I knew that huge numbers of hidden art therapists have toiled over the years in relative anonymity; there are many that do so today. They are immensely crucial to the furtherance of the profession, because art therapy's credibility in large part rests on them—how they are seen and experienced by the community, by patients and clients and by other mental health professionals. As art therapists they have practiced in schools, clinics, hospitals, institutes of psychotherapy and all too many have remained "invisible." This history is dedicated to the thousands not mentioned in this book.

I taught art therapy for almost 40 years and was Chair of the Clinical Art Therapy Program at Loyola Marymount University in Los Angeles for a number of those. In all that time, I listened to and tried to answer my student's urgent questions about their beloved profession. I believed then, as I do now, in the touchstone concept that understanding one's professional ancestors and the happenings and vicissitudes of one's profession—both accidental, and intentional—gives form, content and thrust to one's own practice, direction and developing history as a art therapist. After all these years, I am still primarily concerned with the fascinating and innovative mental health discipline that is art therapy, with its history and with its future. They are inexorably intertwined with mine.

The Modern History of Art Therapy in the United States is my effort to answer my student's questions in a way that is useful to them and to all art therapists while remaining true to the history as I see it. Writer Amy Tan says: "Writing to me is an act of faith, a hope that I will discover what I mean by truth"

(2003, p. 323). In this book, I attempt to bring fresh insights and knowledge from my long career in art therapy to a history that continues to intrigue and compel me. Art therapy has been a gift in my life.

The development of the art therapy profession is a story about a special breed of *person* who discovered the profound and unique power in the integration of art and psychology and had the energy and drive to create the new field. It is also a story about the people who encouraged and supported them. Beginnings are exciting and stressful. Art therapy is well past its beginnings; it has become a legitimate mental health discipline. But in its very legitimacy, problems may flourish and creativity dim. I believe the new generations must reclaim the courage, force and vision of the early pioneers to push art therapy forward—now, more than ever. As the Talmud says: If not now, when?

MAXINE BOROWSKY JUNGE, PHD, LCSW, ATR-BC, HLM
December 2009
Whidbey Island, Washington

ACKNOWLEDGMENTS

My first thanks go to Myra Levick for the Foreword to this book and for her support, encouragement and humor along the way. I am grateful to my many art therapy and expressive therapies colleagues who graciously and quickly answered my questions and often provided extensive information and always good stories. Part of the fun of doing this history was meeting (through email) Bernie Stone. With my request for information from him, he began to write down memories of his impressive art therapy career and his ideas about the profession. He ended up sending me many letters–handwritten on paper torn from yellow pads–of fabulous memories, all of which I enjoyed. I hope he will turn them into a book so other art therapists can gain from them as I did. His published papers and copies of artwork I retain as treasures.

I thank those who wrote important sections for this book. I am particularly indebted to Frances Kaplan who described and critiqued art therapy assessments and came in before deadline. Michelle Winkel, the new Director of the British Columbia School of Art Therapy interviewed the founder Kay Collis and Ellen Greene Stewart told the story of her achievement of a license in New York. Both Michelle and Ellen were my students a long time ago.

I thank Ed Kaplan for his obstinateness and humor.

My son Benjamin was my computer consultant again and Jason Calk produced the CDs and other technical material necessary. I am grateful to both. With these two, I had the technical back-up staff I needed. Benjamin also took the photograph for my author's picture.

My publisher Michael Thomas of Charles C Thomas has been ever helpful and quick to answer my questions. I feel I know him quite well and look forward to meeting him some day other than through email. We have worked together on a number of books and, from my point of view, we have had a wonderful relationship–very rare for a publisher/author.

I am deeply indebted to those who granted permission to print the figures in this book. Their names follow:

Art Resource

The Topeka Capital-Journal

Marilyn Ault

Harriet Wadeson

Vija Lusebrink

Don Jones

Judith Rubin

David Henley

Myra Levick

Helen Landgarten

Katherine Williams

Byword, Bethesda Hospital

CONTENTS

PART II. ART THERAPY DEVELOPING

PART III. ART THERAPY EXPANDING

PART IV. ART THERAPY IN THE LAST YEARS

THE MODERN HISTORY
OF ART THERAPY
IN THE UNITED STATES

We can't really travel to the past, no matter how we try.
If we do it's as tourists.
—Margaret Atwood, *Moral Disorder*

I write stories because I have questions about life,
not answers.
—Amy Tan, *The Opposite of Fate*

Part I

EARLY DAYS

Chapter 1

INFLUENCES

The influence of the arts on the evolution of society and culture manifests and predicts a developing structure of consciousness (Gebser, 1985). The arts go far back in prehistory and so it can be said that art therapy, like the visual arts themselves, has deep roots in the past. Since prehistoric people drew images on cave walls to explore, express and master their world, the arts have played a crucial role in human history and in consciousness. Visual art representing therapeutic rituals can also be found in the distant past: Relevant examples are the art of Native American tribes on the North American continent, African sculptures found in various locales and art rituals in which whole communities gathered together to create something to memorialize and remember the dead. The AIDS Quilt is a contemporary example of this mode of expression. Other present-day archetypes are the creations of writing, artwork, flowers and objects left at the scene of an accident or the home or other representative place of a victim of violence, or at the site where a person has died. Sometimes these offerings are left by people who may not have known the deceased but who wish to commemorate the life lost. The current outpourings for pop singer Michael Jackson exemplify this mode of memorial.

The formal profession of art therapy is usually thought to have begun and flowered in the Northeastern part of the United States; for example, Margaret Naumburg and Edith Kramer, arguably the major theoreticians of the field, both spent most of their time in New York City. Margaret Naumburg, usually called "the mother of art therapy" gave a name to the new profession in 1940, by calling her work "dynamically oriented art therapy." She first published in 1943. Edith

Kramer, considered the other major art therapy theoretician, published her first book in 1958.

After the dissemination of Freud's influential ideas, many people in Europe and across this country became fascinated with the integration of the visual arts and the psychological. Psychiatrists found that the art images created by their patients could be used as diagnostic revelations of the unconscious which they claimed manifested visually deep portions of the human personality. It came to be believed that created art could be used to expand talk psychotherapy into more hidden arenas of the psyche. Early on a number of psychiatrists, many of whom were artists themselves, used the arts in their analytic work. Hans Prinzhorn, a Heidelberg psychiatrist published a collection of artwork of psychiatric patients and the insane in Germany in 1922. It contained over 5000 pieces of artwork by psychiatric patients. A picture book, few words were necessary and its influence was broadly felt before it was finally translated into English in 1973.

From the 1940s[1] on, there were many people in the United States beginning to use the arts not only as assessment and diagnosis but as *treatment* or *therapy*. These early *art therapists* typically started as visual artists themselves and often studied art in university or art school through a graduate degree. Personally preoccupied with the intensity and profound nature of the arts, they began to apply their knowledge of fine arts to work with psychiatric patients. Often alone, (or so they thought,) and in different geographic areas of America, they went about experimenting and inventing the theory and methods of art therapy.

GROWING INTEREST IN THE INTERSECTION
OF ART AND PSYCHIATRY

By the 1960s, the practice of art therapy was growing across the United States from East coast to West coast. Art therapists came from art, psychiatry and from art education, the threads of which remain prevalent in the field today. Many fledgling art therapists were hungry

---

1. Part of the incentive for my 1994 history of art therapy was that when I began to teach art therapy in 1974, all I could find of art therapy history and literature, was a monograph titled "The History of Art Therapy in the United States" which cited Naumburg, Kramer, Ulman and Kwiatkowska as the pioneers. It was credited to Ulman, Kramer & Kwiatkowska. Even as a relative novice, I knew there was a lot more to the story than that.

for psychiatric training and sought out psychiatrists and other mental health professionals for help. Or they were sought out by them. Art therapy was an idea whose time had come.

By 1925, Nolan D. C. Lewis, a psychiatrist who would later mentor and hire Margaret Naumburg at the New York State Psychiatric Institute was fascinated with art created by his patients in his psycho-analytic practice. Psychiatrists like Prinzhorn and Lewis discovered the compelling *aesthetics* and innate power of psychiatric art. Like Psychologist Tarmo Pasto in Sacramento, California, many collected artwork by psychiatric inpatients, exhibited it and propelled a whole new interest in the graphic outlay of dysfunctional psychiatric patients. The mystery of a creative spirit that did not seem to be dimmed by mental disorders, and in fact sometimes seemed enhanced by it, sur-prised the mental health community and artists alike.

Distant from New York City, Harriet Wadeson (then Sinrod) came

Figure 1-1. Martin Ramirez, "Soldado With American Flag," Hemphill Collection, Smithsonian American Art Museum, DC/Art Resource. First collected by Tarmo Pasto.

to the National Institute of Mental Health in Bethesda, Maryland as an apprentice to Hanna Kwiatkowska in 1960 and in 1963 Myra Levick in Philadelphia began work as an art therapist.

There was a great deal of interest in fine arts in the Midwest at the Menninger Foundation Clinic spurred by Karl Menninger, who hired Mary Huntoon in the 1930s and encouraged her to start an art therapy program. Don Jones came to Menninger's in 1950 and later in 1960 trained Robert Ault who is known as one of the five founders of the American Art Therapy Association. In Ohio, by 1967-68 there were 12 art therapy programs in clinical sites, many of them started by psychiatrist Pedro Corrons. In Houston, Texas, Felice Cohen, influenced by Irving Kraft, Chief of Psychiatry at Houston State Psychiatric Hospital who had read Margaret Naumburg, was establishing art psychotherapy.

Psychiatrist Irene Jakab, a founder of the International and American Societies for Psychopathology of Expression, mentored a young painter named Bernard Stone. At the time Jakab found him, Stone was a Fine Arts major at Kansas University. In 1967, he was hired by psychiatrist Pedro Corrons to be an Art Psychotherapist in the Ohio state hospital system. Trained by Curt Boenhiem (the only psychoanalyst in Columbus, Ohio) and Corrons, Stone integrated art into psychotherapy and the institutions in which he worked received insurance reimbursement for his services.

In California, Tarmo Pasto, Professor of Art and Psychology at Sacramento State College (originally called California State College at Sacramento) received an $80,000 grant from the National Institute of Mental Health to conduct research on the graphic imagery of hospitalized psychiatric patients and prisoners in the State Department of Corrections (Holden, 1965.) Pasto was instrumental in the careers of two art therapists, Don Uhlin and Cay Drachnik. Drachnik became a President of the American Art Therapy Association and Uhlin established the art therapy graduate program at Sacramento State College. In 1967, Helen Landgarten began work as an art therapist on an adolescent unit of the Los Angeles County General Hospital. (Later, Landgarten single-handedly would invent "Clinical art therapy" with the innovation of the art therapist as primary therapist, and not merely adjunctive or a member of a treatment team led by a psychiatrist.)

In Louisville, Kentucky in 1957, Roger White initiated the first art therapy in America. Located in both the Psychology Department and the Art Department and despite not having an art therapist as Director, the program graduated two students, then closed in 1959 and became inactive for 10 years until 1969 when the American Art Therapy Association was initiated on the University of Louisville campus and a 25-year-old art therapist named Sandra Kagin (now Graves-Alcorn) was asked by Roger White to direct the program. Two years before it opened again, Myra Levick established her graduate art psychotherapy program at Hahnemann Medical College and Hospital in Philadelphia situated in a health sciences center.

On the art education side of the profession, in 1920, Florence Cane began as an art instructor at Walden in her sister, Margaret Naumburg's progressive school in New York City. Cane's first and only book, *The Artist in Each of Us* was published in 1951. Viktor Lowenfeld's book *Creative and Mental Growth* was published in 1947. In this book, Lowenfeld, an influential art educator, connected children's art and development in a convincing model and made a strong case for the importance of art in a child's education.

In the 1950s, when I was 12 years old, I attended an art class taught by Eula Long on Saturdays at the Kann Institute of Art in Los Angeles. Fascinated by Gestalt philosophy and psychology, Long's model eschewed the teaching of skills or technique in favor of providing an encouraging, supportive environment in which, she hoped creativity would flourish. Long changed my life and helped me find the artist that I am and the therapist that I became. Later, when I taught art to children, adolescents and adults, I successfully used Eula Long's model and that of Florence Cane's which I had discovered in her only published book. This model of art education and "art as therapy" retains a powerful place in the field of art therapy and many who practice it are now called "art therapists."

This book, *The Modern History of Art Therapy in the United States* is intended to capture the spirit and daring deeds not only of the important and pioneering Northeastern art therapists, but also art therapists across the country, even some of the "hidden" ones who may not have published their work and thus may be lost to us today.

Following, I describe some issues and events in the world that influenced and contextualized the development of art therapy as a profession in the United States. First are influences from psychiatry and psychology, outsider artists, the International and American Societies for Psychopathology of Expression, supporters of art therapists, psychological tests and, last, influences from art education. The chapter concludes with significant names, events and dates that the reader should know and study questions which are intended to create a thoughtful and critical approach to the material provided.

PSYCHIATRY AND PSYCHOLOGY
FREUD AND JUNG

Art therapy, as a mental health discipline has as its primary ancestors Freud, Jung and others of this ilk. In particular, the theories and techniques of psychoanalysis provided the bedrock from which the profession evolved. (And although art therapy has proven adaptable to many contemporary theories, many people continue to believe today–wrongly–that art therapy is primarily Freudian and psychoanalytically based.)

Nevertheless, Freud's powerful concept of the unconscious and his still-pervasive ideas about the unconscious' expression in dreams through symbolism remains, in my opinion, the main conceptual framework for the practice of art therapy. Through visual imagery which can sidetrack defenses and "reality" and by tapping directly into the unconscious, the art therapist effectively gains a visual portrait of the client's[2] thoughts, feelings and memories in the here-and-now and so does the client. Freud wrote: [A dream] "is predominantly a question of images. Part of the difficulty of dreams is due to our having to translate these images into words. 'I could draw it,' a dreamer often says to us, 'but I don't know how to say it'" (Freud, 1963, p. 90).

Freud was personally interested in artwork and kept antiquities artifacts on a table in his consulting room. He was fascinated with artists and often wrote about them, but he focused his analysis of their art, *on their life.* He believed that it is in the *life history,* not in the artwork itself, that clues to creative expression may be found. He was sometimes wrong (cf. Leonardo da Vinci). His notion that creativity was close to

---

2. The words "client" and "patient" are used interchangeably in this section. Because of the prevalence of a medical model, the word "patient" was used until about 1975 for most people who came to mental health agencies seeking help. The designation of "patient" indicates a doctor as the therapist (along with all the unspoken tacit meanings of the doctor/patient relationship). After this time, the word "client" tended to be used, which implied less adherence to a medical model and often more social equality between therapist and the person who came for help. In fact, dating from about the mid 20th century, most psychotherapy practitioners *are not* medical doctors.

madness, although disproven, is still prevalent today and many–including artists–generally believe it and are excused all manner of bad behavior because of it.

Carl Jung, first a disciple of Freud, developed many ideas that have greatly influenced art therapy because he gave centrality to the image itself, rather than as a clue to be unraveled through psychoanalysis as had Freud. He also created art imagery himself.[3] He disagreed with an allegiance to science and believed in a less rigid, more spiritual idea of personality. Jung's concept of the "collective unconscious" as a universal, cross-cultural form of symbolism transmitted generationally struck a chord. Freud never asked his patients to draw their dreams or fantasies, but Jung did. He was interested in psychological meanings of his own images and those of his patients. He wrote: "To paint what we see before us is a different art from painting what we see within" (1954, p. 253). Of special interest to Jung was the *mandala* ("magic circle" in Sanscrit) which has found its way into contemporary art therapy practice as an wholistic circle, which can provide comfort in structure and boundary to a psychiatric patient or client struggling with personality chaos or disintegration.

INFLUENCE OF OUTSIDER ARTISTS

Art of psychiatric patients and self-taught or "Outsider" artists at the early part of the twentieth century influenced later art therapists. But even before then, European psychiatrists Lombroso, Tardieu and Simon noticed and wrote about their patient's art. Many scholarly books and journal articles were published on the art of the insane and non-Western cultures; children's art was also described and interpreted (Harris, 1963). There exist several specific and detailed biographies of art created in psychiatric settings. These include MacGregor (1989), Kiell (1965), and Anastasi and Foley (1940, 1941a & 1941b).

While many in the European psychiatric community considered art by patients to have primarily aesthetic value, there were others who viewed psychiatric art as having a potential to provide diagnostic clues to the clinician about the inner problems of the patient. Hans

---

3. Author's note: The recent publication of Jung's *The Red Book* contains Jung's journal and extensive artwork during a psychological crisis.

Prinzhorn, a Heidelberg art historian and psychiatrist, famous for his collection of artwork by psychiatric patients is one who appreciated the artistry and aesthetics. Prinzhorn never considered the therapeutic potential of art for psychiatric patients, either as diagnosis or treatment. He was fascinated by the art itself and its sometimes bizarre imagery. In *Insania Pingens* (Cocteau, 1961) another European publication, two directors of psychiatric hospitals and a professor from the Academy of Plastic Arts in Munich, presented the art of psychotics. Artist and filmmaker Jean Cocteau wrote the introduction. While most of the discussion concerned the aesthetic merits of the works, in his section, Bader ("The Pictorial Work of Psychotics—A Mirror of the Human Soul") extends his interpretation to the possibilities of art as diagnostic and reflective of the interior psyche (Cocteau et al., 1961).

In the 1960s, psychologist Tarmo Pasto conducted a research project funded by the National Institute of Mental Health. In his investigation he categorized the visual imagery of hospitalized psychiatric patients, California Youth Authority clients and also adult prisoners. He is noted for discovering the obsessive, bizarre and fascinating artwork of Martin Ramirez—a noted Outsider Artist. Ramirez, a laundry worker in Mexico who became homeless and indigent in the United States, was discovered by Pasto at the De Witt State Mental Hospital in Auburn, California where Ramirez lived as a patient for more than 30 years (Figure 1-1). Although artwork was generally confiscated and burned at the hospital, Ramirez hid his drawings and, in 1954, presented Pasto with a large group of them. Pasto began bringing Ramirez art materials and organized the first show of his work (Tuchman & Eliel, 1992).

Pasto argued that artists had stopped providing "the one great means of experiencing emotion," but that in children's art and the art of the insane, inner meaning could be expressed (Pasto, 1962, p. 73). He wrote: "A true work of art functions on several psychological levels . . . [and] provides for ego-development through the conscious effort required in manipulation of both images and materials (Pasto, 1962, pp. 73-74).

Pasto was a Professor of Art and Psychology at the California State University at Sacramento. Through his interest in the psychology of art, Pasto met Don Uhlin,[4] also a Professor there. Collaborating with

---

4. In 1973, Don Uhlin established an art therapy master's program at Sacramento State College. It was one of the first such programs on the west coast and one of the few in a public university. (Drachnik in Junge & Wadeson, 2006)

Uhlin, Pasto became interested in art therapy although he admitted "One can see that the art therapist is dealing with many complex things. Often both he[5] and the patient will forever remain in the dark as to what the art expression means, or why art expression assisted the patient to recovery" (Pasto, 1962, p. 76). As with art, with art therapy much remains, rightfully so, a mystery.

THE INTERNATIONAL SOCIETY FOR PSYCHOPATHOLOGY OF EXPRESSION AND THE AMERICAN SOCIETY FOR PSYCHOPATHOLOGY OF EXPRESSION

Established in 1959 in Verona, Italy by psychiatrist Irene Jakab, the International Society for Psychopathology of Expression[6] and the American Society incorporated in 1964 in Topeka, Kansas were tremendously influential in the later formation of the art therapy profession by providing a gathering place and forum for many emerging art therapists. The society mainly focused on the nature of pathology in artwork and included many mental health disciplines as members, but the recognition that art could be integrated into psychotherapy and that patient artwork could offer an unparalleled window to the psyche and to the unconscious, were essential encouraging factors to the development of the art therapy profession. The Societies were dominated by psychiatrists and Don Jones referred to its "caste system" and to the art therapists there as "invited guests," Irene Jakab (1968, 1969, 1971), President and founder championed many art therapists, invited their presentations in the Societies and published their papers, thus legitimatizing art therapists as experts in the psychopathology of art and, I speculate, giving them confidence in their own drive to create an organization which emphasized treatment as well as pathology. The societies for the Psychopathology of Expression continue to this day and sponsor a yearly conference. Jakab is President and lives in Brookline, MA.

Many early art therapists were members of the Society for Psychopathology of Expression, attended and presented at their con-

---

5. Author's note: Within some quotes, the sexist language of the times is evident. I have not changed it. It is particularly ironic in that most art therapists then and now, are women.
6. The International Society for the Pathology of Expression changed its name to include art therapy. It is the International Society for the Pathology of Expression and Art Therapy.

ferences. They also published their works in volumes by Jakab (1969)[7] and Tarmo Pasto, Marge Howard and Elsie Muller were officers of the Association. An important side effect of the Society's conferences was that art therapists who attended came to a central place; there, they met each other, heard each other speak and encountered each other's common interests. According to art therapist Bernard Stone, the American Art Therapy Association (AATA) "has never admitted the very strong influence of the Societies of Psychopathology of Expression . . . Felice Cohen, Marge Howard, Judith Rubin, Harriet Wadeson, Elinor Ulman, Myra Levick and many other early AATA members were first ASPE participants and authors" (B. Stone, Personal communication 2009). The Societies for Psychopathology of Expression were a driving force in the establishment of the American Art Therapy Association (AATA). The Society's influence on the profession of art therapy was so important that Rubin calls Irene Jakab "the fairy godmother" of art therapy (Rubin and Wadeson, 2006, p. 103).

SUPPORTERS OF ART THERAPISTS

Without encouragement and mentoring by a number of psychiatrists and some psychologists who were significantly fascinated with the juxtaposition of art and psychiatry, it is doubtful that pioneering art therapists would have been able to achieve what they did. Many of these men (and they were usually men) are mentioned in other sections in this book, mentoring the art therapists they supported. A major exception to the "male" rule is Dr. Irene Jakab who was a founder of the International Society for the Psychopathology of Expression and the American Society for the Psychopathology of Expression which contributed in many ways to the new mental health discipline of art therapy. She is discussed above. In many cases, these well-regarded mental health professionals were responsible for art therapy training programs, because they had the "institutional clout" to get things done and could instigate the art therapy programs they supported–usually insisting that the head of the program be an art therapist. Importantly, they recognized the talents of the art therapist to be. There is no question that art

---

7. Papers in this volume were by Margaret Howard, Elsie Muller, Bernard Stone, Donald Uhlin, Tarmo Pasto and Harriet Wadeson.

therapy pioneers deserve to be saluted, but many had important help along the way which must be saluted as well.

A family friend, whose wife was the first-ever woman Mayor of Beverly Hills, California was asked what it was like to be her spouse. He replied: "Behind every working woman is a tired man." While the work of pioneer art therapists—not all of them women—is described in future chapters, the names of the "tired mentors"—not all of them men—who helped them along and championed the new profession are listed here. This list includes some supporters and mentors of art therapists who began in the 1960s: Nolan D.C. Lewis (Margaret Naumburg); Viola Bernard (Edith Kramer); The Menninger Brothers and Karl Menninger in particular (Mary Huntoon, Don Jones and Robert Ault); Pedro Corrons, Curt Boenheim, Irene Jakab (Bernard Stone); Lyman Wynne (Harriet Wadeson); Irving Kraft (Felice Cohen); Tarmo Pasto (Don Uhlin & Cay Drachnik); Roger White (who initiated the first art therapy educational program in the country and later hired Sandra Kagin Graves-Alcorn); Morris J. Goldman and Paul Fink (Myra Levick); Saul Brown (Helen Landgarten); Fritz Perls (Janie Rhyne); Thelma Alper, Margaret McFarland and Marvin Shapiro (Judith Rubin). Much earlier than the 60s, Friedl Dicker mentored Edith Kramer in Austria and Prague and Viola Bernard in New York called her an "art therapist."

PSYCHOLOGICAL TESTS

Many psychological tests have been discredited because of their lack of scientific validity, disregard for cultural influences and usually an all-white sample. Nevertheless, they are still prized by psychologists in clinics and private practice and—updated—are still taught in psychology training programs. Projective psychological tests were influential precursors to the practice of art therapy because they proclaimed that imagery and patient drawings could give clues to personality. They typically used visual imagery to stimulate and evoke associations which were regarded as indicators of personality manifestations. Leonardo da Vinci is often regarded as the first to envision an associative projective test in his *Introduction to the Painter*. Viewing a mark made upon a wall by a sponge, Leonardo wrote: "Various experiences can be seen in such a blot, provided one wants to find them in it–human heads, various animals, battles, cliffs, seas, clouds or forests and other things" (quoted in Zubin, Eron & Shumer, 1965, p. 167).

The Rorschach Inkblot Test, first established by Hermann Rorschach in Europe in 1921, was introduced in the United States four years later. The interpretative system primarily used in the United States was by psychologist John Exner (2002). The famous *Rorschach* provides a series of inkblots ambiguous in nature and asks the patient to respond to them with associations which presumably have researched meanings to give a window into the personality of the patient. *The Rorschach* is often used in psychological evaluation. Also widely used is *The Thematic Apperception Tests (TAT)* published in 1938 which required that the patient respond with imagined stories to a series of pictures on cards as stimuli.[8]

In the 1940s, projective tests based on patient drawings were developed. In 1926, Florence Goodenough developed an intelligence test–the *Draw-a-Man.* This was based on the idea that the number of *details* in a drawing of a man could indicate a child's intelligence (i.e., the greater number of details portrayed in the drawing, the greater the intelligence). Goodenough and other clinicians began to note that the *Draw-a-Man* test appeared to be revealing personality traits as well as intellectual ability. Buck's *House-Tree-Person* procedure was published in 1948 and Machover's *Draw-a-Person* test in 1949. Buck and Machover had been working with established intelligence tests, but with the evolution of their new projective tests proposed that drawing could be used as a clinical tool to plumb and reveal hidden depths of the human personality.

Unlike psychologists who tend to use projective testing as a "one-shot" indicator, art therapists who use these tests today, typically employ them as a *sequence* of drawings. Projective drawings cannot be used as "truth" but as a speculative hypothesis which may provide insight for the clinician into personality structures or may not. One method of use today may be to gather projective test data at times of change during art psychotherapy. In this way, the clinician can acquire a group of projective tests *over time* which may help in the concretization of the therapy and the marking of important changes for the client. See Chapter 24 "The Question of Art Therapy Assessment and Assessment Procedures" for more information on projective tests and their use in art therapy.

---

8. Groth-Marnat (1990) in *Handbook of psychological assessment* (2nd ed.) provides a detailed history and description of projective tests including the *Rorschach* and *TAT.*

EDUCATION AND THE ARTS

Progressive Education

Beginning late in the nineteenth century for the first time, educators and psychologists, studied childhood using scientific methods. Their observations proposed that children evolved through a series of developmental stages which were evident in behavior and artwork and which could be predicted. Writers such as Maria Montessori, John Dewey and Jean Piaget advocated that schools should be created for *the individual needs of children* rather than using the method of rote memorization that had been prevalent and the Progressive Education movement was born.

The philosophy of Progressive Education is usually primarily attributed to John Dewey who, with his wife, began the Laboratory School at the University of Chicago in 1896. Progressive Education focuses on *the whole child* and has as its guiding principle that humans are social creatures who learn best in real-life experiences with other people. "Learn by doing," is the major proposition of Progressive Education. Important is that within Progressive Education, a child's creativity is encouraged and an emphasis on the creative arts is respected and included. These emphases encouraged a plethora of new teaching techniques in modern education.

These days, as the education pendulum has swung in a drastically different direction–unfortunately, in my view–the current educational philosophy emphasizes *how much children learn* as measured by standardized testing, not *how they grow.* This philosophy, along with the all-but complete disappearance of the arts in the public schools today, has created an environment which I believe, does not suit many children's learning styles.[9]

In the late nineteenth century, Progressive Education was established as a reaction to the alleged narrowness and formalism of traditional education: "One of its main objectives was to educate the

---

9. Author's note: I felt so strongly about Progressive Education, that before I ever heard of art therapy, I sent my two children to a progressive elementary school, Westland, in Los Angeles, California. (Westland was established in 1949.) Both successful adults, my children tell me that this form of education remains a major influence in their life today. Examples of colleges following a progressive philosophy are Goddard College in Vermont and Antioch University. (I have taught art therapy at both.) The Bank Street College of Education in New York, a famous center of teacher training in the United States, follows progressive principles.

"whole child". . . . Creative and manual arts gained importance in the curriculum, and children were encouraged toward experimentation and independent thinking" (Encyclopaedia Britannica, 1980, VIII, p. 232).

Margaret Naumburg, acknowledged as the "mother of art therapy" founded a Progressive school in New York City in 1915–The Walden School. Her older sister, Florence Cane came to teach art there. These two remarkable sisters form the two poles of what would come to be known in the art therapy profession as "art as therapy" and "art psychotherapy." Can we call this sibling rivalry? (See Chapters 3 and 4.)

Modern Art Education and Viktor Lowenfeld

In the early part of the twentieth century, psychology was accepted as a social science and began to be integrated into universities and artists and art educators began to be interested in the psychological aspects of children's art. Franz Cizek (1865-1946), an Austrian, was the first to encourage spontaneous artistic creativity in children in his school and to recognize that child art not only revealed the inner workings of a child's mind as psychologists proposed, but also had about it aesthetic and creative properties. His beliefs about art and children spread to the United States and influenced child educators. In 1904, Cizek became director of the Department of Experimentation and Research at the University of Applied Arts in Vienna (Viola, 1936).

Viktor Lowenfeld, (1903-1960) a widely-read art educator, studied psychoanalysis in Vienna before he came to the United States. Cizek was Lowenfeld's mentor. In 1938 Lowenfeld, a Jew, fled with his family to the United States. During World War II, he taught psychology at the Hampton Institute in Virginia where he established the art department. In 1946, Lowenfeld became Chairman of Art Education at Pennsylvania State College, now "University" where he remained until he died (Efland, n.d.).

With his 1947 publication of *Creative and Mental Growth*, Viktor Lowenfeld wrote the single most influential textbook in art education. His book was grounded in constructs from psychology and from growth stages of children. He strongly believed that art was crucial in education because a child's intellectual development was integrally connected to creative development. Lowenfeld stated:

The process of drawing, painting, or constructing is a complex one in which the child brings together diverse elements of his environment to make a new meaningful whole. In the process of selecting, interpreting and reforming these elements, he has given us more than a picture, he has given us a part of himself. (1964, p. 1)

Lowenfeld conceptualized that a child evolves through six stages, each of which is revealed in the specific nature and detail of the child's drawing. These stages are: Scribbling Stage (ages 2-4), Preschematic State (4-7), Schematic Stage (7-9), Gang Stage (9-11), Pseudo-Naturalistic Stage (11-13), and the Period of Decision: The Crisis of Adolescence. From scribbling as a 2-4-year-old, to more advanced attempts to represent the natural world, the child moves through a series of sequential drawing stages as they grow and mature into adolescence (Lowenfeld, 1964).[10]

Along with his stage theory, Lowenfeld also worked with mentally and physically disabled children. His chapter "Therapeutic Aspects of Art Education" appeared in the third edition of *Creative and Mental Growth* (1957) but was omitted from later editions. (Much later this chapter was published in the *American Journal of Art Therapy* (1987), Junge, 1994.) The integration of psychology, psychoanalysis and art gave important impetus to the new profession of art therapy.

Erik Erikson and Children's Developmental Stages

Although he did not designate art stages, the vastly influential stage theorist Erik Erikson published his seminal book *Childhood and Society* in 1950. In his conceptualization, Erikson expanded the five stages designated by Freud's theory of personality to eight based on a central crisis in each. Erikson, a Dane and an immigrant to America was a student and teacher of art in Vienna and England and also studied the Montessori method of education. According to Levick, Erikson was hired by Anna Freud to teach art to the children she was caring for from the London Air Lift: "She convinced him to become an analyst and was his analyst. When he asked why an artist, she said 'psychiatry

---

10. According to art therapist Linda Gantt, Lowenfeld was not the first person to innovate a predictable stage theory in child art: Cook had first published on the subject in 1885 and in a 1905 book, Kerschensteiner organized drawings into three stages. (L. Gantt, Personal communication, 1991.)

needs people who can see'" (M. Levick, personal communication, 2009). Erikson completed his psychoanalysis at the Viennese Psychoanalytic Institute and with the advent of Hitler, immigrated first to Denmark and then to the United States where he became an American citizen and remained the rest of his life practicing as a child therapist and reworking his stage theory of human growth and development. (See Chapter 12, "Judith Rubin" for more on Erikson's influence.)

IMPORTANT DATES AND EVENTS

Late nineteenth century–The philosophy of Progressive Education is developed and in 1904 John Dewey and his wife establish the Laboratory School at the University of Chicago.

1904–Franz Cizek becomes director of the Department of Experimentation and Research at the University of Applied Arts in Vienna. Cizek is influential in recognizing the importance of child art.

1913–Freud's *The Interpretation of Dreams* is published in the United States

1916–Jung's *Psychology of the Unconscious* is published. This version was translated by Beatrice Hinkle, a Jungian who became Florence Cane and Margaret Naumburg's analyst.

1921–*The Rorschach Inkblot Test* is first published in Europe. It is brought to the United States in 1925.

1922–Hans Prinzhorn's book *Bildnerei Der Geistranken (Artistry of the Mentally Ill)* is published in Europe.

1926–Florence Goodenough designs an intelligence test for children, the *Draw-A-Man.*

1936–Viola's book *Child Art and Franz Cizek* is published.

1948–John Buck designs the *House-Tree-Person* test.

1947–Viktor Lowenfeld publishes *Creative and Mental Growth.* In it he proposes six stages of children's drawing sequences. This volume becomes the most influential book in art education and is important to many art therapists.

1949–Karen Machover's *Personality Projection in the Drawing of the Human Figure* published.

1950–Erik Erikson's *Childhood and Society* is published. A reworking of

Freud, Erikson postulates a series of developmental stages each with its own crisis.

1959–Irene Jakab founds the International Society for Psychopathology of Expression.

1966–Jakab founds the American Society for Psychopathology of Expression. Art therapists present at these conferences and publish in Jakab's proceedings of the conferences.

STUDY QUESTIONS

1. Compare the contributions of Freud and Jung to art therapy.
2. Why were outsider artists influential in the development of art therapy?
3. Discuss the goals, nature and uses of projective tests for art therapists.
4. Describe the contribution to art therapy of Viktor Lowenfeld. Include his influence on art education.

Chapter 2

THE 1950s, THE UNITED STATES AT THE TIME OF THE FORMATION OF THE ART THERAPY PROFESSION

To grasp the cultural thrusts providing impetus and form to the fledgling profession of art therapy, it is essential to understand the sociological, economic and intellectual forces helping to create organized art therapy and enhancing its development as an important innovative mental health discipline.

THE GREAT DEPRESSION AND THE WORKS PROJECT ADMINISTRATION

In the 1930s, within the despair of the deepest economic depression ever to occur in the United States, Franklin D. Roosevelt created a remarkable social experiment. Under Henry Hopkins, on April 8, 1935 as part of Roosevelt's "New Deal" the Works Project Administration (WPA) was established. Although less than one percent of the WPA budget went to artists, arts projects employed 40,000 American artists. The WPA was essentially a relief program for indigent citizens, but for the first time artists were included in an influential social and economic movement. This essential grounding in broad national issues gave a useful philosophical and practical drive to the new profession of art therapy. The WPA arts projects included the Federal Art Project (creating murals in public buildings, among other things,) the Federal Music Project, the Federal Writers Project and the Federal Theater. The intention was to provide work, not develop culture for the American people, but develop culture, they did. I wrote: "For example, many playwrights, actors (such as Orson Wells) and technicians who became central to the American theater received their start and vital experience in the Federal Theater"[1] (Junge, 1994).

Mary Huntoon, a pioneering Midwestern art therapist returned home from Europe in 1931 and, in 1934 became Kansas Director of the Federal Art Project. She remained as Director until 1938. Her model of an artist/activist grounded in the realities of the arts integrated with the social and economic milieu, provided her an important history on which to later build art therapy at the Menninger Foundation in Kansas. The significant realization of the authority and power of the arts to transform community lives on as an important part of the modern art therapy profession. We hear an echo of this narrative in the many who want to become art therapists "to use my art to help people." Other indications are the art projects by art therapists bent on healing that grew out of the destruction of New Orleans and the Gulf Coast by Hurricane Katrina.

POST-WORLD WAR II POLITICAL CLIMATE: FERVENT ANTI-COMMUNISM[2]

Although the Soviets had been our allies during World War II, the Cold War brought on fears of Communism infiltration and "subversive activities" in the federal government and elsewhere. The House Unamerican Activities Committee (HUAC), an investigative committee of the U.S. House of Representatives and Senator Joe McCarthy, Republican from Wisconsin conducted investigations into the *possibility* that Communism and the American Communist Party had secretly become spies in the WPA, Federal Theater Project and Federal Writers project, among others. (Hallie Flannagan, head of the Federal Theater was called to testify.) Typically without evidence or substantiation of any kind, these inquiries resulted in the Hollywood Blacklist in which the motion picture industry was thought to be involved in the creation of Soviet propaganda. Many buckled to the tremendous pressure. The "Hollywood Ten" was a group of writers who refused to testify before HUAC, were convicted of "contempt of Congress" and sen-

---

1. My mother worked as a set and costume designer for the Federal Theater.
2. Information from en.wikipedia.org. Retrieved December 17, 2009.

tenced to prison.

It is hard to imagine the aura of fear that enveloped the United States at that time. Despite the obvious "witchhunt" nature of the investigations in the Hollywood entertainment industry and other places, many were fired, left the country to avoid prison and some went to jail. Numerous careers were ruined and very few were able to be resurrected. The secrecy surrounding the process made it difficult to fight back. Geogheghan in the *Harvard Crimson* wrote: "In the 50s the most effective sanction was terror. Almost any publicity from HUAC meant the "blacklist." Without a chance to clear his name, a witness would suddenly find himself without friends and without a job" (February 24, 1969). The Hollywood Blacklist continued for many years. The few writers that could get work and usually living in Europe wrote under pseudonyms; some connected with "front" writers who acted as the writer of the work with motion picture studios and producers. The Blacklist was not effectively broken until 1960, when one of the Hollywood Ten was publicly recognized as the writer of *Spartacus* and *Exodus*. Many remained unable to work for years afterward.

By 1957, when McCarthy died, he had been censured for his actions by the U.S. Senate. But it was not until 1959 that HUAC was denounced by former President Harry S. Truman as "the most un-American thing in the country today." The main character of Barbara Kinsolver's recent novel, *The Lucuna,* an innocent writer of novels about Mexico is hounded by the Committee and commits suicide at age 34.

SIGMUND FREUD AND JOHN DEWEY

Psychoanalysis Provides a Relevant and Fertile Ground for Art Therapy

At the beginning of the twentieth century with the publication of Freud's *The Interpretation of Dreams,* psychoanalysis, and later psychotherapy, began its evolutionary journey in the United States spreading through the intellectual community; many people, including artists, grew convinced of its use and became fascinated with "free association." Based on Freud's innovative dynamic psychology and personality theory, psychoanalysis and psychodynamic psychotherapy became dominant treatment methods throughout much of the century. Before *The Interpretation of Dreams* appeared in 1909, Freud spoke at Clark University. A. A. Brill began to translate his writings which were then published in the United States.

While Freud's notions have been largely discredited in many houses of contemporary psychotherapy, old paradigms with such potency don't easily die out of the culture. Instead, they leave remnants of this predominant manner of thinking long after it has presumably disappeared and Freudian thought is prevalent today in American culture. As a mother questions the misbehavior of her young child by saying "why did you do that?" we hear Freud in the cause and effect query.

Freud's significant rationale that symbols and images in our dreams have meaning and act as disguised messages which can unlock the deep recesses of the unconscious, offered an important motivation and impetus for the development and evolution of art therapy. Art therapy as the combination of visual arts imagery and psychology was a practice which could offer a uniquely effective way to access a person's unconscious. The medium of psychoanalysis is an abstraction already distant from real experience. Often more efficient than words, the use of art imagery in treatment had the ability to cut through defenses and ephemera and open the "royal road to the unconscious" (Freud, 1963).

PROGRESSIVE EDUCATION: A PHILOSOPHY PROVIDING INCENTIVE TO ART THERAPY

Based largely on John Dewey's philosophy, Progressive Education focuses on the "whole child." Abandoning the Cartesian mind/body duality, in favor of the "whole child," Progressive Education emphasizes experiential learning through doing. The classroom is viewed as an ideal democratic community model in which the child learns to live a life, rather than to simply gain intellectual information (which social activist Paulo Friere calls the "banking model of education"). Meaningful experience including the creative arts is central to the child's growth. According to Dewey, education must be relevant to life, practical and process focused (Dewey, 1958; Johnson, Dupuis & Johansen, 1973).

While all-but-abandoned in mainstream educational settings today, this philosophy played a major role in the widespread educational reforms of the 1960s and 1970s which called for an "open classroom."

There are many today who think this approach is the appropriate one for many children.

DEVELOPMENT OF THE BIRTH CONTROL PILL

Despite opposition to birth control by the Catholic church and others, in the summer of 1957, the Federal Drug Association (FDA) approved the use of Enovid. Prescribed by doctors for menstrual difficulties, bottles were required have a label stating that the pill prevented ovulation. Although President Dwight D. Eisenhower stated that the federal government was not in the business of birth control, it began to be recognized over the years that more and more women were using Enovid for birth control. In the 1960s, extensive use of the pill would provide a great deal of new freedom for women and would impact American culture in many ways.

THE MENTAL HEALTH CLIMATE

A Time of Innovation Provides a Climate for Art Therapy

The profession of art therapy was born at a time of change and innovation in mental health in the United States. In the first part of the twentieth century, Freud's European ideas focused in the past took on a kind of American pragmatism as they spread across the country integrating into the many new therapies designed to treat returning veterans after World War II. Psychotherapy grew into what many called the "secular religion" of the United States.

One innovative form of psychotherapy was *the group* evolving from the necessity to manage and help the many damaged veterans who emerged from the War with mental problems. This acknowledgement of sometimes seriously distressed people has been called "battle fatigue" "combat stress" among other things, and now "Post-Traumatic Stress Disorder," but that one side-effect of war can be significant mental disorders, has long been known (Yalom, 1985).

Carl Rogers (1902-1987)[3] developed a "Client-centered" approach

---

3. The information on Carl Rogers was culled from the Wikepedia entry. It is listed specifically in "References" at the end of this book.

(originally called "non-directive") which helped to forecast the Human Potential movement of the 1960s situated at places like the Esalen Institute in Big Sur, California and aiming to promote human growth. Rogers is considered one of the founders of the Humanistic Psychology movement and is widely thought to be a founding father of psychotherapy research.

Rogers argued that humans strive to actualize themselves in order to realize their innate potential. He believed that therapists should use a technique of "positive regard" with their clients, which many translated to mean that the client was the driver in the work, and the therapist should reflect back the client's verbal utterances and behaviors. Rogers' philosophy is well-regarded and is centrally taught in many contemporary psychotherapy training programs, especially those educating counselors (Rogers' influence on art therapy can be found in Chapter 19).

In the 1950s after World War II, another major influence on psychotherapy culture, were the ideas of B. F. Skinner (1904-1990). Skinner called his theory "Radical Behaviorism." He maintained that such things as feelings and other interior musings were useless for human change; he believed that it was exterior and quantifiable behavior that mattered.

Skinner invented a series of experimental milieus such as the "operant-conditioning-chamber" through which he could conduct experiments and establish behavioral laws. In a recent survey, B. F. Skinner was listed as the most influential psychologist of the twentieth century. His ideas and those of other Behaviorists dominate most current-day psychotherapy programs. Cognitive Behavioral Therapy is a contemporary adaptation of Skinner's ideas.

Family Therapy was another type of therapy evolving in the 1960s. Based in systems theory which argued that it was the "whole" that was the essential unit of treatment and that the whole was more than the mere sum of parts, the individual was no longer considered the major unit of treatment. Instead of drawing boundaries at the individual as had psychoanalysis and psychodynamic psychotherapy, family therapy focused on the whole family and its *interpersonal* relationships. In that, it was not unlike the relatively new innovation of *group* psychotherapy. In family therapy, the social context was considered an important factor in treatment.

Development of the Major Tranquilizers
to Treat Psychopathology

The use of medications to treat people with problems is so ubiquitous today that it is easy to believe they have always existed; this was not the case. In 1954, the invention of the major tranquilizers suddenly ushered in a whole new approach to the treatment of psychiatric illness. All of a sudden, it was thought that patients who had spent years on the back wards of sometimes inhumane institutions could be stabilized on medication and moved into their community. The idea was that even the most difficult of patients could receive medication and outpatient treatment in their local milieus, while living at home or in some other appropriate non-hospital facility, but not imprisoned forever behind the forbidding walls of an institution. This significant change was thought to be vastly more cost-effective as well as more humane. Oliver Sacks, Professor of Neurology and Psychiatry at Columbia, in his 2009 article "The Lost Virtues of the Asylum" reminds us of the more positive and humane intentions and actualities of early psychiatric hospitals to provide "asylum" for the insane: "The old term for a mental hospital was 'lunatic asylum' and 'asylum' in its original usage, meant refuge, protection, sanctuary" (p. 50). Psychiatric hospitals intended to provide *protection* for mentally afflicted people.

John Kennedy's "Federal Mental Health Act of 1963" which began the closing of mental hospitals also had worthy and humane intentions. It offered the financial means to establish community mental health centers and storefronts which, in concert with the new antipsychotic medications, were intended to service large numbers of people in their own communities, using short-term and crisis treatment. Long-term treatment programs often lost funding. In reality, the idealist notions of these years were not often realized and mental health problems today are generally and rightfully viewed as too complex for any simplistic solution. We are left with great numbers of people with serious mental health problems, usually uninsured, unable or unwilling to find treatment and living on the streets or in jails. We are left with enormous numbers of homeless and, as Sacks (2009) calls them "sidewalk psychotics" (p. 51).

The Mental Health Culture of Art Therapy's First Years

The era in which art therapy was born, after World War II, was a time of tremendous hope, remarkable optimism and the sense of a potentially very effective whole new approach to mental health issues in the United States. The spread of psychotherapies across the United States resulted in ever-increasing numbers of people fascinated with psychology and entering education to become mental health professionals. Interest in the use of art imagery as a psychological tool propelled art therapy into the mainstream.

Money seemed plentiful. Community mental health centers were being built around the country; they were hiring new and talented staff as job markets expanded. New treatment innovations were sought out. Art therapy, with its innate ability to quickly cut through layers of defenses and provide a concrete record for the client and the therapist, proved a formidable "new kid on the block," particularly helpful, it was thought, for the popular briefer clinical treatments.

Art therapy's unique synthesis of art and psychotherapy offered a powerful contribution to already established mental health disciplines. As it expanded its perimeters over the next decades in the United States, the evolving profession of art therapy would formalize requirements, standards, ethics and education. And it would become a significant, if sometimes little understood form of psychotherapy.

IMPORTANT DATES AND EVENTS

1904–John Dewey and his wife establish the Laboratory School at the University of Chicago using the philosophy of Progressive Education.

1900–Psychoanalysis and psychotherapy spread across America. Some call it the "secular religion."

1930s–Because of the Great Depression in the United States, President Franklin Roosevelt creates the Works Project Administration (WPA).

1938–Originally called the "Dies Committee," the House Unamerican Activities Committee is formed. Although it loses much of its power after the 1950s, it continues until 1975.

1939-1945–During and after World War II, innovations are sought in mental health; group therapy developed.

1945–F. D. R. dies and Harry Truman becomes President. Bertalanffy presents General Systems Theory.

1950s–B. F. Skinner: Radical Behaviorism. Family Therapy begins. Important names are Bowen, Whitaker, Bateson, Haley, Jackson, Ackerman, Boszormenyi-Nagy, Satir and Minuchin.

1950s–Communist witchhunts of the 50s. HUAC and Senator Joe McCarthy conduct investigations intended to root out Communist spies and subversives in the Federal government, Hollywood and elsewhere. This is the era of the Blacklist in Hollywood. With virtually no evidence, a tremendous aura of fear is created. Folk singer Pete Seeger, among others, is a victim, is kept off radio and TV and has only been allowed to perform on TV relatively recently.

1951–Carl Rogers publishes *Client-Centered Therapy*.

1954–Development of the major tranquilizers–the first "new wave" of antipsychotic drugs.

1957–Summer. The FDA approves the use of Enovid for the treatment of severe menstrual problems. The label states that the drug will prevent ovulation. Many women begin to use Enovid for birth control.

1960s–Progressive Education is widespread in the educational philosophy of the "open classroom."

1963–John F. Kennedy's Federal Mental Health Act enacted, with the goal of taking patients out of psychiatric hospitals and treating them in their home communities in community mental health centers.

STUDY QUESTIONS

1. Describe the culture of the United States at the time of the development of art therapy. Why was this a fertile ground for art therapy?

2. Describe the specific events and milieu of mental health which helped to establish the art therapy profession.

3. Create an image in the spirit of the culture of the times.

Chapter 3

FLORENCE CANE (1882–1952) AND THE WALDEN SCHOOL

Most art therapists regard Margaret Naumburg as the "mother" of art therapy. One calls her "The mother of us all" (Rubin in Junge & Wadeson, 2006, p. 5). Florence Cane was Naumburg's older sister. An artist and teacher, she came to teach art at the Walden School in New York City (originally called the Children's School) a progressive school which her sister had established in 1914. It is said that Naumburg invited Cane to teach in 1920 after Cane criticized how art was taught at the school. According to Cane's daughter she felt that "creativity and individuality were being crushed" (Robinson, 1983, p. ii).

Influenced by the psychoanalytic ideas and intellectual climate of the times, especially prevalent in New York City, Cane underwent a Jungian analysis with Beatrice Hinkle as did her sister Margaret. In a time when most art teaching involved instruction in techniques and skills, Cane believed that the person and the product should be integrated. She looked to the emotions as the wellspring for creativity and had as her goal the liberation of creativity and free choice. She aimed to "loosen defenses, evoking a type of free association . . . tapping into fantasies and the unconscious" (Junge, 1994, p. 15). Cane was influenced by Gurdjieff, a Greek-Armenian spiritual teacher who emphasized dance, music, movement, innovative group work and writing as avenues for increased self awareness and growth. She also read and used Eastern Philosophy and thought.

As an 8-year-old, Cane began a diary called "Things My Mother Does to Me That I Won't Do to Children." Later at the Walden School, she developed methods to help free children's defenses including movement and sound which, along with their art expression, often released unconscious imagery. Cane also developed the scribble technique thought to tap into the child's unconscious processes through art making. The scribble method is largely attributed to Cane's sister, Margaret Naumburg who later employed it in art therapy.

As an art teacher, Florence Cane had patients referred to her by psychiatrists and analysts aware of the importance and uses of art imagery as therapeutic. She never called herself a therapist but relied on her role as a psychologically-informed art teacher. Along with her teaching at Walden, for 14 years Cane was Director of Art at the Counseling Center for Gifted Children of the School of Education at New York University in Manhattan. Because of her knowledge of and intentions toward the revelation of the unconscious through art imagery as healing, she was a tremendous influence on art education and a remarkable, if somewhat hidden influence on art therapy.

Mary Cane Robinson, Florence Cane's daughter wrote:

> I recall a picture I made in the mid-1920s when Florence was teaching at The Walden School and I was a 16-year-old student in her class. It was called "Despair." Each member of the class was to act it [despair] out through movement and gesture; make sketches of it; find the colors and environmental forms or shapes; express this feeling; then organize all this into a painting . . . it was a *whole* experience using the three functions—movement, feeling, thought. (Robinson in Detre, Frank, Kniazzeh, Robinson, Rubin & Ulman, 1983, p. 11)

Within the philosophy of Florence Cane, art therapists will hear echoes of a later dominant art therapy theoretician, Edith Kramer and in the integration of many arts, the sounds to come of "creative arts" therapies.

In 1951, Florence Cane published her first and only book, *The Artist in Each of Us.*[1] She died in 1952. Her book, long out of print, was finally republished in 1983. With its reprinting, Florence Cane takes her

---

1. In the late 1960s when I began teaching art to children in the community room of a local market in Los Angeles, I read everything I could find on art teaching. It was an era of change with many revisionist ideas about teaching in general, such as those of Kozol and Holt. I found *The Artist in Each of Us* at the library and adapted many of Cane's methods in my teaching. It was a book that changed my life.

rightful position as an intriguing and important influence on artists, art educators and art therapists. It is strongly recommended that all art therapists read this book. Cane stated:

> This awakening [of the spirit cannot] be won in the method adopted by some moderns . . . the teacher's role becomes that of a lover and student of human beings, whose aim is to release the essential nature of the child and to let that nature create its own form of expression, beginning in play and growing into effort. The integrity of the child is preserved and the art produced is genuine, primitive, and true. (Cane, 1929, p. 12)

IMPORTANT DATES AND EVENTS

1882—Florence Cane is born.

About 1910—As a young woman, Cane undergoes Jungian analysis with Beatrice Hinkle.

1914—Margaret Naumburg establishes the Children's School (later renamed "Walden") a Progressive Education school in New York City.

1920—Cane arrives to teach art at the Walden School; it is said she criticized how art was taught there and was invited by her sister Margaret Naumburg to teach. For 14 years, Cane is also Director of Art at the Counseling Center for Gifted Children of the School of Education at New York University.

1951—Cane's only book *The Artist in Each of Us* is published.

1952—Cane dies at age 70.

1983—Long out of print, *The Artist in Each of Us* is republished.

STUDY QUESTIONS

1. Discuss the intellectual milieu which influenced Cane's art teaching.
2. Discuss the principles of Cane's teaching and how it differed from the usual art instruction of the day.
3. Create an art image in the spirit of Cane.

Chapter 4

MARGARET NAUMBURG (1890–1983) CREATOR OF THE ART THERAPY PROFESSION AND THE FIRST MAJOR THEORETICIAN

Figure 4-1. "Margaret Naumburg."

Although other art therapists had written about art therapy and called themselves art therapists,[1] Margaret Naumburg was the first to define art therapy as a separate mental health profession and a different form of psychotherapy in 1940 when she wrote of "dynamically oriented art therapy." There are generally thought to be two poles in art therapy, one, art psychotherapy evolving from the psychothera-

---

1. For example, Mary Huntoon became an art therapist at the Menninger Foundation in 1935.

py arena and the other art *as* therapy emerging from art education. The concept of the art therapist as a special form of psychotherapist (with a history in psychotherapy and art) arrives with the theories, practices and techniques of Margaret Naumburg.[2]

Naumburg lived in the thriving intellectual climate of New York City and was influenced by a variety of disciplines. She underwent both a Jungian and a Freudian analysis and studied with the great visionaries of psychotherapy and education such as John Dewey and Maria Montessori. She graduated from Barnard College, New York in 1912 after attending Vassar College. Rubin calls her "comfortably eclectic and open-minded in her approach to both education and therapy," (Rubin in Junge & Wadeson, 2006, p. 5).

In 1914, Naumburg founded the Children's School in New York City. (In 1915, it changed its name to the Walden School.) The school focused on the arts and the intellectual stimuli arising from psycho-analysis. With a Progressive Education philosophy, Naumburg created a school in which children could pursue their own interests and through this process, learn math, reading and the like. Her older sister Florence Cane taught art at Walden from 1920. In 1928, after leaving Walden School, Naumburg wrote her first book, *The Child and the World,* about her progressive school and children's education. Much later, Naumburg insisted that art therapist to be Judith Rubin read that book because as she said "the roots of art therapy were all there" (Rubin in Junge & Wadeson, 2006, p. 7).

As a personality, that Margaret Naumburg was difficult is well known. If the word had been in usage then, she might have been called a "diva." At an early meeting to form the American Art Therapy Association, apparently angry that she was not elected to the original board of directors, Naumburg–79 years old by this time–banged her cane on the floor when she disagreed with anything. At some point she became furious and "stormed out of the room," saying "I'm not through with you!" (Ault in Junge & Wadeson, 2006, p. 70).

In a perhaps apocryphal story told to the author, in 1938 Margaret Naumburg visited the Menninger Foundation to give an invited presentation on art therapy. She clashed with Karl Menninger, clinic

---

2. Although, art psychotherapy and art as therapy sometimes overlap, in their original forms they carried different philosophies and definitions of art therapy. The other side of the continuum from Naumburg–art as therapy–comes from art education and is usually attributed to the theory of Edith Kramer. Kramer's ideas are discussed in Chapter 5.

founder and angrily left before she gave her presentation. At Menningers', she met and talked with Mary Huntoon. Soon after she returned from her visit, Naumburg began to refer to what she did as "Dynamically Oriented Art Therapy" thus naming art therapy as a separate profession. There is the possibility that Naumburg used the term that Huntoon had created to describe art therapy (R. Ault, 1985, Personal communication). In 1954, a second interaction between the two women took place: Naumburg invited Huntoon to send patient artwork for an exhibition she was organizing called "Use of Spontaneous Art in Psychotherapy." When the exhibit opened, none of Huntoon's patient artwork was included. According to Naumburg there was "no space" for them (Huntoon Archives, no date).

Many of the early art therapists were mentored or supported by psychiatrists. Margaret Naumburg was no exception. Through her connection to Nolan D.C. Lewis, she propelled her clinical knowledge and established her theory. After writing her book about the Walden School, bearing a son—Thomas—and divorcing her husband Waldo Frank,[3] Naumburg met Nolan D.C. Lewis who was then Director of the New York State Psychiatric Institute. Naumburg knew of Lewis' interest in and use of his patient's artwork in psychoanalysis. She later noted that he was "the first psychiatrist to employ analysis of the art productions of patients either singly or in series. . . (Naumburg, 1950, p. 13). She wrote:

> I asked [Lewis] whether he might be interested in an experimental research program in the use of spontaneous art in therapy with some of the behavior-problem children in his hospital. His immediate and sympathetic response to this idea was based on his own experience as to the value of spontaneous art with his own patients. (Naumburg, 1966, p. 30)

Naumburg went to work for Lewis at the New York Psychiatric Institute from 1941-1947. Her clinical work ranged from dynamically oriented art therapy with children to spontaneous art with schizophrenic adults. She published her first art therapy book in 1947, *Studies of the "Free" Expression of Behavior Problem Children as a Means of Diagnosis and Therapy. Schizophrenic Art: Its Meaning in Psychotherapy*, was

---

3. Most of the information about Naumburg's personal life cited in this chapter is from her son, Thomas Frank's memories in Detre, Kniazzeh, Frank, Robinson, Rubin & Ulman, 1983.

published in 1950 and *Psychoneurotic Art: Its Function in Psychotherapy* in 1953. Naumburg's book *Dynamically Oriented Art Therapy: Its Principles and Practice* which was extraordinarily important to the evolving field of art therapy[4] was first published in 1966. In this deceptively thin volume and using a series of case histories, Naumburg described her theory of art therapy and laid out essential principles for a fledgling practice that would last through the twentieth century and into the twenty-first and that would prove not only powerful and lasting, but influential and formative to generations of art therapists to come.

During the 1950s, Naumburg spread the word about art therapy and her vision of it, by giving training seminars in New York, Philadelphia, Washington and Cambridge, MA, to medical students, psychiatric hospital staff members and other mental health professionals, thus inspiring the next generation of art therapists.[5]

At age 93, Margaret Naumburg died in her sleep in 1983. Her son, Thomas Frank wrote:

> I have clear memories of my mother as a fighter against the establishment, against the inevitable resistance to new ideas and concepts . . . I recall her telling often how she had to fight established psychiatry's opposition to her research with patients. She was forever pointing out that art therapy, with its use of symbolic language and imagery was often a more effective road to the unconscious than the usual verbal approach of psychoanalysis and dynamic psychotherapy. (Frank in Detre et al., 1983, p. 114)

After her death, many tributes were published, but none more telling than that of Rudolph Arnheim, well-known psychologist of art and Professor Emeritus, Harvard University, who said: "Perhaps it is in the nature of a new discipline that it starts with a great figure of a founder whom nobody in particular has taught the things he or she will teach the first generation of regular professionals" (Arnheim, 1984, p. 3).

---

4. For an extensive reference list of Naumburg's publications, including many of the case studies in her books, the reader is referred to the References list.
5. Elinor Ulman, who initiated the first art therapy journal, arranged Naumburg's lectures in Washington, D.C. (see Chapter 7) and Hanna Kwiatkowska attended (see Chapter 8).

NAUMBURG'S THEORY OF
PSYCHODYNAMIC ART THERAPY[6]

Margaret Naumburg integrated the theory and techniques of Freudian psychoanalysis with her own ideas about the uses of art and symbolism in psychotherapy to provide an important basis for the practice of art therapy. While the beauty and simplicity of her theory are such that it can be adapted to many different ideas of psychotherapy and to the changing notions embodied in contemporary concepts, there are many who falsely still believe that the limits of classic psychoanalytic and psychodynamic psychotherapy remain today the limits of art therapy.

With Freud, Naumburg recognized that the unconscious speaks in images. But unlike Freud who never asked his patients to draw that we know of, Naumburg encouraged her patients to spontaneously draw their fantasies, associations, fears and dreams. She said: "Art therapy recognizes that the unconscious . . . can be projected more immediately in pictures than in words" (Naumburg, 1966, p. 3). In that statement the reader can hear the entire basis for the field of art therapy.

Naumburg believed that imagery was an *outward projection* of the patient's inward intrapsychic processes. She called this projection "symbolic communication" between patient and therapist (Naumburg, 1966, p. 1). Through her clinical casework, Naumburg found that the use of spontaneous imagery could speed up the therapeutic process because it does not rely on speech, is less familiar than words and could slip by what Freud called the mind's "censor."(Later generations of art therapists experienced this speed to be true, but also found it to be a potential problem in that the created image can escape the boundaries of repression and offer a concrete image that may be confrontational and even overwhelming to the patient.)

Art Therapy Within the Transference Relationship

Like psychoanalysis, Naumburg's art therapy takes place within a *transference relationship.* However, unlike traditional psychoanalysis

---

6. In this description of Naumburg's theory, I have tried to hit "the high points" and capture the important concepts; nevertheless, the reader is strongly urged to pursue Naumburg's original writings. I believe reading the primary source material should be an important part of any art therapist's education.

which encourages regression to enhance the development of transference, Naumburg insisted that the patient–rather than lie on a couch– sit up and take an active role in the therapy through art making. Within Naumburg's framework, *the patient* interprets the imagery themself. In traditional psychoanalysis, the analyst generally controls the interpretations and it is both a common mistake by art therapists and a broad assumption in the general public that art interpretation is solely the domain of the therapist. Herein lies the concern, verging on fear by the client and the public that the art therapist can "read" the artwork, even though the person who made it, may not be able to understand the inherent meanings.

Naumburg focused on the patient's transference *to the artwork itself* rather than to the psychotherapist, and considered it the third important element in the therapy (therapist, patient and art). She believed that eventually the patient would come to recognize the imagery as a "mirror" through which the patient's inner process was revealed and which the patient could learn to interpret. In this way, Naumburg believed the patient retained important independence within the therapy. These notions of expressive activity, independence and patient control represent an extreme departure from traditional psychoanalysis.

Interpretation

One of Naumburg's most important theoretical ideas was that the patient should free associate to their spontaneous artwork which could then lead to their making their *own interpretation* of the meanings of the imagery. In this way, the patient could feel a control over their artwork that they could not feel if they "turned over" the job of interpretation to the therapist. This stringency about who interprets the artwork in Naumburg's theory is essential in that it recognizes the personal, individual meaning of artwork and that this can vary person to person. Rather than experience the confronting nature of the "all-knowing" therapist's interpretation, Naumburg's method of handling interpretation can help the patient gain independence through control of the art product, the alleviation of fears and the development of a supportive and containing environment.

The Importance and Meaning of Art in Naumburg's Theory

Margaret Naumburg clearly focused on the *therapy* part of art therapy. She viewed the art therapist as another form of psychotherapist—one who had studied, understood and used the tools of psychodynamic psychotherapy and one who understood and practiced art and the creative process.

In Naumburg's form of art therapy, no emphasis was placed on the aesthetic product itself; she encouraged her clients to make even basic expressive marks to aid in symbolic communication. For Naumburg, the art product itself was not valued as "art" nor viewed aesthetically in any way; nor was it important as a technical accomplishment. Her theory places art *in* psychotherapy, not art *as* therapy. This lack of emphasis on art wrongly implied to some that *anyone* can practice this form of therapy, even a non-artist and that even "unfinished" imagery is valuable. Within Naumburg's, theory, that the art product is de-emphasized has contributed to criticism that art used in this way is merely another tool for verbal psychotherapy.

Naumbug deemphasis on the art product reflects her concept that the *locus of change* in therapy is innate to the patient/art/therapist relationship and in the patient's increasing ability to use their art as a mirror for self understanding. It is there that the helping lies and not in the creation of the artwork itself nor in its value as a creative, aesthetic product.

The Verbal Nature of Naumburg's Art Therapy

Within Naumburg's framework, words play a very important part as they do in traditional psychoanalysis and psychotherapy. Making an expressive image is not enough. The patient creates an image which is then associated to, analyzed and interpreted verbally by the patient. Words provide an extension for art. For Naumburg, art had the capacity to considerably speed up psychotherapy and the art image represents a concrete picture to which the patient can return time and again. But this art-making process must be also considerably extended through the use of words. The therapist acts as a witness to the patient's process, offering support, encouragement, direction and at times education and confrontation.

IMPORTANT DATES AND EVENTS

1882–Margaret Naumburg is born in New York City.

1914–Naumburg establishes the Children's School, based on Progressive educational philosophy and psychoanalytic principles.

1915–The name of the Children's School is changed to the Walden School.

1925–Nolan D. C. Lewis, Director of the New York State Psychiatric Institute and psychiatrist, uses free painting with his patients.

1928–Based on her experiences as an educator, Naumburg publishes her first book: *The Child and the World.* Much later, she says it contains all her ideas about art therapy.

1938–Naumburg visits the Menninger Clinic in Topeka, Kansas and meets with Mary Huntoon. In a huff, she leaves before giving her planned presentation.

1940–Naumburg defines "dynamically oriented art therapy" thereby establishing art therapy as a separate mental health discipline. This is perhaps the most important occurrence in the early history of art therapy.

1941-1947–Naumburg meets Nolan D. C. Lewis and initiates a research program at the New York Psychiatric State Institute, using art therapy with children and adults.

1947–Naumburg publishes her first art therapy book: *Studies of the "Free" Expression of Behavior Problem Children as a Means of Diagnosis and Therapy.*

1950–Naumburg's *Schizophrenic Art: Its Meaning in Psychotherapy* is published.

1950s–Naumburg gives training seminars to mental health professionals and staff about dynamically oriented art therapy in the major cities of the eastern United States.

1953–Naumburg's *Psychoneurotic Art: Its Function in Psychotherapy* is published.

About 1957–Naumburg presents at the Art Therapy Masters Program at the University of Louisville. She infuriates the faculty in both the art and psychology departments where the program resided and, after graduating two students, the program closes until Sandra Kagin (Graves-Alcorn) is hired to reopen it in 1969.

1966–Naumburg's description of her theory, *Dynamically Oriented Art Therapy,* is published. She is 84 years old.

1970–Naumburg receives the first Honorary Life Membership, the highest award given in art therapy by the new American Art Therapy Association.

1983–At age 93, Margaret Naumburg dies in Boston.

STUDY QUESTIONS

1. Describe the influence of psychoanalysis on Margaret Naumburg's ideas of human development.
2. Describe ideas from Progressive Education in Naumburg's theory at the Walden School and as an art psychotherapist.
3. Briefly outline Naumburg's concepts of art psychotherapy.
4. Explain the uses and limits of the art product in Naumburg's theory.
5. Create an image in the spirit of Margaret Naumburg.

Chapter 5

EDITH KRAMER (b. 1916)
SECOND ART THERAPY THEORETICIAN:
ART AS THERAPY

In a second viewpoint for art therapy and differing from Naumburg, Edith Kramer conceptualized that it is the creative process itself and the successful making of the art product that can bring change and healing for the patient. She vehemently stated that she was not a psychotherapist, but was like a psychologically-informed art teacher with a different goal than the development of increasing technique and method for her clients. Unlike Naumburg who viewed art made in art therapy as *symbolic communication* between therapist and patient, for Kramer it is the *art product* that is essential and which contains the mysterious potential for healing. For Naumburg "therapy" resides in the totality of the art psychotherapy experience. For Kramer, "therapy" emerges from the client's creation of the art product itself. In *A History of Art Therapy in the United States* (Junge, 1994) I suggested that Kramer, in her focus on the art in therapy may represent the viewpoint of Naumburg's sister and art teacher, Florence Cane and thus be an example of a form of sibling rivalry. Kramer calls the division between herself and Naumburg "The Historic Rift" and suggests that it still survives today. She singles out the *talking aspect* of art psychotherapy as different in the two theories and writes "They seemed to feel that a session where interesting art was produced was insufficiently "therapeutic," (Kramer in Junge & Wadeson, 2006, p. 19).[1] Nevertheless, recent-

---

1. For a more extensive discussion of this split and its symbolism and meaning within the art therapy profession, the reader is referred to "Reconsidering the Wars Between Art and Therapy" in my book *Mourning, Memory and Life Itself, Essays by an Art Therapist* (2008).

ly Kramer establishes the difference between the two as "more to do with the age group and social environment of the individuals under our care. She states [at times] "our approaches were very similar . . . but the supposed rift in our field persists" (Kramer in Junge & Wadeson, 2006, p. 20). Articulating the crucial notion that the therapy should be adjusted to enhance growth and change for each unique and specific client, Kramer forecasts the concept of differential diagnosis and specific treatment planning.

Edith Kramer was born in Austria in 1916 into an artistic family. In 1938, at the age of 22, she fled Hitler's Germany and arrived in New York City. She wrote: "Ever since I can remember, the center of my life was the making of art: drawing, painting and sculpting (Kramer in Junge & Wadeson, 2006, p. 11).[2] Today, in her 90s, Kramer continues to lecture and to paint in New York City and in the Austrian mountains where she resides each summer. She says: "My task remains to paint and sculpt the world around me with humility, vigor and truthfulness: to depict both the horrors and the beauty of our world. . ." (Kramer in Junge & Wadeson, 2006, p. 28).

Growing up in Austria, at the age of 13, Kramer became an art student of the well-known teacher and artist, Friedl Dicker. (Many of Dicker's approaches to art teaching seem much like Florence Cane's in that she used sound, rhythms and movements.) As a Communist in Hitler's *Reich,* Dicker was arrested by the Nazis. After her release she immigrated to Prague where the now 18-year-old Kramer followed her to become her disciple. She helped Dicker teach art to the children of political refugees: "It was during this work with uprooted children that I first experienced how art could help them regain their emotional equilibrium (Kramer in Junge & Wadeson, 2006, p. 12). Dicker, a Jew, was later deported to "Theresienstadt [Terezin]" where she famously[3] taught art to children. In 1944, Dicker was gassed at Auschwitz/ Birkenau. Kramer stated:

> To this day I honor Friedl's memory. Her work has had a profound effect on my life as an artist, a teacher of children and eventually as an art therapist. Indeed, all art therapists should know of Friedl's story and

---

2. Much of Edith Kramer's biography is from her memoir in Junge & Wadeson's *Architects of Art Therapy, Memoirs and Life Stories.*
3. Artwork from Terezin has appeared in an influential and important book portraying traumatized children's art, *I Never Saw Another Butterfly,* 1994.

respect her as one of the earliest art therapists and the "grandmother" of art therapy. (Kramer in Junge & Wadeson, 2006, p. 13)

Kramer left Czechoslovakia just before the arrival of the Nazis and came to New York City. She began to work as a shop teacher at the Little Red School House, a progressive school in Greenwich Village. During World War II, she was the only woman machinist in a tool and die shop in the So Ho District of New York where she learned to operate the various machines, read blueprints and prepare the metals for tool and die workers.

Kramer realized she could not make a living solely as a painter and looked around for another method to support herself. She also needed money to continue the psychoanalytic treatment which she had started in Prague. She made contact with Viola Bernard, a psychoanalyst on the board of the Wiltwyck School for Boys, who arranged for Kramer to be hired there. Kramer writes: "It was also Dr. Bernard who pronounced me an 'art therapist' rather than teacher, as few art teachers at the time would work with such disturbed children. . . . It was at Wiltwyck that I began to develop my ideas that would later become Art as Therapy" (Kramer in Junge & Wadeson, 2006, p. 15). Bernard told Kramer that everything that was done at Wiltwyck was therapy; therefore she must be an art therapist.

Figure 5-1. "Edith Kramer at Wiltwyck School for Boys, 1950s."

Kramer viewed her variety of art therapy as a special form of art class. Her clients were called "students" and she wrote that the art therapist must be a skilled artist, teacher and therapist: "The art therapist . . . communicates with his students[4] via the students' paintings and this communication has therapeutic value . . . But he is no psychotherapist" (Kramer, 1958, p. 5).

At Wiltwyck, for seven years, Kramer kept a diary of her work which later was turned into a book outlining her theory, *Art Therapy in a Children's Community*,[5] published in 1958. Kramer's was the first book after Naumburg's 1947 *Studies of the "Free" Expression of Behavior Problem Children as a Means of Diagnosis and Therapy* to describe art therapy with emotionally disturbed children. One reviewer wrote that the book provided "New insight into the process of art therapy by linking psychoanalytic knowledge with her . . . ability as an artist" (Kramer in Junge & Wadeson, 2006, p. 17). In a later book, *Art as Therapy With Children* (1971), Kramer described her art therapy programs in a children's ward of a psychiatric hospital, in residential treatment and in a day school for emotionally disturbed blind children.

Soon after her first book was published, Kramer received a fan letter from Elinor Ulman, later the founder of the first art therapy journal. The two established a close friendship, resulting among other things in Kramer's long association with the George Washington University Art Therapy Masters Program which Ulman and psychologist Bernard Levy developed. It may be that Kramer was influential in encouraging Ulman to start the first art therapy journal, the *Bulletin of Art Therapy* in 1961. Both Kramer and Ulman were against the creation of a professional organization (the American Art Therapy Association) believing it was too early in art therapy's development.[6]

During the 1960s, Kramer taught university and college courses based on her clinical experience with disturbed children. At New York University she was asked to form the graduate degree program in art therapy in 1973 but refused its Directorship because she thought herself much more at home in the art studio and because she was "intolerant of the politics of full-time academia" (Kramer in Junge &

---

4. The sexist language of the day is retained in certain quotations.
5. For an extensive list of Edith Kramer's publications, the reader is referred to References in this book.
6. For a fuller description of this controversy, see Chapter 11, "Myra Levick (b. 1924) and the Formation of the American Art Therapy."

Wadeson, 2006, p. 23). The NYU program is well known for its singular adherence to Kramer's theory, its immersion of students in art and its refusal to engage in the adjunct of "talk therapy" or art psychotherapy. In 2005, she retired from New York University. At a celebration for her retirement, Kramer "exhorted . . . [art therapists and students] to continue to make their own art: To curb the burnout that comes with exhausting clinical work, by restoring our zest and identity through the joys of creative work" (Kramer in Junge & Wadeson, 2006, p. 27).

No one who has seen Edith Kramer at the annual conferences of the American Art Therapy Association can forget her formidable presence: In Birkenstock sandles and with a long braid down her back, she rises from her chair to challenge the audience to engage in their own creative process, often criticizing the imagery of the conference program as stereotypical and meaningless. She notices that issues of the art therapy journal contain less and less art and more and more graphs and wonders where the art in art therapy is going.

Figure 5-1. Edith Kramer at an American Art Therapy Association book signing standing beneath her painting "3 Art Therapists."

EDITH KRAMER'S THEORY OF ART AS THERAPY

Edith Kramer's theoretical focus is art *as* therapy rather than art *in* therapy as was Naumburg's. For Kramer it is *the art process itself* that is the healing agent of change. Kramer's perspective proposes a focus opposite that of Naumburg and established a belief system which has many followers today. She maintained that art therapy was "an essential component of the therapeutic milieu and a form of therapy which complements or supports psychotherapy *but does not replace it*" (Kramer, 1971, p. xiii, emphasis added).

Training programs in art therapy, often innovated and directed by art therapy pioneers, tended to attach to and promote either Naumburg's or Kramer's theories. Kramer maintains she was not a psychotherapist, had no real training as such, and no interest in being one. Like many of her most vocal followers, Kramer came from art education. She was called an "art therapist" rather than an "art teacher" almost by accident and many of her concepts come from Progressive art education. But art education traditionally focused on the development of enhanced technical and expressive possibilities. Instead, the primary goal and focus of Kramer's model of art therapy, is *personality change and healing through the vicissitudes of the creative process.* For Kramer, the healing potential of the creative act itself depends on the psychological processes activated through creativity.

Theoretical Basis of Kramer's Ideas

Kramer's concepts are based in Freudian psychoanalytic thinking about human growth and development. Her art therapy fosters ego growth, enhances the development of the sense of identity and encourages the individual's maturity and maturation processes in general.

Interpretation

Interpretation has little, if any, importance in Kramer's theory. While Kramer acknowledges an individual unconscious like Freud, she believes that the art therapist "will not, as a rule, directly interpret unconscious meaning, but . . . will use his knowledge to help the child produce art work that contains and expresses emotionally loaded material" (Kramer, 1971, p. 34).

Sublimation

The integration of sublimation with the creative process and the art product is Kramer's most important theme and *enhancing the process of sublimation through the use of art* is Kramer's primary contribution to theory. Sublimation was first defined by Freud as a defense mechanism of the ego in which a primitive, anti-social or asocial expression is *transformed* into a socially acceptable act. Later Freud's daughter Anna and the ego psychologists redefined and documented sublimation not as a defense but as the one normal unconscious process of the ego. Edith Kramer retained Freud's original definition.

Differentiating sublimation from substitution, Kramer, with Freud, defines substitution as the channeling of "actions and emotions without changing their nature [it] remains a safety valve throughout life. When we strike a table with our fist, we express anger, substituting table for person . . . but this alone is not yet sublimation" (Kramer, 1971, p. 70).

Edith Kramer proposed that the visual imagery of the completed art product represents the transformation of the object, the goal and "the kind of energy through which the goal is achieved" (Kramer, 1971, p. 71). The art therapist assists the client using their skills and insight and encourages a "high level of artistic performance within the limitations of the student's talents." In Kramer's art therapy theory, the characteristics of the created aesthetic product indicate the "depth and strength" of sublimation (Kramer, 1958, p. 23). Whereas Naumburg's theory de-emphasized the art product and called it "symbolic communication" between patient and therapist, Kramer believes that it is the art product itself that is the visible indicator of the success or failure of therapy: The more fully realized and expressive the aesthetic product is, the more successful the sublimation. Thus Kramer helps her clients create "good art." Her definitions of "good art" are "evocative power, inner consistency, and economy of artistic means." According to Kramer "the harmony of art is attained through the integrations and balance of tensions. . . . In psychoanalytic terms this harmony is identified with the process of sublimation" (Kramer, 1971, p. 67). There are those that argue that this notion of Kramer's connection of the art image is not sublimation. They assert that sublimation cannot be achieved through art making, but that art making is a simple form of substitution and nothing more.

The Use of Words

Kramer criticizes the art psychotherapy camp for being too "wordy." She attempted to establish the art studio as a kind of "sanctuary" and said she avoided words because she felt they might emerge as loud and raucous argument with the particular population she was working with. She asserted that during the intense making of art, her clients did not want to be interrupted to engage in discussion and often refused her attempts. According to Kramer, after they had finished their art and were washing brushes or doing other finishing tasks, more discussion was possible. Moreover, Kramer states honestly: "It's also maybe a question of temperament" (Kramer in McMahan, 1989, p. 112).

> I've come to feel that more talk can be included in art therapy than I have included and that there is a place for more psychotherapy in art therapy (under certain circumstances). And I have certainly always felt that one needs psychoanalytic understanding in order to do art therapy; that plain being an artist and a nice person does not suffice to be an art therapist; that you must know what you're dealing with; you must understand the implied and hidden messages. You must know something about illness and health and psychic processes and the unconscious in order to deal with the material you're getting. . . . (Kramer in McMahan, 1989, p. 112)

AN EXAMPLE OF THE TWO THEORIES IN CLINICAL ART THERAPY PRACTICE

In the mid 1970s at Immaculate Heart College in California, Helen Landgarten innovated the idea of the art therapist as the primary therapist carrying responsibility for the whole case and working as an equal staff member in the clinic. (Previously, art therapists had typically been adjunctive members of the treatment team.) Coining the term "clinical art therapist," Landgarten focused on the therapist's ability to evaluate the patient's needs, including differential uses of art media. She taught her students to decide on specific treatment and goals for the unique patient enhanced by the use of media. Depending on the patient's needs at the time, the therapist might veer closer to art psychotherapy theory or art as therapy theory, thus allowing for the integration of the two within art therapy clinical treatment.

Years ago as a faculty member in Landgarten's program, I gave a day-long workshop at the annual American Art Therapy Association Conference. Attending were a number of students who were in the New York University and George Washington University art therapy programs. I remember how they were trained in Edith Kramer's theory of verbal silence during art therapy and how hungry they were to learn how to use words to extend the art process.

IMPORTANT DATES AND EVENTS

1916–Edith Kramer is born in Vienna, Austria.

1930s–As a disciple of Friedl Dicker, Kramer conducts art classes in Prague for children who are refugees of Nazi Germany. In these classes, she recognizes the importance of art to alleviate trauma and stress. She calls Dicker the "grandmother of art therapy."

1938–Fleeing the Nazis, Kramer–age 22–immigrates to the United States and settles in New York City.

1939-41–Kramer teaches shop at a Progressive school, the Little Red School House in New York City.

1947–Kramer goes to Europe and tours France on a motorbike. She sees the cave paintings at Lascaux and becomes more convinced of the "eloquent communication" powers of art without written or spoken words (Kramer in Junge & Wadeson, 2006, p. 20).

1950-57–Kramer teaches at the Wiltwyck Home for Boys, a residential treatment center in upstate New York. Rather than an art teacher, she is called an "art therapist." She keeps a diary for seven years which will result in her first book outlining her theory of art therapy.

1958–Kramer's first book *Art Therapy in a Children's Community* is published. She is 42 years old. In this book, Kramer establishes a second theory for the art therapy field, based on the importance of the creative process and product and the psychological properties unleashed by the engagement in art making. Soon after the publication of her first book, Kramer, lectures on art therapy at the New School for Social Research in New York City, Turtle Bay Music School and at other universities and institutions.

1964–Kramer initiates a therapeutic art program for blind children at the Jewish Guild for the Blind in New York City.

1971–*Art as Therapy with Children* is published. In this book, Kramer addresses the problem of quality in art. "When artistic efforts become fully formed, there is a greater likelihood that sublimation will be achieved. . . . I believe . . . [this] is one of my foremost theoretical contributions to the field" (Kramer in Junge & Wadeson, 2006, p. 23).

Early 1970s–Kramer responds to New York University to form a graduate degree program. She does not want to be Director because of "academic politics" but continues to teach adjunctively at NYU until 2005 when she formally retires. Because of her strong friendship with Elinor Ulman, she also regularly teaches at George Washington University's art therapy program (established by Ulman and Bernard Levy).

1971–Edith Kramer is the second person to receive the highest award in art therapy (Honorary Life Membership) from the American Art Therapy Association.

1979–*Childhood and Art Therapy* is published.

2000–*Art as Therapy: Collected Papers* is published (with L. Garity as Editor).

2005–A formal retirement celebration is held for Edith Kramer at New York University. She urges the audience of students and art therapists to continue making their own art.

2006–Kramer publishes a memoir of her life in Junge & Wadeson's *Architects of Art Therapy, Memoirs and Life Stories.*

2006–Now almost 90, Kramer continues her artistic life and her lectures.

STUDY QUESTIONS

1. Explore the cultural/social experiences in Nazi Germany which gave rise to Kramer's perspective on art.
2. Describe Edith Kramer's theory of art therapy.
3. Describe *sublimation* and its use in Kramer's theory of art therapy.
4. Explore the problem of quality in art according to Kramer's concepts.
5. Compare Naumburg and Kramer's ideas of art therapy.
6. Create an image in the spirit of Edith Kramer.

Chapter 6

ART THERAPY IN THE MIDWEST

THE MENNINGER FOUNDATION, TOPEKA, KANSAS

Far away from the East Coast art therapy happenings, in the 1930s and early 1940s art therapy was beginning to sprout on the plains of Kansas. Sheltered by the Menninger Foundation and Karl Menninger[1] in particular, the Foundation was established in the 1920s in Topeka, Kansas as an innovative psychoanalytically-based therapeutic milieu—one of the very first. Previous to this, in 1919, Dr. C. F. Menninger and his son Karl founded the Menninger Clinic for the practice of general medicine and psychiatry. Later Will Menninger, who was the Chief of Psychiatric Services for the army during World War II, joined the Clinic and Foundation.

It is difficult to understand now, the importance of the Menninger Clinic in the history of psychiatry but their form of treatment which later became known as "milieu" therapy (or the use of the total environment to treat mental illness) was an important beacon of hope. At a time when long-term custodial care and life-time exile in asylums seemed the only options, the Menningers believed that a person with mental difficulties could be treated and helped. This was a radical notion at the time. In 1946, the School of Psychiatry was formed at Menningers'. Driven by a post-World War II demand for psychiatrists to treat returning war veterans, it became the largest training center in the United States. Over the years, much psychotherapy research was done at the clinic and foundation; included were psychotherapy with

---

1. Karl Menninger was a painter who after his retirement painted every day, sometimes with Bob Ault. Menninger died in 1990. (R. Ault, Personal communication, 1995)

children, adolescents, adults and many mental illnesses.

Karl Menninger was a psychiatrist who was devoted to art and music. He helped acquire an important collection of contemporary art—including such a luminaries as Henri Matisse—for the Foundation. His interests in the arts spurred that of other staff members to include the potentialities of the arts in therapy treatment and to investigate their uses as therapeutic methods. From its inception, inpatient treatment at Menningers' included non-interpretive music and art therapy as an "activity" along with psychodynamically-based psychotherapy.

In 1937, Jeanetta Lyle[2] and Ruth Faison Shaw published an article which can be considered an early art therapy publication. Their study postulated that a child's finger paintings and drawings revealed the inner life and could be used both to understand the interior experience and to externalize internal feelings, particularly hostility. "A child may say in pictures what he [sic][3] cannot or will not say in words," Lyle and Shaw wrote, "and the analyst can then interpret these drawings in the light of his knowledge of the history of the child's situation" (Lyle and Shaw, 1937, p. 78).

In the 1950s, 60s and 70s, the Menninger Foundation Clinic continued to hold to Freudian ideas and psychoanlysis as the best theory and treatment approach. It was thought by many to be the best milieu treatment in the country. More psychiatrists and other mental health professionals were trained there than any place else in the world.

> They had top talent, lectures, publications, research—movie stars and the wealthy came for treatment and hospitalization. . . . Topeka [Kansas] was a unique place for psychiatry. . . . the city was crawling with psychiatrists, psychologists, medical interns and many patients . . . there was a psychiatrist behind every tree. (B. Stone, personal communication, 2009)

In 2002, Menningers' affiliated with Baylor College of Medicine and the Methodist Hospital in Texas and in 2003 it moved from Topeka to Houston, Texas where it continues today. I was told that the old Menninger campus in Kansas is now empty, the buildings wobbly and it is looking for a buyer.

---

2. Jeanetta Lyle later married Karl Menninger (Friedman, 1990, p. 156).
3. The sexist language of the day is retained in original quotations.

Well before Menningers' went to Texas, art therapy pioneers Mary Huntoon had died, Don Jones had gone to Harding Hospital in Ohio to open his own program and Robert Ault had founded "Ault's Academy of Art," a storefront in Topeka, Kansas where he taught art, practiced art therapy, created and exhibited his own art and enjoyed himself very much until his death in 2007.

Mary Huntoon (1896–1970)

Figure 6-1. "Mary Huntoon to Direct Revamped Studio Gallery, Mary Huntoon and Bernard Stone." *Topeka Capital Journal,* A. P. Photo, c. 1960.

Because of his belief in the power of the arts to heal, Karl Menninger was fond of hiring artists to work at Menningers' and the other institutions to which he consulted. Born in Topeka, Mary Huntoon first became an art therapist at the Veterans' facility called "Winter General Hospital." Many staff from Menningers' worked at the Veterans Hospital after World War II. Huntoon named what she did "dynamically oriented art therapy." By this she meant, paying attention to the patient's psychodynamics.[4] Thus it was probably Mary

---

4. Robert Ault told me the following story about Huntoon being the first to name "dynamically oriented art therapy. Ault said that Margaret Naumburg was invited to give a presentation at Menninger's in 1938 and met and talked with Huntoon. Naumburg returned to New York City in a huff having not given her planned presentation. However, soon after, in 1940, she defined "dynamically oriented art therapy" which gave a name to the emerging profession of art therapy as a separate mental health discipline (R. Ault, personal communication, 1992).

Huntoon who contributed the definition that is commonly used today and which was put into broad usage later by Margaret Naumburg.

Huntoon became an art "instructor" at what was then called the "Mennninger Sanitarium" in about 1935 (Hagaman, 1986). In 1949, her job description became "therapist" and in 1956 she was called "manual arts therapist" (Junge, 1987b). Huntoon had a great deal of rich experience and many responsibilities with returning World War II veterans: "I doubt Naumburg had anywhere near such a case load" (B. Stone, personal communication, 2009).

Throughout her life, Huntoon's work intensely focused on the integration of art and the social milieu; this combination reflects a strong thrust in art therapy today—and is sometimes called "community arts." Mary Huntoon can be termed an early day artist/social activist and her Works Project Administration (WPA) social awareness provided her with a model from which she would develop her form of art therapy.

Mary Huntoon, a trained artist and printmaker, was born in Topeka, Kansas in 1896. She graduated from Washburn University in Kansas and moved to New York City where she studied painting at the Art Students League. Robert Henri and George Bridgeman were among her teachers. She went to Paris to create etchings and stayed for five years, having her first one-person show there. In 1931, after 10 years in Europe, Huntoon returned to Topeka; there she became Director of the Federal Arts Project (Works Project Administration of the New Deal[5]) where she remained until 1938 (Junge, 1994).

In 1935, with Karl Menninger's sponsorship, Huntoon developed a visual arts focus for patients at Winter Veterans' Hospital (Hagaman, 1986). As part of the Psychiatric Training Program, Huntoon established the Department of Art, Physical Medicine, and Rehabilitation at Winter and stayed on there in various roles until the late 1950s. According to Hagaman (1986), first Huntoon was known as an "art teacher"; she was an art teacher for three years at Menningers' in about 1935. Later she became an "art therapist." Throughout, her job title was never "psychotherapist"; she functioned as a "recreational therapist" and was part of the "activity" program at Menningers'. In

---

5. WPA or "Works Project Administration" was created by Franklin Delano Roosevelt as part of the New Deal to alleviate the Great Depression. By 1935, 40,000 artists, writers, musicians and theater people were employed.

her work, art and rehabilitation were connected perhaps for the first time.[6]

In an undated memo in the Huntoon Archives at the University of Kansas in Lawrence, Mary Huntoon outlined her approach to art therapy: It included diagnosis through art and art therapy "as release of the creative process." She wrote that the patient could express feelings through art and thereby gain improved insight and awareness through the painting of the "idea or problem." Huntoon believed that a person's creativity remained intact and unchanged, despite severe mental illness problems. In a letter to a friend, she said: ". . . I have built up the art shop so that it is considered one of the leading efforts in the particular field. I handle almost two dozen mediums . . . and correlate my department with the psychiatric and psychology departments of the hospital" (Letter dated August 21, 1947, Huntoon Archives).

Mary Huntoon published a number of papers in the late 1940s and 1950s. Her first paper (soon after Margaret Naumburg's first book and almost ten years before Edith Kramer's first publication) was "The Creative Arts as Therapy" (1948).[7] There are many original ideas in her publication—such as "[the creative arts enhance] the externalization and mastery of subjective thoughts and emotions"—which would sound very familiar to today's art therapists (p. 202).

Huntoon retired from Menningers' in 1960 and died of cancer in 1970 at age 74. Her retirement predated the founding of the American Art Therapy Association and therefore she is not as well known as she should be, but she was a founding member of the American Association of Rehabilitation Therapists (AART) and presented on art therapy at its initial conference.

Don Jones (b. 1923)

Don Jones intended to be a minister and at times functioned as one. Early on, he hoped to find a way to combine his interests in art and theology. He wrote: [As a child] "peacemaker became a way of life,

---

6. It would be many years until art therapists at Menningers' were designated "psychotherapists" and even then hierarchical issues would still hold sway. (cf. Ault in Junge & Wadeson, *Architects of Art Therapy*, 2006)

7. A more complete list of Mary Huntoon's writings is in the References section of this book. Her first appearance in Ulman's *Bulletin of Art Therapy* was in 1961, the year it was established.

Figure 6-2. "Don Jones' Self-Portrait 'Portrait of an Artist Posing as an Artist.'"

not only as negotiator, but as therapist for my extended family. . . . My guide was Gandhi. . . . My philosophy became 'I am not my brothers' keeper, I am my brother!'" (Jones in Junge & Wadeson, 2006, pp. 40-41). Registering as a Conscientious Objector during World War II, Jones was assigned to Marlboro State Psychiatric Hospital in New Jersey where he stayed for almost four years: "This experience became my 'university of psychiatry.' [Marlboro State Hospital] contained 2800 beds and during the war was almost entirely staffed by C.O.s We worked alone in cottages housing 150 patients, twelve-hour shifts, six days a week" (Jones in Junge & Wadeson, 2006, p. 41). Jones noticed the importance that art held for the patients at Marlboro and began to collect their artwork. "I immediately became intrigued by the many graphic productions and projections of patients which literally covered the walls of some rooms and passageways" (Jones in Levick,

1983, p. 6). Using the collected artwork and adding drawings of his own, Jones published *PRN[8] in a Mental Hospital Community* in 1946.[9] Painting throughout his years at Marlboro, Jones' manuscript, *Tunnel,* contained his artwork about the patients he had worked with at the hospital.

After the second World War, Jones came to Rossville, Kansas to function as an "artist-pastor." He began to teach art classes in Topeka where some of his students were social workers, psychiatrists and other mental health staff from the Menninger Clinic. Through this connection he met Karl Menninger who wanted the *Tunnel* artwork for Menningers'. Jones wrote: "Menninger said 'I must have these paintings for the Menninger Museum.' I wrote Dr. Karl a letter saying that you must have Don Jones also if you're going to have his paintings. . . . You need me to do art therapy, whatever that is" (Jones, 1975).

Jones began employment at the Menninger Clinic in 1951 and stayed until 1966. Menningers' was focused on Freudian ideas and believed that psychoanalysis was the best treatment. Colleague and art therapist Bernard Stone wrote:

> Don Jones once shared with me a significant exchange he had with a young psychiatrist who challenged Don: "When are you going to get past all those symbols and metaphors and get to the truth and the facts?" Don answered: "The metaphors *are* the truth and facts." (B. Stone, personal communication, 2009)

During his time at Menningers', Jones also maintained a part-time position at a rural Methodist church and during the summers continued and completed his seminary studies:

> My original one easel in the [Menninger] clinic's Occupational Therapy shop was replaced by degrees with a creative arts building including studio spaces for all the arts and stipends for art interns. . . . Through the arts, I introduced a concept of "process versus content-analysis." I taught and promoted the idea that even the most psychotic artworks created in art therapy were "affect images" and important attempts at self healing. . . . First as Co-Director of the Creative Arts Division and later as Co-Director of the Adjunctive Therapy Department, I wrote and presented

---

8. "PRN" is an abbreviation of a medical term meaning "when necessary."
9. A selection of Don Jones' many publications can be found in the References section of this book.

many position papers to the staff. (Jones in Junge & Wadeson, 2006, p. 44)

Maloney, writing of Don Jones' significance wrote:

> With the support of Dr.s [sic] Karl and Will Menninger, Don Jones became a significant leader in retooling the treatment methods used in VA, state, and private psychiatric hospitals. Don lectured and presented this new philosophy of the sociotherapeutic milieu system throughout the United States. (Maloney, in Junge & Wadeson, 2006, p. 44)

In 1967, Jones went to Harding Hospital[10] in Worthington, Ohio where he set up a milieu program similar to the one he had innovated at Menningers'. He remained at Harding for 22 years until 1988. He was one of the major founders of the American Art Therapy Association in 1969 and in 1975 became its fourth president. He received the highest award in art therapy, the Honorary Life Membership of the American Art Therapy Association in 1988.

Don Jones has been a practicing painter throughout his life and career as an art therapist and currently works in his studio every day. He paints,[11] exhibits his work, mentors art therapists and sees art therapy clients in his private practice. His thinking about art therapy, manifested through his milieu programs at Menningers' and Harding Hospital, along with his own continuing artwork have continuously been presented at conferences of the American Art Therapy Association and have been immensely significant to the evolving profession of art therapy.

Jones' spiritual journey continues alongside art and, among other things, he has founded two Unitarian churches. He reminds us that "Doing art is a phenomenal expediter of expression of insight. . . . The aesthetic spirit is life saving and life-giving. My hope is that it will be beauty and poetry that may help to save the world" (Jones in Junge & Wadeson, 2006, p. 48).

---

10. The art therapy program at Harding Hospital, under Don Jones, in 1967 was the first hospital-based education program to receive "Approval" from the American Art Therapy Association.
11. For some of Don Jones' artwork, see his chapter in *Architects of Art Therapy* (Junge & Wadeson, 2006).

ART THERAPY IN OHIO

Pedro Corrons (b. 1931)

Pedro Corrons, a painter and guitar player, was interested in the arts and psychiatry. He is the only psychiatrist extensively described in this book, but his innovation of art psychotherapy in Ohio must be underscored because it was early and important. Today, he practices art psychotherapy in a psychiatric hospital and in private practice in Madrid, Spain. By 1967-1968 there were art psychotherapy programs at 12 sites in Ohio established by Corrons.

In 1959, Corrons started in Ohio what Bernard Stone calls "our nation's first state-supported Art Psychotherapy Department." Stone calls Corrons "a great teacher" (B. Stone, Personal communication, 2009). Corrons' art therapy program was intended to train state employees of all mental health disciplines with art background. His philosophy of art psychotherapy mandated a clinical setting, differential diagnosis, physician referral of the client and a team approach.

Around 1959-1960 preparing to open an Art Psychotherapy Department at Columbus State Hospital, Corrons visited Mary Huntoon at Menningers'. He took notice of her coordinating her work with the psychiatric staff and was impressed by her in-depth understanding of the psychodynamics of her clients and her enthusiasm and personal warmth.

Corrons opened a program within the Ohio Department of Mental Health at Columbus State Hospital. He collected and exhibited artwork of psychiatric patients and developed a large data base of client artwork. Corrons hired Bernard Stone in 1966, one year after Stone received his Masters of Fine Arts degree from the University of Kansas in Lawrence, Kansas. Among his writings, Corrons published "Psychotherapy Through Art" in 1967. In 1973, Corrons presented his book, *Colors of the Mind*.[12]

---

12. Author's note: As far as I can tell, this book was never published in the United States. According to Pedro Corrons (personal communication, 2009), he is getting it ready now to finally publish it in Europe.

Bernard Stone (b. 1934)

Figure 6-3. "Introducing . . . Mr. Stone and Art Therapy." *Byword,* Vol. 11, 1, Spring 1978. Bethesda Hospital, P. R. Department, Zanesville, Ohio.

Bernard Stone, from Ohio, was at the founding meeting of the American Art Therapy Association and was elected to its first Executive Board as Membership Chair. Don Jones writes of Stone:

> A young man came as a fine painter to ask about becoming an art therapist. . . . When I came to Ohio [to Harding Hospital in 1967] he was there. Bernard Stone had trained with Dr. Pedro Corrons and they had established in the state hospital system a very sophisticated art psychotherapy training program. (Jones, 1975)

In his days in Topeka, Kansas, Stone opened the "Studio Gallery," the first commercial exhibit space for regional artists. The first show in the new gallery was Robert Ault's work and Mary Huntoon worked in the gallery after she retired from the Veterans' Administration Hospital in 1960.

Bernie Stone remembers his childhood in Washington state during World War II:

> I got up before daybreak to catch a school bus along Highway 5. I stood under a big sign with a sailor-soldier-marine-air force—all figures in uni-

form asking for volunteers. . . . The school house was in the woods–a three-story frame structure. . . . They called my brother and me "Oakiees" [sic]. . . . We were like depression invaders from the Dust Bowl. . . . Dad left for Ft. Lewis. My mother and we three brothers had to work as migrant laborers to raise money to survive. (B. Stone, Personal communication, 2009)

Stone was a member of the International Society for Psychopathology of Expression before the American Art Therapy Association was established and published his work in Irene Jakab's books (Jakab, 1971, 1969, 1968). He calls Jakab "my first mentor in art therapy."[13]

She showed me the initial publications of A.S.P.E. [American Society for Psychopathology of Expression] when I was a graduate Fine Arts major at Kansas University. . . . She eventually put me in contact with Dr. Pedro Corrons, psychiatrist, in Columbus, Ohio, where I was hired into our nation's first state supported "art psychotherapy department." Art therapy had been practiced there since 1959.[14]

Like Pedro Corrons, Bernie Stone vehemently defines art therapy as (1) being in a clinical setting, (2) needing referral from a physician, (3) having "an identified client" and (4) coordinating with the patient's physician, nurses, social work staff and psychologists. He would not be likely to accept other definitions. In Ohio state hospital settings, Stone's art therapy services were reimbursed by insurance and he was possibly the very first art therapist to achieve insurance reimbursement for his work.

Pedro Corrons hired Stone at Columbus State Hospital in 1966. In 1967 he was appointed Director of the Art Psychotherapy Department. Stone also worked at Cambridge State Hospital, Good Samaritan Medical Center and the Bethesda Hospital Association all in Ohio.

To this day, Bernard Stone remains angry at the American Art Therapy Association which he found full of politics, deviousness and exclusionary practices. He wrote: "AATA [American Art Therapy Association] was very self defeating in not following a sound *clinical*

---

13. Judith Rubin called Irene Jakab the "godmother of art therapy."
14. Quotes from Bernard Stone are from personal communication, 2009.

model and standards from the start."

Bernard Stone is now retired, and living in Delaware. He is still making and exhibiting artwork at 75 years old. His last art therapy position was at the Upper Shores Community Mental Health Center in Chestertown, Maryland where he worked for 12 years. "It's been a challenging journey and I've had thousands of referred clients. . . . I was validated where I worked . . . the hospital life was real [and] tangible. . . . I rest in my work with clients."

After a series of arguments with Elinor Ulman, the Editor of the first art therapy journal and after Ulman removed footnotes from his article and added others of her choosing, Stone refused to publish there (For more on the first art therapy journal and Ulman, see Chapter 7). He said "I felt she [Ulman] was attempting to control the history of art therapy" (B. Stone, Personal communication, 2009). Some of his writings on art psychotherapy are "Escape into Space, The Graphic Expression of Anaclitic Anxiety" (1971), "Sequential Graphic Gestalt, An Accelerated Art Therapy Technique for Ending Recurring Nightmares" (1975), "The Graphic Expression of Blackbirds as an Omen of Suicide" (1983), and "The Harlequin Complex Indicated by Graphic Expressions of Sex-Death Fantasies Among Acute Psychiatric Inpatients" (with D. Smith, 1984), which was presented at Harvard University. Bernard Stone never received the Honorary Life Membership from the American Art Therapy Association.

THE BUCKEYE ART THERAPY ASSOCIATION

The Buckeye Art Therapy (BATA) Association was established in 1967 and is a precursor to the American Art Therapy Association.[15] Co-founders were Bernard Stone and Don Jones who, in 1967, had moved from Menningers' to Harding Hospital, in Worthington, Ohio (a suburb outside of Cleveland). Originally, the group met under the auspices of psychiatrists Curt Bonheim and Pedro Corrons to discuss clinical applications of art. Its mission is to support the art therapy field and support the use of art in therapy. Jones was the Buckeye Art Therapy Association's first president.

---

15. Although its constitution came later in approximately 1968–69 (G. Miller, personal communication, 2009).

In 1969, Stone and Jones both attended the formation meeting for the American Art Therapy Association. Pioneer art therapist, Robert Ault later talked of the irony that if Jones hadn't left Menningers' for Harding Hospital, one of them would have had to stay at Menningers' to keep the program open. As it was, both Ault and Jones were able to attend the formation meeting as representatives of their art therapy programs and went on to be elected to the new Ad Hoc Committee to form AATA and to be Presidents[16] of the American Art Therapy Association; they were extremely instrumental in the development of the profession. Both Jones and Stone were members of AATA's first Executive Board.

Many members of the Buckeye Art Therapy Association did not see a reason to join the American Art Therapy Association nor to gain Registration from AATA as art therapists. Stone says that of the original members, only three gained Registration with the American Art Therapy Association. Today, the Buckeye Art Therapy Association is an affiliate of AATA. It is more than 40 years old and, in 2009, had expanded its membership to 200.

IMPORTANT DATES AND EVENTS

1896–Mary Huntoon is born.

1919–Menninger Clinic is founded by Dr. C.F. and his son Karl for the practice of general medicine and psychiatry.

1923–Don Jones is born in Towanda, Pennsylvania.

1925–Menninger Sanitarium is founded.

1931–Mary Huntoon, a printmaker and artist, returns to Topeka after 10 years of study and exhibiting in Europe. She becomes Topeka Director of the Federal Works Project Administration formed by Franklin Roosevelt during the Great Depression to give artists employment.

1934–Bernard Stone is born in Freemont, Nebraska.

1937–At Menningers', Jenetta Lyle and Ruth Faison Shaw publish "Encouraging Fantasy Expression in Children" about finger painting. This paper can be considered an early art therapy publication.

1942-1946–During World War II, Don Jones becomes a Conscien-

---

16. Ault was the second President of AATA and Jones, the fourth.

tious Objector and is assigned to Marlboro State Psychiatric Hospital in New Jersey. There he recognizes the importance of art to the patients and begins to collect it. He publishes a book of patient art titled *PRN*.

1946–With Karl Menninger's help, Mary Huntoon founds an arts program at Winter Veterans Hospital in Topeka, Kansas. She also begins work at the Menninger Sanitarium doing what she called "dynamically oriented art therapy." She remains there until 1960.

1946–The School of Psychiatry is founded at Menningers'. Driven by the need to train psychiatrists to treat veterans returning from World War II, it becomes the largest training center in the country.

1948-1949–Huntoon publishes "The Creative Arts as Therapy." Mary Huntoon's job description at Menningers becomes "therapist."

1950-1966–Jones is assigned to be a pastor in a rural Methodist church in Rosswell, Kansas. He also teaches art and has in his classes many staff members from Menningers'. Through them, he meets Dr. Karl Menninger and comes to work at Menningers'. He develops his sociotherapeutic theories of milieu therapy and presents them nationally and internationally. He continues being a pastor and finishes seminary training.

1956–Huntoon's job description becomes "manual arts therapist."

1959–Pedro Corrons, a Spanish psychiatrist, establishes the first state supported art psychotherapy department at Columbus State Hospital in Ohio.

1960–Huntoon retires from Menningers'.

1960–Robert Ault comes to Menningers' where he is trained by Don Jones.

1966–Corrons hires Bernard Stone as an art therapist at Columbus State Hospital. Stone had recently graduated with an Masters of Fine Arts degree from the University of Kansas.

1967–Don Jones goes to Harding Hospital in Worthington, Ohio where he sets up a milieu program based on the one he had developed at Menningers'.

1967–Jones and Stone co-found the Buckeye Art Therapy Association (BATA). Jones is BATA's first President.

1968-1969–Jones is a founder of the American Art Therapy Association. Both Jones and Stone are members of AATA's first Executive Board.

1970–Mary Huntoon dies at age 74.

1973–Pedro Corrons first presents his book, *Colors of the Mind.*

1975–Jones becomes fourth president of the American Art Therapy Association.

1988–Jones receives the highest award granted in art therapy, the Honorary Life Membership from the American Art Therapy Association.

2002–Menninger Foundation affiliates with Baylor College of Medicine and Methodist Hospital.

2003–Menningers' leaves Topeka and relocates to Houston, Texas.

2006–Jones publishes a memoir of his life in Junge & Wadeson's *Architects of Art Therapy, Memoirs and Life Stories.*

2008–Jones is retired, living in Ohio, painting, exhibiting, seeing private patients and mentoring art therapists.

STUDY QUESTIONS

1. Describe the early influence of the Menninger Foundation on the development of art therapy. What about its philosophy of treatment made the arts a natural there?
2. Describe Mary Huntoon's role in art therapy.
3. What are Don Jones' contributions to art therapy?
4. Explore the integration of serious art making and art therapy in Huntoon and Jones' work.
5. State the importance of Corrons' and Stone's art psychotherapy in Ohio to the developing profession of art therapy.
6. Describe the reasons for the founding of the Buckeye Art Therapy Association.
7. Create an image in the spirit of Huntoon, or Jones, or Stone or art therapy in the Midwest as a whole.

Chapter 7

ELINOR ULMAN (1910–1991)
AND THE FIRST ART THERAPY JOURNAL

Figure 7-1. "Elinor Ulman."

In 1961, Elinor Ulman of Washington D.C., edited and published (with her own money), the first art therapy journal, the *Bulletin of Art Therapy*. In 1970, it changed its name to the *American Journal of Art Therapy (AJAT)*. The name change caused a good deal of controversy in that Ulman's journal, although it seemed to be, was never connected to the American Art Therapy Association. It was always a free-standing journal completely controlled by Ulman. Her "wielding of the pen" made her a remarkable and important force in the evolving field of art therapy and was an important milestone enabling the profession to move forward.¹ In 1963, Ulman conducted a survey of art therapists in the United States and Canada; she found only 30.

The *Bulletin of Art Therapy* was first conceived of as a Newsletter by Ulman and her colleague Bernard, Levy, a psychologist, who, later in 1970 with her, established the George Washington University art therapy graduate program—one of the first. Quickly the Newsletter became a journal. Ulman wrote: "Edith Kramer agreed to do a lead article for the first issue. We found one book to review and that's how we started" (Ulman, 1975). Ulman's *Bulletin* allowed art therapists and art teachers with a psychological bent, many of whom had been working completely alone in different parts of the country and making it up as they went, to communicate, to argue their ideas and to gain feedback within an ostensibly open forum.

Ulman intelligently recognized the potential of art therapy and its swift-occuring movement toward a professional organization. She cited this as part of her motivation for establishing the journal:

> . . . I decided that I would like to be an organizer rather than an orga-
> nizee. What was partly in the back of my mind in founding the journal
> was that writing and editing were close to my heart. I also thought cor-
> rectly that it would put me in a position . . . it would put me in the mid-
> dle of things. (Ulman, 1975)

She was right about being in the middle of things.

Ulman was often known as a figure of controversy (typically align-ing with Edith Kramer) and in many ways her vehemence and strong views created the reputation of the American Art Therapy Associa-tion's early days as being an organization of fights and fighters. Ulman stated:

> I think I have a reputation of being a fighter. In fact, I was accused of
> liking to fight, and I don't think I like to fight. But when doing what I
> want to do involves a fight, I'd rather go down fighting then give up. If

---

1. Ulman's journal was always an individual endeavor. In 1983, after 22 year of existence and a bit-ter and unsuccessful battle in which a group wanted the American Art Therapy Association to take over publication of Ulman's journal, it moved to Norwich University in Vermont.(At that time, AATA established its own journal *Art Therapy, Journal of the American Art Therapy Association*.) Ulman continued as editor of AJAT for a time. Later, Gladys Agell, who had been a student and mentee of Ulman's edited the *American Journal of Art Therapy* until 2002 when it ceased publication. The first art therapy journal existed from 1961 to 2002, 41 years.

I lose a battle, I lose a battle. But if I don't fight, then I always think I might have won. . . . I enjoy being sarcastic when I'm really angry. . . . (Ulman in Jordan, 1988, p. 109)

Ulman was seen by many as an obstructionist with strong views who attempted to divide. Williams who wrote about her in *Architects of Art Therapy,* said she had "fierce energy" and "Elinor's reputation for fierceness was not unfounded. She did not suffer fools and could ignite instantly when one of her passions was challenged" (Williams in Junge & Wadeson, 2006, p. 5).

For 12 years, Ulman's journal was the *only* one in art therapy. For art therapists working alone and lonely, the journal became a lifeline which in many ways, created the instrument that enabled the innovative profession to expand and move forward as a reputable and respected mental health discipline. Helen Landgarten said

One of the residents at the county hospital told me there was a *Bulletin of Art Therapy.* I back ordered all the issues. I had another friend doing a little art therapy and I thought we were the only ones in the world until I got the journal and found out there were people on the East Coast doing the same thing I was doing. . . . [The *Bulletin*] was my lifeline. (Landgarten, 1975)

That Elinor Ulman's origination and innovation of the *Bulletin of Art Therapy* was an immense contribution to art therapy cannot be underscored enough: Without her journal the profession of art therapy would have taken a good deal longer, if at all, to congeal. Almost singlehandedly[2] through the *Bulletin,* Ulman established a legitimacy and a visible national presence for the profession that expanded art therapy to include ever-wider populations as clients, enabled art therapists to find each other—sometimes across large distances—and attracted many others to the field as students and mental health professionals. Ulman's contribution propelled the profession forward into arenas of practice which would have greatly surprised her. The person who wants to make an impact should pay attention to Ulman's example.

Ulman graduated Phi Beta Kappa from Wellesley College with a

2. As mentioned before, Ulman financed most of the journal herself. Subscriptions did not cover expenses and she refused to raise subscription costs to "break even." She sustained personal financial losses for much of the duration of the journal (L. Gantt, personal communication, 1991).

Bachelor of Arts in English Literature. She studied art with painters George Grosz, Maurice Stern and Othon Coubine and Chinese brush painting for two years in Beijing. Her paintings were exhibited at the 1939 World's Fair in New York, the Corcoran Gallery in Washington D.C., at the Baltimore Museum of Art and at the Phillips Gallery. She intended to be an art teacher. From 1934-1940, Ulman painted and taught private students.[3] She fell in love with landscape architecture, earned a Bachelor of Science degree from the University of Iowa and became a landscape architect. From 1942-1953, Ulman worked as a draftsperson, cartographer and technical illustrator: "While beginning to explore the process of teaching art to handicapped children and offering art materials to participants at an alcoholic rehabilitation program" (Williams in Junge & Wadeson, 2006, p. 5).

In the 1950s, Ulman arranged Margaret Naumburg's lectures about art therapy in Washington, D.C. and in 1957 taught "Introduction to Art Therapy" at the Washington School of Psychiatry. She established art therapy at D. C. General Hospital and developed the Ulman Assessment Procedure, perhaps the first art-based assessment instrument.[4] In 1971, with Bernard Levy, she founded the George Washington University art therapy Masters program.

Although Ulman wrestled with the problem of the definition of art therapy among other things, and as editor published two anthologies of articles from the journal, her tremendous focus on the journal was at the cost of her own individual publishing (Ulman & Dachinger, 1975 and Ulman & Levy, 1980). She claimed she had "writer's block."

In 1978, with Edith Kramer and Hanna Yaxa Kwiatkowska, Ulman wrote a monograph titled *Art Therapy in the United States.* Although it claimed to describe "art therapy in the United States," the monograph in reality, solely focused on three art therapists from the eastern part of the country. Nevertheless, this monograph essentially functioned as a history of art therapy for the field until in 1994, I broadened the national scope by including the many more art therapists from other areas of the country than the east in my publication with Paige Asawa,

---

3. Much of the biographical information for Elinor Ulman is from Williams in Junge & Wadeson, 2006.

4. Barry Cohen and colleagues' later assessment, based on the Ulman Assessment Procedure is discussed in depth in Chapter 24, "The Question of Art Therapy Assessment and Assessment Procedures."

A History of Art Therapy in the United States.
After Ulman's death, Kramer said of her:

> Alas, Elinor spoke too seldom. Suffering from severe writer's block, she
> never wrote the books she ought to have written . . . a loss to the pro-
> fession. The block, however, made her a superb editor. It was the gain
> of the many who contributed to the *Bulletin* and later AJAT [*American
> Journal of Art Therapy*] as well as the gain of the countless students whose
> papers she mercilessly corrected. (Kramer, 1992, p. 67)

IMPORTANT DATES AND EVENTS

1910–Elinor Ulman is born in Baltimore, MD.

1930–Ulman graduates from Wellesley College, Phi Beta Kappa with
a Bachelor of Arts in English Literature.

1932-1934–She paints in France.

1934-1936–She studies Chinese brush painting in Beijing.

1936-1940–Ulman paints and instructs private students in art.

1942-1953–She works as a draftsperson, cartographer and technical
illustrator. During this time, Ulman teaches art to handicapped children and to alcohol rehabilitation patients.

1950s–She coordinates lectures in Washington, D.C. for Margaret
Naumburg.

1955-1965–Ulman establishes art therapy at Washington D.C.
General Hospital and develops the Ulman Assessment Procedure.
She establishes a strong friendship with Edith Kramer.

1961-Using her own money, Ulman creates and edits the first art therapy journal, *Bulletin of Art Therapy* (which later changes its name to
the *American Journal of Art Therapy*).

1969–Ulman creates controversy with her strong-held views that it is
too early for the art therapy profession to initiate a professional
organization. Nevertheless, she is a member of the Ad Hoc Committee to Form the American Art Therapy Association. Despite her
opposing maneuvers (as many said), the American Art Therapy
Association is created.

1970–The *Bulletin of Art Therapy* changes its name to the *American
Journal of Art Therapy* causing some controversy in that it sounded
as if it was published by the American Art Therapy Association,

although, in reality, they were never connected.

1971–With psychologist Bernard Levy, Ulman establishes an art therapy Masters program at George Washington University.

1972–Ulman is the third person to receive the highest award in art therapy, the Honorary Life Membership from the American Art Therapy Association.

1975–Editors, Ulman and Dachinger publish *Art Therapy in Theory and Practice,* an anthology of articles from Ulman's journal.

1978–With Kramer and Kwiatkowska, Ulman publishes *Art Therapy in the United States.* Arguably, this book stands as the most comprehensive description of the history of American art therapy for 16 years.

1980–Ulman and Claire Levy edit and publish another anthology of articles from the journal: *Art Therapy Viewpoints.*

1991–Elinor Ulman dies in Washington, D.C.

STUDY QUESTIONS

1. Describe a major reason for Ulman's creation of an art therapy journal.

2. Discuss the contributions of the Ulman's journal to the art therapy profession and to the history of art therapy in the United States.

3. Create an image in the spirit of Elinor Ulman.

Chapter 8

HANNA YAXA KWIATKOWSKA
(Deceased, 1980)
THE INVENTION OF FAMILY ART THERAPY

Figure 8-1. "Hanna Yaxa Kwiatkowska"

Hanna Yaxa Kwiatkowska was born in Poland into an aristocratic family and studied art in childhood. As an adult, she became a sculptor and married a Polish diplomat, Alexander Kwiatkowska. On assignment, they lived in China. Then Alexander joined the Polish Free Forces against the Nazis during World War II. Hanna (pronounced "Hanya") waited for her husband in Brazil.

Kwiatkowska was educated in Switzerland, Austria and Warsaw, Poland, spoke seven languages and when her husband rejoined her in

Brazil after the War, came with him to the United States. She eventually met Margaret Naumburg and became her first student. In New York, to gain solid psychiatry and psychoanalytic training, Kwiatkowska studied at the William Alanson White Institute with such teachers as Erich Fromm and Clara Thompson.

Her husband joined the State Department in Washington D.C. and in 1955 Kwiatkowska began work as an art therapist at St. Elizabeth's Hospital, a large psychiatric facility. She wrote: "With no official title, I was given the freedom to design my own programs" (Kwiatkowska, 1978, p. xiii). At St. Elizabeth's, Kwiatkowska designed and carried out a research inquiry on the graphic productions of schizophrenic patients using chlorpromazine (Thorazine). In 1958, she joined the staff of the National Institute of Mental Health (NIMH) Kwiatkowska stayed for 14 years until 1970. There, virtually alone, she invented family art therapy. Levick states: "Hanna Kwiatkowska really did the seminal work in quantitative research. Her family evaluation had a very elaborate scoring system and was really good. The problem was it was so complex it was hard to use" (M. Levick, personal communication, 2009).

The late 1950s and 60s were an exceptionally expansive and innovative time for family studies at the National Institute of Mental Health. In particular, were the studies of schizophrenic families which became a main thrust of the burgeoning family therapy movement in the United States. Murray Bowen, one of the major founders of family therapy, worked first at Menningers' and then came to the National Institute of Mental Health in the early 1950s. He set-up the family studies project there to study the family unit and arranged for whole families with a schizophrenic patient to be hospitalized together. Lyman Wynne succeeded Bowen at NIMH and directed Kwiatkowska's research.

At the beginning, Kwiatkowska treated and researched individuals. Harriet Wadeson writes: "Family art therapy began accidentally when family members visited patients and attended their art therapy sessions" (Wadeson in Junge & Wadeson, 2006, p. 56). When she saw the patients with their family, Kwiatkowska realized that art could help family members communicate better and recognize and understand their particular family dynamics. As other clinicians at NIMH began to be familiar with the value of art with families, art therapy became a usual part of family evaluation.

For family evaluation at NIMH, Kwiatkowska was invited into a family session by other mental health professionals to assess through her valuable specialty—the use of art. Kwiatkowska developed a six-step procedure for family evaluation which she believed needed to be done in the correct sequence. According to Kwiatkowska, with its six individual drawings, the procedure involved movement from freedom to structure. Kwiatkowska claimed that by comparing the first "free" picture with the last, the therapist could assess how the family handled the stress of the session. The drawings of the six-step procedure are:

1. A free picture
2. A picture of your family
3. An abstract family portrait
4. A picture started with the help of a scribble
5. A joint family scribble
6. A free picture (Kwiatkowska, 1978, p. 86)

A "free picture" was one where no subject was given and the scribble technique followed Florence Cane's model. Except for No. 5, all the pictures were individually done by family members working on a separate easel. But after every drawing, family members were encouraged to make comments about each others work, which helped create a whole family dynamic. By including the family's primary therapist in the session and suggesting that they participate in the verbal portion, Kwiatkowska introduced visual exploration into the treatment.

Although she published a number of papers and research studies beginning in 1959,[1] Kwiatkowska's book outlining her family evaluation protocol was not published until 1978 as *Family Therapy and Evaluation Through Art.* As an artist, she exhibited her work in Switzerland, Brazil, Manchuria, Austria and the United States (L. Gantt, personal communication, 1991). She was awarded three Fulbright travel awards to Brazil where she lectured on art therapy and gave a family art therapy presentation using as an example a Brazilian family with a schizophrenic child.

Kwiatkowska taught in the art therapy graduate program at George Washington University beginning in 1970 and at the Catholic University of Rio de Janeiro, Brazil. She was Research Chair on the

---

1. See References for a complete listing of Kwiatkowska's published work.

first Executive Board of the American Art Therapy Association and was awarded the American Art Therapy Association's fourth Honorary Life Membership. She would never tell anyone her age, so although it is known that she died of cancer in 1980 in Washington, D.C. her date of birth is unknown. I remember meeting her in Los Angeles. She was an elegant-looking woman who had difficulty walking and used a cane; she walked very slowly and carefully so as not to fall and spoke with an accent. But Hanna Kwiatkowska had a warmth about her, a smile, and an interest in others which made her physical difficulties become all but invisible.

IMPORTANT DATES AND EVENTS

Around 1910–Hanna Yaxa Kwiatkowska is born in Warsaw, Poland. As an adult, she becomes a sculptor and marries a Polish diplomat. The couple live in China for a few years. During World War II Kwiatkowska moves to Brazil to await her husband who is working for the "Polish Free Forces" and fighting for England. After World War II, the couple is reunited in Brazil and move to New York City. There, Kwiatkowska, becomes Margaret Naumburg's first student. Recognizing her need for training in psychology, psychotherapy and psychoanalysis, she studies at the William Alanson White Institute. With her diplomat husband, she moves to Washington, D.C.

1955–Kwiatkowska begins work at St. Elizabeth's (a large psychiatric hospital).

1958–She joins the staff of the National Institute of Mental Health and, "by accident," invents family art therapy there.

1969–Kwiatkowska is on the first Executive Board of the American Art Therapy Association as Research Chair.

1970–Through Elinor Ulman who began the program, Kwiatkowska becomes a professor in the George Washington University Masters art therapy program in Washington, D.C.

1972–Kwiatkowska leaves NIMH.

1973–Kwiatkowska receives the Honorary Life Membership Award from the American Art Therapy Association.

1978–Her book, *Family Therapy and Evaluation Through Art,* is published.

1980–Hanna Yaxa Kwiatkowska dies.

STUDY QUESTIONS

1. Describe Kwiatkowska's "accidental" invention of family art therapy.
2. List Kwiatkowska's procedure for a family evaluation.
3. Create an image in the spirit of Kwiatkowska.

Chapter 9

A BRIEF HISTORY OF ART THERAPY IN GREAT BRITAIN AND CANADA

GREAT BRITAIN

Art therapy in Great Britain has developed much as in the United States. Like the United States, the English tradition has been for artists to become art therapists, rather than medical people or mental health professionals. Waller (1991 & 1992b) is a well-established writer on the history of art therapy in Britain. Ten years later in 2001, Hogan wrote a history of British art therapy. Despite being about English art therapy, it is mistitled *Healing Arts, the History of Art Therapy.*

Waller states that the term "art therapy" began to be used in the United Kingdom as early as the 1930s and art therapy is included in England's National Health Service. Adrian Hill, a professional artist, after World War II was recovering in a tuberculosis sanatorium and is usually credited with coining the term "art therapy" in 1942. Hill turned to his own art for therapy and subsequently received permission to "introduce painting to other patients" (Junge, 1994). Hill also mounted patient art exhibitions. About the same time as Hill used the term, in 1940 American Margaret Naumburg defined "dynamically oriented art therapy" thereby identifying art therapy as a separate mental health discipline. Much like those of the United States, British art therapy origins are in psychoanalysis, developmental psychology, occupational therapy and art education (Waller, 1992b).

In 1942, a British commercial artist Rita Simon, conducted outpatient groups under the auspices of social psychiatrist Joshua Bierer who had begun "social psychiatry clubs." Waller (1992b) writes: "Simon quickly became aware of the potential for using art as a means of expression and communication and entered her own psychoanalysis in order to understand more about the therapeutic process" (p. 8).

In 1946, the artist Edward Adamson was hired at the Netherne Psychiatric Hospital. His task was to help the medical staff research the effects of leucotomy on patients' visual perception. ("Leucotomy" is another word for "lobotomy." It is defined as a "surgical interruption of nerve tracts to and from the frontal lobe of the brain [and] often results in marked cognitive and personality changes.")[1] Adamson said: "It was suggested that I might help the patients to paint for themselves. I was dubious but I resolved to try" (Hogan, 2001, p. 203). Like many, the artist Adamson was employed to do research and discovered the uses of art as therapy on his own. Adamson later established a gallery of patient artwork and developed paintings for diagnosing specific psychiatric disorders. In *Art As Healing* (1984) Adamson describes his experiences. His research was the first "rigorous attempt in British psychiatry to ascertain the usefulness of art as therapy" (Hogan, 2001, p. 80).

Carl Jung's ideas dominated much of art therapy in Great Britain. A Jungian psychoanalyst Irene Champernowne and her husband, Gilbert, who had been a theologian, founded The Withymead Centre for Psychotherapy Through the Arts in Devon, England; Withymead was the first therapeutic center devoted to art therapy. The Champernownes moved into Withymead House in 1942 four years after their marriage. It began as a home and gradually expanded into an institution housing up to 40 patients. The influence for the arts at Withymead came directly from C. G. Jung who emphasized the need for a development of creativity for psychiatric patients. Withymeade provided a great impetus for the development of art therapy in Great Britain during the 1940s and '50s.

The British Art Therapy Association was founded in 1964. Waller (1992b) describes British art therapy in the 1960s and early 1970s as:

> . . . art therapy practice was not unlike a sensitive form of art teaching–similar to that of the best art colleges where the therapist took care to encourage the patients to develop their own form of visual expression and . . . [enter] into a supportive, non confrontative [sic] relationship. . . . Although some found art therapists had experience of psychotherapy

---

1. Retrieved September 16, 2009 from wordnetweb.princeton.edu/perl/webwn

themselves or had some training in psychology, it was not until the late 1970s and early 1980s that some . . . developed a stronger orientation toward psychodynamic practice. (p. 89)

Hogan (2001) asserts that the adherence to a Jungian paradigm as the major theory base for art therapy in Great Britain provided a decidedly spiritual and pseudo-religious orientation; she criticizes Waller for not acknowledging this. Writing about contemporary art therapy in Britain, Hogan states:

Art therapy today is a small profession with less than 2000 registered members in the UK. Training to become an art therapist is now a two-year, full-time post-graduate diploma. . . . The attitudes of many art therapists practicing today are not dissimilar from those of the pioneer art therapists, though the spiritual emphasis so characteristic of early art therapy as become rather muted. The dominance of the Jungian approach in general has dwindled . . . some art therapists seem to think that art therapy developed exclusively out of psychoanalysis. (2001, p. 315)

Books describing the history of art therapy in Great Britain are Waller's 1991 *Becoming a Profession* and Hogan's 2001, *Healing Arts, The History of Art Therapy.*

CANADA

According to Lois Woolf Barch (2003) in "Art therapy in Canada: Origins and Explorations"[2] art therapy in Canada had four pioneers: Psychiatrist Martin Fischer in Toronto, Selwyn and Irene Dewdney in London, Ontario and Marie Revai in Quebec. Most training programs in art therapy were established outside academic institutions as free-standing institutes. The exception is the Masters program at Concordia University in Montreal founded by Revai in 1983.

Canadian art therapists followed the educational and practice guidelines set up by the American Art Therapy Association and were often members of AATA. In 1972, Revai received Registration (ATR) by the

---

2. From the keynote address given at the Canadian Art Therapy Conference, Toronto, Ontario, Canada, 2003.

American Art Therapy Association. Kay Collis, who was the founding President of the British Columbia Art Therapy Association in 1978, attended the meeting in 1969 in which the American Art Therapy Association was formed.

Kay Collis was an art student at the University of Victoria, British Columbia when she was invited to develop an art program at the Victoria Mental Health Center, an outpatient institution which was part of a psychiatric hospital. Following is an interview with Kay Collis by Art Therapist Michelle Winkel, MA, ATR, who is the new Director of the British Columbia School of Art Therapy.

Interview with Kay Collis by Michelle Winkel, MA, ATR

MW: How did you start the work of art therapy?

KC: I had a nurse friend who worked in psychiatry at the local mental health center. . . . She said, "Kay, do you think you could help me with my patients at the hospital?". . . The population I was asked to work with were mainly suffering with schizophrenia . . . . I worked unpaid for four years at the Victoria Mental Health Centre. . . . I would meet with social workers, psychiatrists, nurses and discuss patient progress. I taught many of the staff to look at and understand the artwork of patients.

KC: In 1969 I had no idea what art therapy was. I was only a volunteer teaching art to people with schizophrenia! A good friend of mine was visiting the Menninger Clinic in Topeka, Kansas. She told the staff there "We have one of what you have" (meaning art therapist.) The Menninger brothers requested slides of the work I was doing . . . I sent slides and progress notes . . . this was before medication was common for patients with schizophrenia. For my Masters thesis, I categorized it [art] into the stages and phases of disintegration within the acute and chronic [schizophrenic] framework. Robert Ault [see Chapter 12 of this book] wrote back [from Menningers'] and said "You are an art therapist." It was somewhat of a revelation to know that I could call the work I did "art therapy." I was invited to attend the founding meeting of the American Art Therapy Association in Louisville, Kentucky. . . . I was the only Canadian attending . . . I became an active member just by being present at the founding in 1969.

Regarding the status of Canadian art therapy today, Barch (2003) writes: "While we are still pioneering this work, while we still do not have too many jobs advertising for art therapists. . . . There are more of us . . . a growing presence across Canada" (p. 6).

IMPORTANT DATES AND EVENTS

1930s–Waller (1992b) writes that the term "art therapy" is used in Britain since the late 1930s.

1940–Margaret Naumburg in the United States defines "dynamically oriented art therapy" establishing art therapy as a separate mental health discipline.

1942–In Great Britain, artist Rita Simon conducts "social psychiatry clubs," groups for outpatients under the auspices of social psychiatrist Joshua Bierer. Adrian Hill credited with coining the term "art therapy." Irene Champernowne and her husband Gilbert move to Withymead House in Devon and found the Withymead Center for Psychotherapy Through the Arts–the first therapeutic center dedicated to art therapy. Both Champernownes are Jungians.

1946–Artist Edward Adamson is hired as an art therapist at Netherne Psychiatric Hospital.

1950s–Canadian Marie Revai teaches art to psychiatric patients at Alan Memorial Institute, Montreal in the outpatient department.

1949 & 1954–Canadians Selwyn and Irene Dewdney work as art therapists at Westminister Veterans Hospital in Ontario.

1964–The British Art Therapy Association is founded.

1960s & 1970s–According to Waller (1992b) art therapy of this period is a sensitive form of art teaching.

1960s–Toronto psychiatrist Martin Fischer initiates residential treatment for children and adolescents.

1967–Fischer establishes the Toronto Art Therapy Institute.

1969–At the invitation of Robert Ault, Kay Collis–a Canadian art therapist–attends the founding meeting of the American Art Therapy Association. She is the only Canadian there.

1977–The Canadian Art Therapy Association is founded by Marie Revai.

1978–The British Columbia Art Therapy Association is established. Kay Collis is Founder-President. The Ontario Art Therapy

Association established.

Early 1980s–Canadian Marie Revai founds the graduate art therapy program at Concordia University in Quebec. For many years it is the only art therapy education program within an academic institution. First it is a diploma program, with Michael Edwards as director. Then it becomes an MA in Art Education with a specialization in Art Therapy. Concordia received the first international "Approval" from the American Art Therapy Association in 1985.

1982–Quebec Art Therapy Association founded.

STUDY QUESTIONS

1. Describe the important differences between art therapy in Great Britain and America.
2. Name the important Canadian milestones in the development of art therapy in that country.

Part II

ART THERAPY DEVELOPING

Chapter 10

THE 1960s: THEIR INFLUENCE ON
THE DEVELOPMENT OF ART THERAPY[1]

The 1960s were turbulent years in America, full of potential and actual change and at times, full of rage. Moving away from the conservative 1950s, the United States embraced revolutionary ways of thinking, many of which continue to evolve today. Andy Warhol and Pop Art became popular; Marshall McLuhan wrote about technology as an important driver of modern society. Many consider that Rachel Carson with her book *The Silent Spring,* jump-started the modern environmental movement and Truman Capote changed journalism and the novel forever with his *In Cold Blood,* a true story about the murder of a family in Kansas.

Many young people turned to eastern mysticism and religion. At Harvard, Timothy Leary and Richard Alpert (who later became Baba Ram Dass, a Hindu spiritual leader) experimented with the use of psychedelic drugs on human subjects. They were fired for it. (Alpert wrote a book called *Be Here Now.*) The hippie movement, originally a youth movement which spread worldwide, was born—advocating free love, community and higher consciousness through drugs; Woodstock occurred in August of 1969. The 60s was the era of folk/protest songs, Elvis and the Beatles. Marijuana use increased and respect for authority declined. John F. Kennedy was inaugurated President in 1961 and created the Peace Corps soon after.

---

1. The information in this history of the 1960s is collected from Kclibrary.lonestar.edu/decade60.html-103k, www-VL:history:United States-1960-1969/1960 history, www.Thepeopleshistory.com/1960s.html, en.wikipedia.org/wiki/Feminism-393k, en.wikipedia.org/wiki/African-American__ civil__rights__movement__ 1955-1967-293k and Weller, S. (2008). *Girls Like Us.* New York: NY: Atria Books.

Kennedy's 1963 Community Mental Health Act created a fertile ground for innovation and expansion in mental health and offered an important opportunity for the new field of art therapy. Under the umbrella of the National Institute of Mental Health, it provided grants to states to create community-based care for people with psychiatric problems. In 1954, the new major tranquilizers such as Thorazine emerged which made possible the release of many patients from psychiatric hospitals. The intention of Kennedy's bill was to deinstitutionalize patients who had been warehoused in psychiatric hospitals some for years, and create instead community-based care. The infusion of large amounts of money into local communities and the building of community mental health centers helped drive the formation of art therapy as an important mental health discipline.

With the incentive of World War II and the new forms of therapy used to treat the veterans of that war, the 60s was a decade in which many new psychological theories and philosophies emerged; it was a time in which Humanistic psychology and innovative and experimental methods to help psychiatric patients heal were encouraged. Art therapy was one of these. Unfortunately, the results of the Community Mental Health Act were mixed: Some states saw it as an opportunity to close expensive psychiatric hospitals and in many instances mental health services in the community were never established at all.

Kennedy was assassinated in 1963 resulting in intense national mourning, internal reflection and a drive for social change across the United States. Vice President Lyndon Baines Johnson succeeded Kennedy and won re-election on his own in 1964. His Civil Rights Act in 1964, first crafted by Kennedy, making segregation and discrimination illegal, is thought to be a tremendous achievement in this country. But unfortunately Johnson's adherence to the tragedy of the Vietnam War brought him down. College campuses became centers of discourse and argument. Students and many others across the country protested against the draft and the Vietnam War. Johnson refused to run for President again and was succeeded by Richard Nixon who promised to end the War but escalated it. In 1970, four students at Kent State University in Ohio were killed and nine injured by the Ohio National Guard as they protested the War and the American invasion of Cambodia.

For the Civil Rights Movement, the 1960s was a time of great personal courage and forward movement which would eventually, in

2008, result in the first African-American, biracial Barack Obama's election as President of the United States. Congressman John Lewis, age 23 and leader of the Student Nonviolent Coordinating Committee (SNIC) led a march for voter registration in Selma, Alabama. His was the first skull to be hit with a police nightstick. In all, 90 demonstrators were injured. Lewis said:

> Barack [Obama] was born long before he could experience or understand the [civil rights] movement. . . . He had to move toward it in his own time, but it is so clear that he digested it, the spirit and the language of the movement. . . . But at the same time, he doesn't have the scars of the movement, because of how he grew up. He has not been knocked around as much by the past. (Remnick, 2009, p. 22-23)

It is said that when he autographed a photograph for John Lewis at his inauguration, Barack Obama wrote: "Because of you, John" (Remnick, 2009, p. 23).

With the Civil Rights Movement's brave efforts to end discrimination in voting, interstate commerce and segregation in Southern states, the nation saw a series of occurrences in which usually peaceful protestors were ambushed, beaten and jailed by the Ku Klux Klan and others: In Selma, Alabama alone, over 250 were arrested when state troopers and local law enforcement attacked demonstrators. 1960 dawned with Sit-ins at the lunch counters of Woolworth intended to gain the right for Blacks to have a meal alongside whites. Freedom rides occurred in 1961 with Mississippi Freedom Summer in which busloads of mostly white college students came south to work with Blacks on voter registration. In the Birmingham campaign, Americans were shocked at the brutal response to Sit-ins by Police Chief Eugene "Bull" Conner.

In 1963, A. Philip Randolph and Bayard Rustin organized the "March on Washington," a collaborative effort of civil rights organizations, progressive labor and other liberal organizations. Attendees at the March were estimated to be between 200,000 and 300,000 people. It was here that Martin Luther King, the leader of the non-violent wing of the Civil Rights Movement, gave his famous "I have a dream" speech. King received the Nobel Peace Price in 1964 at age 35. He was the youngest man ever to receive it. King's great ally was President Lyndon Johnson. But King's stance against the war in Vietnam caused an irreparable rift between the two.

In 1968, Martin Luther King was assassinated in Memphis as he went to aid the city's sanitation workers. In response, riots broke out in 110 cities nationwide which may have largely destroyed Black business for many years. In the effort to quell what was viewed by the FBI and others as the violent Black power wing of the Civil Rights Movement, many ended up dead or in jail.

African Americans who embraced "Black Power" eschewed King's non-violent means and, following the ideology of Malcolm X and the Nation of Islam, sought to battle inequality "by any means necessary." Malcolm left the Nation of Islam in 1994 advocating against racism of any kind. Less than a year later, in 1965, he was murdered. Martin Luther King had argued for nonviolence as a moral stance which he felt would finally break down the barriers of discrimination. When the morality of desegregation did not win out, African Americans grew impatient and the Black Power movement was born.

Black power advocates, expressed longstanding rage about their treatment, demanded equal rights immediately and set about attempting to make things so difficult for whites, they would have to acquiesce. The Black Panthers, originally a neighborhood organization in Oakland, CA that provided meals for poor children, nationally endorsed revolution as the method to end discrimination and used a black panther as its symbol. Although it is seen as strongly connected to violence, the Black Panther symbol actually had come from a Freedom Political Party of African Americans in the South. The Black Panthers were joined in their approach by the Student Nonviolent Coordinating Committee (SNIC) and other civil rights groups which had first coalesced to support King's brand of nonviolence but especially with his killing, had become impatient and disillusioned.

A scant two months after the assassination of King, Bobby Kennedy, long considered an ally of civil rights and anti-segregation running for President and against the War, was murdered. Then in August 1968, at the Democratic Convention in Chicago, protestors were jailed and gunned down by police and Illinois National Guard. Promising to end the war in Vietnam, Richard Nixon was elected President of the United States in November of 1968.

In 1969, the Stonewall Rebellion occurred. The Stonewall Inn in Greenwich Village, New York was a gay bar consistently raided by police. In June of 1969, when police once again raided, the inhabitants of the bar spontaneously fought back. The Stonewall Rebellion is recognized as the beginning of activism for civil and equal rights for gays and lesbians in the twentieth century.

There is ever-widening use of the birth control pill in the United States. Tyler (1999) writes about "impact on various aspects of social life, women's health, fertility trends, laws and policies, religion, interpersonal relationships and family roles, feminist issues and gender relations, sexual practices among both adults and adolescents" (p. 115). By 1967, 12.5 million women worldwide are on the pill.

Perhaps in part due to the ease and safety of birth control, during the 60s, the Women's Movement was created and flourished, propelling the most important social change of the twentieth century. In 1961, John Kennedy established the first Presidential Commission on the Status of Women and appointed as Chair, Elinor Roosevelt at a time when some women worked outside the home, but received only 63 percent of men's salaries. Ironically, the 60s was also the era of the gigantic success of Barbie Dolls. The Civil Rights Act of 1964 was amended to include gender and the birth control pill became widely available. The congressman who included gender in the bill has called it a joke. Mary McCarthy's *The Group* was published in 1962 and Sylvia Plath's autobiographical *The Bell Jar* appeared in 1963. Both wrote of women's roles outside the home which spelled a departure from the "happy" wife and mother roles of post World War II 1950s.

In 1963, Betty Friedan's controversial *The Feminine Mystique* was published resonating with women across the country and igniting the Women's Liberation Movement. It is widely known as one of the most important and influential nonfiction books of the twentieth century because it recognized the unhappiness of many women of the time who had abandoned their own identity, to find identity through husband and children. In large part, it gave permission and impetus for women to create an identity of their own, as they saw fit—a stunning and essential concept provoking major change in women, in men and in the culture and still playing out in contemporary American culture.

In 1964, Margaret Chase Smith of Maine became the first woman to seek her political party's nomination for President. The National Association for Women (NOW) was created in 1966. Other important movers and shakers of the Women's Movement were Kate Millet, Robin Morgan, Ellen Willis, Kathie Amatniek, Nancy Chodorow, Jo Freeman, Germaine Greer and Gloria Steinem who established *Ms.*

Magazine which became a major instrument for feminist voices in the early 1970s. August, 1970, on the 50th anniversary of women's suffrage in America, thousands of women marched up Fifth Avenue in New York.

Fulfilling President John F. Kennedy's promise, in 1969 a man landed on the moon. Astronaut Buzz Aldrin said: "One small step for man, one giant leap for mankind."

IMPORTANT DATES AND EVENTS

1960–The FDA approves the use of Enovid as a birth control pill.

1960–There are Sit-ins at lunch counters to end racial discrimination across the South. Barbie (dolls) are invented.

1961–John Kennedy is inaugurated President of the United States.

1961–Kennedy establishes the first Presidential Commission on the Status of Women. Elinor Roosevelt is appointed first Chair.

1963–Kennedy's Community Mental Health Act passes.

1963–John Kennedy is assassinated in Dallas, Texas. Lyndon Johnson becomes President.

1963–Plath's *The Bell Jar* published.

1963–Friedan's *Feminine Mystique* is published.

1963–Civil rights march on Washington, D.C.

1964–Lyndon Johnson wins the Presidency of the United States by 61%. Promises to carry out JFK's programs.

1964–Under Johnson, the Vietnam War escalates. College campuses become places of dissent and debate.

1964–Kennedy's Civil Rights Act is passed.

1964–Margaret Chase Smith of Maine is the first woman to seek her party's nomination for President.

1964-1965–Summer riots occur in Black ghettos.

1964–Martin Luther King, age 35, wins the Nobel Peace Prize.

1965–Malcolm X, Black Power advocate, is murdered February 21st.

1965–Under Lyndon Baines Johnson, Medicare and Medicaid begin.

1966–National Association for Women (NOW) is established.

1967–There are 12.5 million women worldwide on the pill.

1968–Because of the Vietnam War March 31st, Lyndon Johnson announces he will not run for another term as President of the United States.

1968–Martin Luther King is assassinated April 4th.

1968–Presidential candidate, Bobby Kennedy is assassinated June 5th.

1968–At the Democratic Convention in Chicago, demonstrators are jailed and shot by police and the Illinois National Guard.

1968–November, Richard Nixon, vowing to end the war in Vietnam, wins the Presidency of the United States.

July 1969–Lunar landing.

1969–Woodstock.

1969–Stonewall Rebellion occurs. From now on gays will work for equal rights.

1970–Four students protesting against the Vietnam War and the invasion of Cambodia at Kent State University are killed by the Ohio National Guard. Nine students are injured.

STUDY QUESTIONS

1. Describe the turbulence of the 60s and their influence on American culture.
2. Discuss the influence of the Civil Rights Movement on the development of art therapy as a separate profession.
3. What are your ideas about the influences of the Women's Movement on art therapy?
4. What was the impact of Kennedy's Community Mental Health Act on the expansion of the field of art therapy?

Chapter 11

MYRA LEVICK (b. 1924)
AND THE FORMATION OF THE
AMERICAN ART THERAPY ASSOCIATION

Myra Levick is fond of saying she established the *first* art therapy program in the country. Technically, she is wrong about this (see below and Chapter 17). But along with her initiation of the Hahneman/Drexel art therapy Masters program, the first graduate art therapy Masters program in the country, what she *did* achieve was the establishment of the American Art Therapy Association (AATA). Her founding of AATA was a huge milestone in the development of art therapy in America. Art therapy could never have become the profession it did without the American Art Therapy Association and for almost 40 years, the American Art Therapy Association *was* art therapy. She didn't do it alone, but it was her courage and consistency which made it possible. The establishment of the American Art Therapy Association is quite possibly the seminal event in the history of the field.

In 1957, Dr. Roger White, a member of the Psychology Department at the University of Louisville, established an art therapy training program located in both the Psychology and Art Departments. Not directed by an art therapist, it graduated two people and in 1959 closed, remaining inactive for ten years until 1969. According to Sandra Kagin (Graves-Alcorn), Margaret Naumburg gave a Grand Rounds presentation which incensed faculties of both Art and Psychology departments, and "the program became dormant" (Personal communication, 2009).

During the time the University of Louisville program was closed,

with the encouragement of psychiatrists Paul Fink and Morris
Goldman, Myra Levick was appointed Co-Director of the first graduate art therapy training program in the country at Hahnemann Hospital and Medical College in Philadelphia (now Drexel University)[1]
where she was hired as a faculty member in the medical school in
charge of developing all aspects of a graduate art therapy training program.[2] She was also "Activities Director" for the mental health center.

Before that Levick had become an art therapist in the usual
serendipitous fashion of the times: As the wife of a doctor with three
young daughters, Levick became a student at the Moore College of
Art in Philadelphia. She graduated with a Bachelor's degree in painting. She applied to Bryn Mawr College for a Masters degree in Art
History but before she could attend she was "waylaid" into art therapy.[3] She writes:

> . . . the director of the first open unit for mentally disturbed patients in
> a general hospital in Philadelphia posted a notice on the bulletin board
> at Moore seeking a graduate to work as an "art therapist." I had no idea
> what an art therapist was but I was intrigued. (Levick in Junge &
> Wadeson, 2006, p. 128)

> . . . [Psychiatrist, Morris Goldman] . . . said that he thought an artist had
> a great deal to offer in working with emotionally disturbed patients and
> if I would bring my art skills, he would teach me how. He told me there
> were art therapists in the country about which I knew nothing. (Levick,
> 1975)

Beginning in 1963, Levick began work as an art therapist at Albert
Einstein Medical Center North:

---

1. The Hahnemann program became "Creative Arts in Therapy." Students could specialize in art
therapy, dance/movement therapy or music therapy. Levick was the Director of all. Hahnemann
eventually changed its name to "Drexel."
2. For the first few months, until his sudden death at the age of 39, Morris Goldman actually held
the title of Director of the art therapy program. After that, Paul Jay Fink took over.
3. Much of Myra Levick's history comes from her memoir in Junge & Wadeson, 2006. Many years
later, after she had become an art therapist, she earned her Ph.D. from Bryn Mawr. Before that, at
Goldman's insistence she had attained a Master's degree in adolescent psychology and education
at Temple University.

[I] had the opportunity to utilize my talent and [art] training as a painter in a 29-bed inpatient unit for adults suffering from moderate neurosis to severe psychosis . . . my job title was "art therapist" and one of my first tasks was to learn what that implied. (Levick 1983, p. 11)

Levick credits Morris J. Goldman with "plucking" her out of painting and offering her the opportunities which opened her pioneering career in the new art therapy field. In 1967, six students were accepted into Levick's new program at Hahnemann Medical College in Philadelphia. She states: "There was no national association, no defined criteria for what an art therapist is" (Levick in Junge & Wadeson, 2006, p. 131). She wrote and received a National Institute of Mental Health grant to train clinical art therapists. This grant is still the only one ever awarded for art therapist training.

Levick's broad experience in art psychotherapy and her contributions to the field extend far beyond her founding of the American Art Therapy Association. Her remarkable career both reflects the expansiveness of the art therapy field itself and helped immeasurably to drive it forward. Nevertheless, Levick's courage, energy and perseverance that helped initiate the American Art Therapy Association may be her major gift–in that what she and a few others created, enabled the development of art therapy into a respected and viable mental health profession. Levick was the first President of AATA.

THE ESTABLISHMENT OF THE AMERICAN ART THERAPY ASSOCIATION–A SEPARATE ORGANIZATION FOR ART THERAPISTS

Beginnings

Art therapists were meeting each other through presenting papers and workshops at psychiatric conferences such as the American Psychiatric Association and the International Society for Psychopathology of Expression (ISPE.)[4] Founded in 1966, the members of ISPE, were primarily interested in pathology and psychology manifested in artwork. Although the Society tended to be controlled by

---

4. ISPE later became "The International Society for Psychopathology of Expression and Art Therapy."

psychiatrists, some art therapists were officers in the Society and art therapists regularly participated (D. Jones, Personal communication, 1993). After ISPE's founding by psychiatrist Irene Jakab in Verona, Italy, art therapists talked of establishing their own organization. Art therapists at those first meetings were: Marge Howard from Oklahoma, who had studied sexually abused children and their art-work, Sandra Kagin (Graves-Alcorn) also living then in Oklahoma and working with retarded children, Tarmo Pasto from Sacramento State Psychiatric Hospital and Elinor Ulman, publisher and editor of the first art therapy journal.

Psychiatrist Irene Jakab, whom Judith Rubin refers to "as the god-mother of art therapy" edited a number of the Society's Proceedings[5] which effectively showcased art therapists and their work. One of Jakab's early volumes (1969), titled *Art Interpretation and Art Therapy*, contains essays by art therapists Margaret Howard, Elsie Muller, Bernard Stone, Donald Uhlin, Tarmo Pasto and Harriet Wadeson.

Why Form a Separate Art Therapy Organization?

Against the background of the 1960s, art therapists participating in other organizations like the International Society for Psychopathology of Expression, wanted to establish their own that would focus not only on pathology in art but also *its treatment*. They wanted an organization in which psychiatrists were not necessarily in control, but where art and therapy and its practitioners–not the established mental health hierarchy–were central. In 1966, Naumburg's book *Dynamically Oriented Art Therapy* was published which defined the theoretical constructs underlying art therapy.[6] Publication of Naumburg's book gave a tremendous impetus to the forward movement of the new profession.

In 1968, a group met in Boston at the American Psychiatric Association to discuss forming a separate art therapy society; Paul Fink of Hahnemann hosted the group. Myra Levick wrote the minutes. Along with Levick, those attending that meeting were Margaret Naumburg, Jane Gilbert, Lynn Flexner Berger, Carolyn Refsness Kniazzeh, Hanna Kwiatkowska and Miriam Dergalis (Junge, 1994).

---

5. Jakab 1968, 1969 and 1971.
6. These had been discussed in Naumburg's previous books and in her nationwide presentations, but this 1966 book formally laid out her theoretical constructs.

Two psychiatrists were also there: Mardi Horowitz, from the University of California Medical School, San Francisco and Paul Jay Fink from Hahnemann Hospital and Medical College in Philadelphia. The attendees talked over the issues regarding a new organization and agreed that its formation would go a long way toward defining art therapy as a separate, important ancillary psychiatric discipline.

Across the country art therapists were beginning to talk about forming a separate organization. For example, Don Jones and Robert Ault, by now working together at Menningers' drank endless cups of coffee and dreamed of a national organization. Ault looked upon Jones as a mentor and father figure. Ironically, Jones left Menningers' for Harding Hospital in Ohio just before the letter came from Myra Levick with an invitation to come to Philadelphia to discuss the formation of a national organization (Ault in Junge & Wadeson, 2006). Thus both Jones and Ault were able to attend the meeting and were central in the formation of the new organization. Robert Ault would be the second President of the American Art Therapy Association and Don Jones, the fourth.

Influences

Along with the previously mentioned occurrences and the publication of Naumburg's seminal book, in my opinion, the following cultural winds in the United States probably helped give impetus to the initiation of a new professional organization for art therapy:

- The Women's Liberation Movement;
- Kennedy's 1963 Community Mental Health Act as part of his New Frontier created an era of flourishing financial expansion and innovation in mental health and the need for increased and talented staff, including art therapists;
- Teachings from the politics of the Civil Rights Movement. The medical hierarchy and its stranglehold on the psychiatric community led to the formation of an organization to further art therapy as a separate discipline.

The Women's Liberation Movement and Art Therapy

Most pioneers from the early days of art therapy are women. (Don Jones and Robert Ault were obvious exceptions and there were some others.) In the era after World War II, cultural edicts commanded that middle-class women stay home with husband and family (and, unless they needed to work for financial reasons, most women did.) It was at this time that, unusual art therapy women stepped out to form the profession of art therapy. They were undoubtedly bright, energetic and driven. They often had support and mentoring by male psychiatrists and psychologists. But it was primarily these women of courage, fighting against cultural and internal tides, who founded the national art therapy profession and the American Art Therapy Association. They soon went on to form art therapy Masters programs to provide education to future generations, in universities and colleges across the United States and, for the most part, managed to survive in the male-dominated academy. Indeed, today, most art therapy Masters programs are directed by women.

Although the vast majority of art therapists are women, art therapy as a women's profession is largely unacknowledged. Exceptions are my own writings in Junge, 1994 and Junge, 2008 where I wrote a chapter called "Art Therapy as a Woman's Profession." In my opinion, the art therapy profession has suffered from the internal and external constraints and oppression of cultural sexism. For example, the early and ubiquitous fighting within the American Art Therapy Association could have been largely due to the strong group of women who found there a safe arena for their heated debates and anger when they had no other in the "outside" world. If this is the case, who can blame them?

The Changing Face of Mental Health Treatment in the United States and John Kennedy's Community Mental Health Act and Art Therapy

The 1963 Community Mental Health Act was President John Kennedy's attempt to deinstitutionalize psychiatric hospital inmates and create care for them in their own communities. Unfortunately, this intention was not always carried out as some states saw the bill as an opportunity to close expensive psychiatric hospitals and the community care aspect did not necessarily follow. Nevertheless, in general, a great deal of funding came to the states for expansion of community services and the development of innovative care. Community mental health centers were originally mandated to serve a "catchment" area of about 200,000 people. Staffing these centers proved to be a ready job market for newly trained therapists, including art therapists.

Community Mental Health Centers were intended to be a nation-wide network of locally-based community care facilities—outpatient clinics for mental health patients who could not afford traditional outpatient services. While resources and programs at the centers varied, they were generally mandated to have outpatient services for children, adolescents, adults and the elderly, 24-hour a day emergency services and screening for psychiatric hospital admission. Most functioned on a "sliding scale" for fees for services. This seldom covered the cost of basic services which was made up by the federal government. They were on the lookout for innovative cost-effective services and talented staff members.

With the notable exception of Margaret Naumburg, up until this time, most art therapists found work as adjunctive therapists—part of a treatment team and "adjunctive" to the psychiatrist leader—in psychiatric hospitals, often working with chronically-ill patients. Employment in a community mental health center gave art therapists new clinical experience with a variety of clients and different problem populations in outpatient settings which expanded their horizons and opportunities. For example, in Southern California where the medical hierarchy was much less stringent than that in the East, with the leadership of Helen Landgarten, many art therapists were hired as primary therapists, equal to other mental health professionals and carrying the full responsibility and decision-making of the case. This was my own experience. Coming into the field just as the community mental health centers were being established, my first and second student internships were in community mental health centers. I was later hired as a staff art therapist at Thalians Community Mental Health Center, Cedars Sinai Hospital in Los Angeles.

The Civil Rights Movement and Art Therapy

The decade of the 60s saw many civil rights activists working to change racial discrimination in the United States. From the lunch counter Sit-ins early in the 1960s, through the award to Martin Luther King of the Nobel Peace Prize in 1964, the Black Power Movement, and congress' Civil Rights Act, the brave struggles and lessons of the Civil Rights Movement are many. Its meaning to the development of art therapy is that it may well have been used as a model for change and growth: The clear message of the Civil Rights Movement was that those who were concerned needed to become activists. As African Americans and others came to see it as their own fight to end discrimination and segregation in the United States, so art therapists quite likely recognized that other mental health professions encumbered with the medical model and hierarchy and having other pursuits and interests would not be "granting them permission" to exist and to flourish. For example, Jones saw the Society for Psychopathology of Expression as "something of a 'caste system' in which the art therapists were 'invited guests." He said that art therapists wanted to discuss treatment options in addition to pathology in art. (D. Jones, Personal communication, 1993). It began to be widely recognized that if art therapy was to become a separate and respected mental health profession, it needed to be accomplished by art therapists themselves. The first step was to initiate a distinct professional organization to further the cause of art therapy and to establish professional standards of practice and education.

In my first book about art therapy history (Junge, 1994) I argued that this self-separation to establish an identity and purpose was often an important first step of a minority groups advancement toward equality. Margaret Naumburg's 1966 publication of *Dynamically Oriented Art Therapy* provided impetus for a new profession in that it carefully laid out a theoretical basis for art therapy. Through forming the American Art Therapy Association (AATA), the field of art therapy would begin to proclaim itself a special and significant field with well-trained practitioners whose skills and expertise were distinctive from other mental health disciplines and which could add immeasurably to them. As I see it, the founding of the American Art Therapy Association was the most important step in the history of art therapy's development and its propulsion toward becoming a legitimate profession.

Levick's Contribution:
The Importance of the American Art Therapy
Association to the Development of the Field

In 1969, with Paul Jay Fink's support, Myra Levick became the driving force and energy that helped create the American Art Therapy

Association. Levick's was a tremendous contribution and *a major turning point* in the development of the field. Levick was elected the first President of the American Art Therapy Association.

With the formation of the American Art Therapy Association, Levick and her colleagues changed the course of art therapy as a profession. As Margaret Naumburg had first done with her declaration of a theoretical basis, with the founding of the American Art Therapy Association, Levick irrevocably emphasized art therapy as a separate mental health discipline with unique standards of practice and a particular training and education of its own. Art therapists felt a burgeoning sense of identity as practitioners of an innovative and different kind of mental health; as the American Art Therapy Association grew, so the growth of identity and self esteem of its members grew. It is my belief that the seminal, course-changing occurrences in art therapy to this time were:

- The creation of two major art therapy theories: Naumburg and Kramer creating a theoretical bedrock for the new profession (ca. 1953 & 1958).
- Ulman's establishment of *The Bulletin of Art Therapy* in 1961, the first and for 12 years the *only,* art therapy journal.
- Margaret Naumburg's definition of "dynamically oriented art therapy" as separate from psychologically oriented art education and art teaching in collaboration with psychiatrists (1966).
- Myra Levick's energy, organizational skills and leadership which, in 1969 pulled people together to create a national organization, the American Art Therapy Association.

Steps to Founding the American Art Therapy Association

As part of her role as Director of the Art Therapy Masters Program at Hahnemann Hospital, in Philadelphia, Myra Levick with Paul Jay Fink created a series of lectures given by prominent art therapists: Elinor Ulman, Hanna Kwiatkowska, Margaret Naumburg, Edith Kramer and Harriet Wadeson were invited. In December 1968, Fink and Levick convened an organizational meeting and invited all the art therapists they could find. Helen Landgarten helped prepare the first list and 50 art therapists attended (80 people in all). The minutes of that meeting report that a decision was made to have *only* art therapists

Figure 11-1. "Ad Hoc Committee to Form the American Art Therapy Association." Back: Robert Ault and Don Jones. Front (L-R): Felice Cohen, Myra Levick, and Elinor Ulman.

as voting members. An *Ad Hoc* Steering Committee was elected consisting of Elinor Ulman, Don Jones, Felice Cohen, Robert Ault and Myra Levick. Edith Kramer and Margaret Naumburg had been nominated but were not elected to the Committee.

Robert Ault described:

[That first meeting was] very heated. Margaret Naumburg was there. She was a very old woman with a hearing loss. She would sit with her cane and every time someone said something she didn't want to hear, she would knock her cane on the floor . . . those initial days, they were something else. . . (Ault, 1975, no page number). When the vote was taken, Margaret was furious, got up, shook her finger at us and announced, "I'm not through with you" and stormed out of the room. I sat there in shock. The grandmother of our profession had just shaken her finger at me . . . but the story doesn't end there. In the following years we exchanged a number of very warm and caring letters. Shortly before her death, she asked me to review her book, and she seemed receptive to my comments about the importance of using what she had created for patients all over the country. I am glad that our paths crossed in this way and there was a different kind of closure. (Ault in Junge & Wadeson, 2006, pp. 70-71)

The *Ad Hoc* Committee was given the task of evolving a constitution and bylaws for the new organization and locating American and Canadian art therapists. According to Levick, there had already been editorials in the *Bulletin* pro and con about starting a separate organization which had galvanized the few art therapists there were. Levick was described as that "redheaded upstart at Hahnemann" (Levick in Junge & Wadeson, 2006, p. 134). Alternately, Ault, upon meeting Levick at the organizing meeting described her as a "very bright, attractive, dynamic woman . . . [who] was determined that we get on with the business of organizing in spite of some real opposition" (Ault in Junge & Wadeson, 2006, p. 70). At the December 5th organizing meeting this exchange occurred:

> Dr. Fink explained that his concept of the meeting was for the art therapists to set up an organization for themselves. He did not think that psychiatrists should be members, and stated that the organization [should be] set up and handled by art therapists. Miss Ulman then emphasized that if art therapy divorced itself from art, it has lost its purpose of being. Miss Naumburg stated that she didn't feel that the group was considering that. . . . She felt that the group was not ready yet. . . . Mrs. Levick argued that the people were there because they wanted to get together to set-up this organization. Mr. Ault went on to say, "The reason people are her [sic] today is because we have been working independently throughout the country." (O'Kane, December 5, 1958. Minutes for art therapy meeting held in Philadelphia. Archives of the American Art Therapy Association. Topeka, KS: Menninger Foundation)

The minutes of the 1968 Philadelphia meeting clearly state that all wanted the new organization to include many definitions of art therapy and to be controlled only by art therapists, not psychiatrists as voting members. Yet Ulman, Kramer and Naumburg, fearful of control by psychiatrists, thought any kind of an organization was premature and that art therapy should be allowed to develop more fully before any organization was established. They vehemently opposed forming a national organization.

Then fearing that the new organization would be dominated by art psychotherapists, Elinor Ulman and Edith Kramer envisioned an art therapy profession that would include venues other than psychiatric. They urged "that art therapists 'look to an independent place in the broad field of special education and rehabilitation rather than limiting their sphere to that of an ancillary psychiatric discipline'" (Silver in Junge & Wadeson, 2006, p. 208). Afraid that the field would be prematurely defined, that it would be too psychotherapeutic in orientation and that it would be controlled by psychiatrists, a group led by Ulman and Kramer did everything they could to slow down or stop entirely the creation of an art therapy organization. In a letter dated May 8, 1969 and signed by Carolyn Refsnes Kniazzeh, Edith Kramer, Hanna Kwiatkowska, Margaret Naumburg and Elinor Ulman, they wrote:

> . . . The future of art therapy will be much brighter if those who formulate the objectives of the first national organization of art therapists look to an independent place in the broad field of special education and rehabilitation rather than limiting their sphere to that of an ancillary psychiatric discipline. (Letter, "To whom it may concern," May 8, 1969. Archives of the American Art Therapy Association. Topeka, KS: Menninger Foundation)

With the formation of AATA, although it had been bubbling near the surface for years, the "war" between art and therapy formally began.[7]

To form a constitution, Robert Ault consulted with William Sears of the Music Therapy Department at the University of Kansas. (In 1954, Sears had been one of the creators of the Music Therapy Association.) Ault also collected constitutions from the American Occupational Therapy Association, the American Speech and Hearing Association and a state art therapy association—the Wisconsin Art Therapy Association (R. Ault, personal communication, 1992). Ault and many others' intention was to create an organization with a strong centralized core. Ulman worked on another model which, according to Ault, had a weak national alliance and strong state units. At a June 27, 1969 meeting at Louisville, Kentucky after arguments that continued until 4 a.m., a constitution with a strong centralized body was adopted and the new American Art Therapy Association was voted into being.

The members of the new organization elected officers and committee chairs. The members of the first Executive Committee of the new American Art Therapy Association were: Myra Levick, President,

---

7. For a more expansive discussion of these "wars" see "Reconsidering the Wars Between Art and Therapy" in *Mourning, Memory and Life Itself, Essays by an Art Therapist,* Junge, 2008.

Figure 11-2. "First American Art Therapy Association Executive Board." Back (L-R): Robert Ault, Ben Ploger, Bernard Stone, Margaret Howard, and Don Jones. Seated: Elsie Mjller, Felice Cohen, Myra Levick, and Hanna Yaxa Kwiatkowska. Floor: Sandra Kagin (Graves-Alcorn) and Helen Landgarten.

Robert Ault, President Elect; Margaret Howard (Oklahoma), Treasurer; Felice Cohen (Texas), Secretary; Elsie Muller (Missouri), Constitution; Sandra Kagin (now Graves-Alcorn) (Kentucky), Education; Helen Landgarten (California), Public Information; Don Jones (Ohio), Publications; Ben Ploger (Louisiana), Professional Standards; Bernard Stone (Ohio), Membership; and Hanna Yaxa Kwiatkowska (Washington, DC), Research (Levick in Junge & Wadeson, 2006).

Edited by Don Jones, the first Newsletter of the newly formed American Art Therapy Association contained the following announcement from President Levick:

For the past 20 years artists have been involved in using their skills to aid in the diagnosis and treatment of psychiatric patients. . . . It is an established fact that an organization must be formed in order to attain professional recognition. And it is with great pleasure that we announce that the AATA was voted into being on June 27, 1969 in Louisville, Kentucky, by a representative group of art therapists from all over the country and Canada. The goals of this new group go far beyond merely formalizing that which has already been achieved. It is hoped that Art Therapy and its relation to mental health and education will be more clearly defined and further developed. (Levick, 1970b, p. 1)

Many on the original Executive Board of the American Art Therapy Association, such as Levick, Ault, Jones, Landgarten and Kwiatkowska are well known as "pioneers" of the profession. Others should be–such as Bernard Stone who ran a very sophisticated art psychotherapy program in Ohio for many years. Some contributed to the field as authors and/or innovators and directors of art therapy training programs; their endeavors are discussed in other sections of this book. But those early volunteers of the first Executive Board, as founding members of the American Art Therapy Association, in essential ways, helped to define the definitions and practice of the art therapy profession in the years to come. It is natural that many early art therapists were primarily clinicians and although their names may not be generally well known and many have passed on, they were extremely important in the formation of art therapy as a separate and enduring field and deserve our appreciation and gratitude.

First Executive Board

Elsie Muller and Margaret Howard

Elsie Muller (1913-1996) and Margaret Howard (1903-1994) were close friends who had both studied with Naumburg in New York. Marge Howard was from Tulsa, Oklahoma and was responsible for the original chartering of the American Art Therapy Association in Oklahoma. She was an active presenter and Treasurer at the American Society for Psychopathology of Expression and did studies of artwork of abused children. For many years, Howard was the art therapist at Children's Medical Center in Tulsa.

Muller practiced as an art therapist in Kansas City, Missouri at Gillis

Home for Children, Ozanam Home for Disturbed Adolescent Boys. She served on AATA's Executive Board from 1969-1973 as Constitution Chair and was Parliamentarian from 1970-1974. (Rubin in Junge & Wadeson, 2006). Rubin writes: "[Muller] was universally liked and admired. . . . She was . . . well regarded by everyone as a stabilizing force in the Association's early, tumultuous years" (Rubin in Junge & Wadeson, 2006, p. 62). She received the American Art Therapy Association's highest award, the Honorary Life Membership in 1976. In 1968, Muller published "Family Group Art Therapy: Treatment of Choice for a Specific Case," a ground-breaking paper which, along with Kwiatkowska's work would provide an important basis for family art therapy.

Ben Ploger

Ben Ploger (1908-1993) who was the first American Art Therapy Association's Professional Standards Chair came from New Orleans, Louisiana. Ploger's focus was toward clinical/patient art therapy. He was an art teacher in Houston in 1935 and became Professor and Chair of the Department of Fine Arts at Delgado College, New Orleans. Interestingly, Ploger taught art to mentally ill cloistered nuns in the religious unit of the De Paul Hospital. He practiced art therapy throughout the hospital and in 1965 became Director of Art Psychotherapy (Levick, 1981, p. 5). Ploger became a consultant in art therapy to De Paul Hospital and to River Oaks Hospital and was an ordained minister.

Felice Cohen

Felice Cohen (1919-2002) was a member of the Ad Hoc Committee to form AATA and founding Treasurer of the American Art Therapy Association. Levick describes her as "mesmerizing with her deep Texas drawl" (in Junge & Wadeson, 2006, p. 123). Cohen was a fourth generation Texan. Her friend, Irving Kraft, Chief of Child Psychiatry at Houston State Psychiatric Hospital read Naumburg's work and convinced Cohen to introduce art to the patients there. By 1968 she was Chief of Art Psychotherapy in the Texas Research Institute of Mental Sciences Family Service Unit. (The Institute later became associated with the University of Texas (Cohen, 1975a).) When mainstreaming laws mandated the integration of "special needs" children into regular

Figure 11-3. "Felice Cohen."

school classrooms, Cohen introduced art therapy into the Houston public school system (Cohen, 1975b) and in 1976, she published a case history on the treatment of a transsexual six-year-old boy (Cohen, 1976). In 1985, with the encouragement of psychologist Loretta Bender, Cohen designed a research study investigating incest markers in children's artwork.

Calling herself a "Sunday Painter" Felice Cohen had attended two years of medical school. But she considered herself a lone art therapist until she found the lifeline of Ulman's *Bulletin* and attended the formation meeting for AATA. She was one of the faction in favor of *not waiting* to establishing a national organization for art therapists. In a rather conciliatory letter to Elinor Ulman, a representative of the other side, Cohen explained: "I believe that the need is so great for the formation of a national society and I also believe that your years of experience, knowledge, integrity and support are of importance. . . . I want us to be a cohesive group with a positive goal. . ." (Cohen, F., April 16, 1969).[8]

---

8. The full text of Cohen's letter to Elinor Ulman appears in Junge, 1994.

Levick describes Cohen's excitement at meeting her heroines Ulman, Naumburg, Kramer and Kwiatkowska for the first time: "She maneuvered her way into having dinner with them. She also told me that somehow they maneuvered her into paying for everyone" (Levick in Junge & Wadeson, 2006, p. 124). With obvious leadership skills, Cohen became the third president of the American Art Therapy Association, after Myra Levick and Robert Ault, and in 1989 received the highest award in art therapy, the Honorary Life Membership given by her peers at the American Art Therapy Association.

Bernard Stone

Bernie Stone, from Ohio, was on the first American Art Therapy Association Executive Board as Membership Chair. (His contributions to art therapy are more fully discussed in Chapter 6, "Art Therapy in the Midwest.") Stone was a member of the International Society for Psychopathology of Expression before the American Art Therapy Association was established and published in Irene Jakab's books (Jakab, 1971, 1969, 1968). He calls Jakab "my first mentor in art therapy."

Distinctly an *art psychotherapist,* Stone found the American Art Therapy Association full of politics, divisions and exclusionary practices. As mentioned before, his unqualified and vehement elements of the definition of art therapy are (1) being in a clinical setting, (2) needing referral from a physician, (3) having "an identified client" and (4) coordinating with the patient's physician, nurses, social work staff and psychologists. In Ohio state hospital settings, Stone's art therapy services were reimbursed by insurance. He was possibly the very first art therapist to achieve reimbursement for his work. He wrote: "AATA was very self defeating in not following a sound *clinical* model and standards from the start" (B. Stone, personal communication, 2009).

Bernard Stone is now retired and living in Delaware. His last job was at the Upper Shores Community Mental Health Center in Chestertown, Maryland where he worked for 12 years. "It's been a challenging journey and I've had thousands of referred clients. . . . I was validated where I worked . . . the hospital life was real [and] tangible. . . . I rest in my work with clients." Stone never received the Honorary Life Membership award.

Sandra Kagin (Graves-Alcorn)

Sandra Graves-Alcorn (Nee Kagin) who had been trained and mentored by Marge Howard was living in Oklahoma working with developmentally delayed children, when, in 1966, she attended a meeting of the International Society for Psychopathology of Expression (Kagin, 1969). There she met with a group of art therapists and talked about forming an independent professional society. Graves-Alcorn attended Levick's formation meeting in Philadelphia[9] and was elected to AATA's first Executive Board as Constitution Chair. She became President of the American Art Therapy Association 1985-87. Within AATA, Graves-Alcorn is acknowledged for finding the compromise which "resolved the argument" and enabled art therapists with a variety of educational and experience backgrounds to achieve professional registration–the ATR (J. Rubin, personal communication, 1994). Graves-Alcorn's contribution to art therapy registration will be discussed in more detail later in this section.

Within art therapy, Graves-Alcorn is perhaps best known for her Directorship of the University of Louisville art therapy training program, technically the first in the country. As mentioned before, the program was first established by Dr. Roger White in 1957. After graduating two people it closed for ten years. In 1969, the program was revived when 25-year-old Sandra Kagin, having just received her Master's degree came to Louisville to meet with others to form the American Art Therapy Association. She called White to inquire about art therapy education. White told her there was none, but immediately hired her to revive the inactive program he had started ten years before.

In 1973, the program at the University of Louisville became an independent entity as the "Institute for Expressive Therapies" within the College of Health and Social Services: "This move toward interdisciplinary expressive therapy studies would prove a point of continuing debate for the field as many would see it as a dilution of what had not yet proved itself as a separate discipline" (Junge, 1994, p. 142). In 1978, with Vija Lusebrink, Graves-Alcorn described an "expressive therapies continuum" establishing, among other things, typical media use at each developmental level (Kagin & Lusebrink, 1978).

---

9. Age 25, she was probably the youngest person there.

In later years, Graves-Alcorn earned her doctorate and became interested in bereavement. She is the co-founder of a Louisville, Kentucky grief counseling agency "Drawbridges" and as Professor Emerita from the University of Louisville in 1994 published *Embracing the Process of Grief,* a book about grief for the lay public integrating art therapy exercises.

The First Conference of the
American Art Therapy Association

Harriet Wadeson writes:

Hanna [Kwiatkowska] was part of a planning committee to select officers. She called me from their meeting in Louisville to ask me to be Financial Chair. I told her I couldn't even balance my checkbook. . . . She insisted on an answer then, so I told her no. (Wadeson in Junge & Wadeson, 2006, p. 97)

The first conference of the new American Art Therapy Association was held at Airlie House in Warrenton, Virginia in September 1970. It was attended by 100 people and the 1969 roster of "Members in good standing" (which probably means dues-paying members) lists 20 people (American Art Therapy Association, 1969).

Professional Standards for Art Therapists

In 1970, at its first conference, the American Art Therapy Association voted to begin awarding the "A.T.R."[10] (Art Therapist, Registered) as certification that the individual met certain established professional standards. A grand-parenting arrangement was passed and registration was offered to those members who had worked in a psychiatric setting for five years or more. Defining standards for art therapy registration proved to be another major battle for the new organization with major divisions and factions.

As state licensing didn't exist in most states, many professional mental health organizations offered certification to their members who were able to meet established professional standards and could pass the required tests. Those who had pushed for the formation of AATA

---

10. In 1993, when it was housed in the newly formed ATCB, it became ATR (without periods).

such as Levick, Jones, Ault and Cohen also pushed for Registration for art therapists. Others, like Ulman and Kramer, felt it foreshadowed a premature narrowing of the field in that it proposed standards of working in a "psychiatric setting." When the 1970 *Newsletter* was published, 52 of 61 "qualified" art therapists accepted registration. However, Edith Kramer, at first, wrote to say she did not want it.[11]

Art therapy registration is not based on demonstrated competencies but on education and professional experience. Requirements for credentialing tend to become more defined and expectations higher as the discipline evolves. This was the case with the art therapy profession. Twenty years after the ATR, in the early 1990s a higher level of certification was established which required the art therapist to pass a national test of art therapy information. This is the "BC" or "Board Certified" status. At the time, the rationale for "BC" was the recognition that further certification for art therapists would help them achieve state licensing or be included in the mental health licensing that was increasingly developing across the United States.

In 1993, in order to separate out professional standards of registration and certification from the membership organization of the American Art Therapy Association, the Art Therapy Credentialing Board (ATCB) was formed as a distinct entity from the American Art Therapy Association. Thus the ATCB manages two tiers of credentialing for art therapists—Registration (ATR) and Board Certification (BC) It assesses applications, developed and conducts national testing and awards all art therapy credentials. Its mission is "to protect the public by promoting the competent and ethical practice of art therapy" (AATA website, March 29, 2009).

Kramer's initial fear that registration would cause a premature rigidity and an unfair enhancement to art therapy in psychiatric settings was argued against in a letter by AATA Secretary Felice Cohen:

> The rationale behind certification and registration was precisely to remove rigidity within the field. Up to this time, art therapy has been quite rigid. There have been so few who were included into what was a rather small group of art therapists. Those art therapists were mostly located in the East . . . there is now diversification in the field. . . . Since

---

11. Kramer eventually accepted the ATR. Janie Rhyne and Arthur Robbins were others who originally turned down registration offered through the grand-parenting arrangement.

the formation of AATA, we have qualified art therapists from practically every state in the country and Canada. (Cohen, 1970, p. 2)

Not only did the two opposing groups disagree philosophically about whether to have standards for registration at all, they battled about what kinds of standards to have and how to assess the many kinds of art therapy experience and training. In 1971, Sandra Graves-Alcorn (nee Kagin) wrote art therapy's Standards of Practice and achieved a compromise that both camps could agree to. Recognizing the sparseness of formal art therapy education across the United States at the time and understanding the tremendous variety of educational and experiential pathways that art therapists followed, Graves-Alcorn proposed a system of *Professional Quality Credits* (art therapist Janie Rhyne nicknamed these "pukies,") which could embrace these differences and promote inclusivity. Her plan was accepted by both camps and remains in operation today more than 40 years later. Graves-Alcorn says "The first people to become ATR's were recorded by my hand in a large leather book" (S. Graves-Alcorn, personal communication, 2009).

The Highest Award in Art Therapy

The highest award in art therapy is given by the American Art Therapy Association and is the "Honorary Life Membership (HLM). It is described as "AATA's most prestigious honor and is conferred upon Professional Members for major contributions that have had a broad influence of the field of art therapy" (http://www.art therapy.org/awardshonors.htm, retrieved March 20, 2009). The first HLM was given to Margaret Naumburg at AATA's first national conference in Warrenton, Virginia. According to Ault, the award to Naumburg meant "We honor you, we respect you, we want you to be a part of us, but you cannot have control of us" (1975). Levick wrote: "Ms. Naumburg thumped her cane in agreement and disagreement" (Levick in Junge & Wadeson, 2006, p. 134).

Having walked out of the organizing meeting in Philadelphia, no one knew whether Naumburg would accept the award. But accept it she did, and gave a warm acceptance speech. According to Levick, the American Art Therapy Association was the only professional organization that Naumburg supported. Her acceptance speech implied an endorsement of the fledgling art therapy organization (Levick, 1975). Myra Levick and Felice Cohen traveled together to the first conference: "One hour out of the city, Felice and I realized we had both forgotten the plaque awarding Margaret Naumburg the first Honorary Life Membership. We returned for it as this presentation to Naumburg was to be the highlight of that meeting" (Levick in Junge & Wadeson, 2006, p. 124).

The Honorary Life Membership is voted on by professional art therapist members of the American Art Therapy Association. It is not awarded every year, but since 1970, it has been awarded to about 30 people who have contributed in many important ways to the field—as clinicians, writers, administrators and those providing endless service (and often all four at once) to AATA.[12] Levick received the Honorary Life Member Award in 1974.

The American Art Therapy Association and its Immense and Enduring Contribution to the Development of the Field

Throughout its history, the American Art Therapy Association has consisted of fierce individualists with strong and passionate perspectives. In 1994, I stated: "The arguments through the years have been substantive, vocal and, at times, difficult and divisive" (Junge, 1994, p. 123). Ulman's[13] account of the first annual meeting of the American Art Therapy Association, printed in her journal, produced a number of angry letters from AATA Board Members who called it "distorted," "biased," and "destructive." Writing to Ulman, Levick said:

> I have read your account of the first annual conference . . . and I must say I am appalled by your biased subjectivity and gross distortions. . . . Your particular criticism of the organization and its officers has been destructive in its attempt to delay progress. (Levick, 1971, pp. 74 & 99)

Judith Rubin, 5th President of AATA said: "The early meetings were so full of passion and discord that I wondered whether I wanted to be part of this noisy group" (1985, p. 30). When I attended the first Art Therapy Educators Conference in 1975 at George Washington

---

12. The list of those who have been awarded the HLM is in AATA's 2004-05 *Membership Roster* and their memoirs can be found in Junge & Wadeson's (2006) *Architects of art therapy, memoirs and life stories.*

13. Ulman's account appeared in the *American Journal of Art* Therapy (1970), Volume 10, No. 1.

Figure 11-4. "Myra Levick Lecturing in Texas."

University and met all the "famous art therapists" I had revered from afar, their vehement and competitive arguments were so upsetting to me that I didn't go to any art therapy event or conference for five years.

Despite the ongoing disputes, the coming together of art therapists within the American Art Therapy Association provided a professional arena in which the issues of the new field could be debated and education, standards and practices could be established. Most likely without AATA, there would not have been an art therapy profession at all. Art therapists expressed their commitment to the new field by the countless volunteer hours they contributed to AATA which propelled art therapy forward and outward. And without Myra Levick's leadership and energy there probably would not have been the American Art Therapy Association. From its first 15 "members in good standing" in 1969, now 40 years old the American Art Therapy Association currently has a membership of about 4000.

Myra Levick lives in Florida and continues to practice art therapy. Her passion for the profession of art therapy and her caring for the American Art Therapy Association which she founded remain central in her life. Along with the Honorary Life Membership Award from AATA (1974), she received AATA's Research Award in 1981. Her contributions to the field are immeasurable and are not limited to the founding of the American Art Therapy Association and the first art therapy Masters program at Hahnemann/Drexel. Since 1967 she has published four books and over 40 articles in psychiatry and psychology journals, medical journals, education journals, art journals and art therapy journals. She taught family art therapy at family therapy pioneer Ivan Boszormeny-Nagy's program and her assessment (see Chapter 24) the Levick Emotional and Cognitive Art Therapy Assessment (LECATA) she says, is the only assessment "based on normal development which consequently immediately identifies abnormalities in development" (M. Levick, personal communication, 2009).

IMPORTANT DATES AND EVENTS

1960s–Influences on the formation of the American Art Therapy Association were the Women's Liberation Movement, President John F. Kennedy's Community Health Center Bill (1963) and Civil Rights demonstrations resulting in the Civil Rights Act of 1964 promulgated by Reverend Martin Luther King and President Lyndon Baines Johnson.

1963–Myra Levick begins work as an art therapist at Albert Einstein Medical Center, North, in Philadelphia.

1966–International Society for Psychopathology of Expression is founded. Many art therapists attend and some are officers. Their meeting each other at these conferences along with Ulman's *Bulletin of Art Therapy* helps lead to the establishment of the American Art Therapy Association.

1967–The first graduate art therapy program in the country opens at Hahnemann Hospital and Medical Center in Philadelphia. Myra Levick is appointed Co-Director with psychiatrist Morris Goldman.

1968–Levick (with Paul Jay Fink) creates a lecture series given by prominent art therapists at Hahnemann Medical School in

Philadelphia.

December 1968–A meeting is convened at Hahnemann to form a national art therapy organization. Fifty art therapists attend. An Ad Hoc Committee is formed to develop a constitution and by-laws for the new organization and to locate art therapists in the United States and Canada.

June 27, 1969–At a tumultuous gathering in Louisville, Kentucky, the American Art Therapy Association is voted into being.

September 1970–First annual conference of the American Art Therapy Association is held in Warrenton, VA. It is attended by 100 people. Margaret Naumburg is awarded the first Honorary Life Membership. The ATR (Art Therapy Registration) is established.

1975–First Art Therapy Educators meeting is held at George Washington University, Washington, D.C.

Early 1990s–BC, art therapy "Board Certification" is established.

1993–Art Therapy Certification Board (ATCB) is incorporated. This organization, separate from AATA, will carry out assessment and awarding of art therapy registration (ATR) and certification (BC).

STUDY QUESTIONS

1. What important events of the 1960s helped in the formation of the American Art Therapy Association?
2. Describe the importance of Myra Levick and her actions to the establishment of AATA.
3. Describe and discuss the nature of the debates about the formation of the American Art Therapy Association.
4. Discuss one of those arguments that continues to this day.
5. Create an image in the spirit of Myra Levick.
6. Create an image in the spirit of other founders, with Levick, of the American Art Therapy Association.

Chapter 12

PIONEER ART THERAPISTS

ROBERT AULT (1936–2007)
THE ART THERAPY MOVEMENT

Figure 12-1. "Robert Ault."

Robert Ault was one of the founders of the American Art Therapy Association and its second president (1971-73). He fashioned AATA's original constitution and helped in its adoption, thus creating a professional organization which furthered the development of art therapy as a profession and of art therapists. Much later he wrote that most art therapists practiced with a number of titles such as counselor, therapist and occupational therapists. It was only after the founding of

Figure 12-2. "Bob Ault With Don Jones and Myra Levick."

the American Art Therapy Association that the name "art therapist" as a professional designation began to be used. Ault received art therapy's highest award, AATA's Honorary Life Membership in 1986.

Robert Ault was born in 1936 and raised in Corpus Christi, Texas. He earned a Bachelor in Fine Arts degree from the University of Texas and a Masters in Fine Arts from Wichita (Kansas) University. He was an art therapist at the Menninger Foundation in Topeka, Kansas for 32 years. Ault considered Don Jones who had come to Menningers' before him a "father figure":

> Don Jones and I spent years working together and sitting in a back room drinking coffee and talking about someday maybe creating a national organization. . . . We had shared [that dream] for a long time . . . we both went to Philadelphia [for the formation meeting of the American Art Therapy Association] to work on a project that we had both wanted as our big life project. (Ault, 1975)

Attending the meeting in which it was decided to establish a professional organization for art therapists, Ault was elected to the Ad Hoc Committee and later to the first Executive Board as President Elect. Ault worked on a constitution for the new organization. For examples, he collected constitutions from the Wisconsin Art Therapy Association, the American Occupational Therapy Association and the American Speech and Hearing Association. Ault also talked with William Sears at the University of Kansas Music Therapy Department who in 1954 had helped write the constitution for the National

Association for Music Therapy. At the same time, Elinor Ulman was also drafting a constitution focusing on strong state units with a weak national coalition. Ault crafted and at the formation meeting for AATA in Louisville, presented a constitution with a strong national alliance allowing for local chapters. Heated debate went on until four a.m. "The next day a constitution was read to the assembled group and adopted" (Ault, 1975). With the help of a graphic artist, Ault designed AATA's first logo.

Robert Ault loved his patients and they loved him. He was a clinician at Menningers' for 32 years and retired from it in 1993 when Menningers' left Topeka for Baylor University Medical School in Texas. Being a therapist at Menningers', Ault stated it was a

> mixed bag. I loved being a part of an excellent hospital and learning environment. I loved the people that I met and my colleagues. I loved the support they gave me as we put together the AATA and when I served on the board, but I hated the institutional prejudice. If you were not a doctor or a psychiatrist, you were a second class citizen. (Ault in Junge & Wadeson, 2006, p. 74)

During Karl Menninger's last years, Ault painted with him nearly every Friday afternoon. Ault initiated the art therapy Masters program at Emporia State University in Kansas which he left in 1995. The American Art Therapy Archives were always Ault's project. For a long while they were housed at the Menninger Foundation. Today they are at Emporia State University and called the "Robert Ault Archives of the American Art Therapy Association." Art therapy and the American Art Therapy Association which he helped create were treasures to him and he called art therapy "A Movement." Recently, a person on the AATA staff told me that she wished Bob Ault were still alive because he was the only person she could think of who could help AATA arise from it's problems and get "the movement" going again. Lovingly and with humor, he encouraged me to endure the nine years it took to create the first history of art therapy in the United States. Without him, it would not have been completed. He discovered and promoted Elizabeth (Grandma) Layton who managed to cure herself of 40 years of bipolar illness by contour drawing. He became fascinated with contour drawing himself and taught many classes in it to art therapists. Of Layton, he said "She was the one I called on Mother's

Day" (in Junge & Wadeson, 2006, p. 79). With Menningers' he produced a number of videotapes–including one about art therapy "Art Therapy: The Healing Vision" (Ault 1986). He innovated the uses of art therapy in management and business, happily spending his last 12 years at Menningers' working with their world-famous Management Institute. He served on the Kansas Arts Commission and in 1985 was chosen Kansas State Educator of the Year.

In 1978, Ault opened his own art school and studio in Topeka, Kansas; He called it "Ault's Academy of Art." There, he taught art, made his own art and practiced art therapy. It is noteworthy that he opened *an art school,* not a private practice for psychotherapy and art therapy. He always identified himself as an artist. In 1977, Ault participated in a panel at a conference for the American Art Therapy Association called "Are You an Artist or Therapist?–A Professional Dilemma of Art Therapists." Ault proclaimed that if awakened in the middle of the night and asked the question, his answer would be "artist." He wrote a chapter in *Advances in Art Therapy* called "Art Therapy with the Unidentified Patient" (Wadeson, Durkin & Perach, 1989). In this, he described people he worked with, who, he thought, came to his art studio seeking therapy in the guise of art classes–those who probably never would have sought out formal therapy. In the "Unidentified Patient" Ault argued for the uses of art as healing growth, whether it was called "therapy" or not. He wrote: "The experience in the art studio has more than proven to me that the world is full of people who can use the experience of art for a better life. . . . I have six art classes and it has always run full" (Ault in Junge & Wadeson, 2006, pp. 81 & 77).

Ault's bibliography contains 89 items, most of them presentations; he loved giving talks and according to art therapy colleague and former student Libby Schmanke, never turned one down. She says "He really did not like writing and did not think it was a strength of his" (L. Schmanke, personal communication, 2009). His writing style, when he did it, was informal and he used personal stories to make the point. Ault wrote a "Commentary" to conclude the chapters on "Integrative Art Therapy" in Rubin's *Approaches to Art Therapy* (2001). He argues that it is the *personality* of the therapist that makes the difference:

> It is not something that is talked about much in theoretical descriptions of clinical work, yet it is there. . . . It is something each art therapy edu-

cator struggles through with each student, for the real core of the work may depend as much on what you *are* as a human being, as on what you *know* of theory and technique. (Ault in Rubin, 2001, p. 340)

Bob Ault had a lovely sense of humor—he collected jokes—but it was the power of his presence—his warmth and generosity—which provided acceptance and encouragement to all he came in contact with and made him a rare human being. The laudatory Yiddish word *mensch*[1] describes Ault. For those who see the significant importance of the therapist's personality and the use of self, Ault gives us a wonderful example of a person who was helpful and healing and most likely would have been that way whatever vocation he chose. But, lucky for us, Ault loved art and art therapy and kept at both through his lifetime.

His artwork—often watercolor—was direct and usually based on the external landscape that he astutely observed in front of him. At Ault's Academy he could run things the way he wanted to without the constraints of politics or hierarchies. At Ault's Academy he undoubtedly helped many people who may never heard of therapy as treatment, nor knew they were receiving therapy from a master. Ault wrote:

[After 40 years] Each new patient is a new course of challenge and exploration. I get to hear the stories and share the deepest of human convictions, conflicts, and spirit. It is an opportunity to create, and to be in the presence of an energy that comes from sharing this. It is the wonderful integration of all I know as an artist and all I have learned as a therapist. (Ault in Rubin, 2001, p. 341)

Ault began his memoir chapter in *Architects of Art Therapy* with a quote from Mark Twain: "I would like to have lived my life so that when I die even the undertaker would be sad." After a long illness, Robert Ault died in 2008 and I have no doubt that the undertaker was sad.

---

1. A *mensch* is a decent, admirable person. Leo Rosten in Wickipedia: "Someone to admire and emulate . . . character, rectitude, dignity, a sense of what's right," (www.answers.com/topic/mensch - 53k.)

Important Dates and Events

1938–Robert Ault is born in Corpus Christi, Texas.

1961-1993–Works as an art therapist at the Menninger Foundation, Topeka, Kansas. Is psychoanalyzed and works with Menningers' Management Institute for his last 12 years.

1968–Attends formation meeting for the American Art Therapy Association. Is elected to the Ad Hoc Steering Committee and crafts the new organization's constitution.

1969–Is elected President Elect of the American Art Therapy Association. Helps create AATA's first logo.

1971-1973–Becomes President of AATA. Is its second President.

1973-1995–In 1973, establishes the art therapy graduate training program at Emporia State University, Emporia Kansas. It is the 5th Masters program in the country and gives a "Masters in Psychology with a Specialty in Art Therapy." Ault retires from this program in 1995.

1977–Participates on a panel called "Are You an Artist or a Therapist?–a Professional Dilemma of Art Therapists" at conference of American Art Therapy Association. Answers the question: if pressed, he would say "artist."

1978–Establishes Ault's Academy of Art, where he teaches art and practices art therapy until he dies.

1985–Is chosen as "Kansas State Educator of the Year."

1986–Receives the Honorary Life Membership from the American Art Therapy Association.

1986–With Menninger's produces "Art Therapy: The Healing Vision," a videotape.

1986–Integrates art therapy and business and publishes "Draw on New Lines of Communication."

1989–Publishes chapter on "The Unidentified Patient in Art Therapy" in *Advances in Art Therapy.*

1993–Retires from Menningers.

1995–Retires from Emporia State University.

1995–Mentors and supervises art therapists and Ault's Academy of Art thrives. Continues to create his own art.

2007–Robert Ault dies in Topeka, Kansas.

Study Questions

1. Discuss Ault's concept of the personality of the therapist as essential in art therapy.
2. Describe Ault's art therapy at the Menninger Foundation and his initiation of the art therapy training program at Emporia State University. What was the importance of these milestones to the Midwest and to the development of the art therapy profession?
3. Describe Ault's contributions to the formation of the American Art Therapy Association.
4. Create an image in the spirit of Robert Ault.

HARRIET WADESON (b. 1931)
AN ECLECTIC APPROACH TO ART PSYCHOTHERAPY

Because she was trained by Hanna Yaxa Kwiatkowska, at the National Institute of Mental Health beginning in 1961, Harriet Wadeson could be called a "second generation art therapist." Actually, however, her art therapy career began in 1949 at St. Elizabeth's Hospital in Washington, D.C. Always fascinated with the combination of art and people and wanting to become a psychotherapist, as a summer college student, Wadeson took over the art groups of the art teacher Prentiss

Figure 12-3. "Harriet Wadeson."

Taylor who had "been socked in the jaw by a criminal patient" and she was hooked (Junge, 1994, p. 228). After the first art therapy pioneers, Jones, Naumburg, Huntoon, Kramer, Kwiatkowska and Ulman, Wadeson (nee Sinrod) is the first author to publish: Her journal article "Communication through Painting in a Therapy Group" appeared in 1964 in the second edition of *Bulletin of Art Therapy,* three years before Levick's first publication and almost 10 years before 1973 when a plethora of art therapy literature began to appear.

Wadeson grew up in Washington, D.C.:

> I drew stories before I could write. I was the cartoonist for my high school paper. (The major challenge was thinking up something funny for each issue.) In college I took more classes in art than in my major, psychology. But I never wanted to become an artist. I didn't think I was good enough. . . . I had no interest in teaching art either. (Wadeson in Junge & Wadeson, 2006, p. 84)

At the age of 14, babysitting for her psychiatrist uncle, she looked through his bookshelf and became fascinated with Freud and dreams. Suffering the typical vicissitudes of adolescence, she wanted to grow up to become a therapist. She attended Cornell University as a psychology major working with the famous researcher Urie Bronfenbrenner. But as a middle-class woman growing up in the 1950s, encouraged by her family to not be a "failure" as a career woman, Wadeson married, bore and raised three children. As was typical of most young women of the time, her identity[2] was attached to her husband and his career. She wrote: "The only thing that was 'different' about me was that I wanted something more" (Wadeson in Junge & Wadeson, 2006, p. 86).

Post World War II, women who had previously handled jobs in the "outside world" ironically moved back into the home and became "stay at home moms." This was Wadeson's story, Levick's story, Landgarten's story and my own. It was also the story of many pioneering art therapists who, fascinated with the mingling of people and psychology, found that staying home to care for children, they wanted *more.* In the Introduction to *Architects of Art Therapy,* Harriet Wadeson and I wrote:

---

2. Researcher and writer Daniel Levinson talks about this attachment by a woman to a man as a specific developmental stage for men in *Seasons of a Man's Life,* published in 1978.

At a time when middle-class women stayed in their homes as wife and mother, before the Women's Movement of the late 20th century, these women ventured out to start the art therapy profession . . . women of this kind often felt isolated and different in their yearnings, but through art therapy and the American Art Therapy Association . . . they discovered a group of professional colleagues and friends who shared their unique aspirations. The evolution of art therapy as a profession was primarily driven by women of courage who were unusual in that they left home and hearth to found a profession of importance and creativity, to educate future generations of art therapists, and to propel their innovative profession toward acceptance in the mental health hierarchy. (Junge & Wadeson, 2006, p. xv)

During her 13 years at the National Institute of Mental Health, Wadeson first co-led adolescent groups with Kwiatkowska. When Kwiatkowska was called away because of a family emergency, Wadeson "without any training" ran the groups by herself. She said: "I wasn't much older than some of the patients who were in their teens and twenties" (Wadeson in Junge & Wadeson, 2006, pp. 87-88). During this time, Wadeson attended classes at the Washington School of Psychiatry. Realizing she needed more than a Bachelor's degree to "do what I had already been doing," she later received an Master of Arts in psychology and art therapy from Goddard College, VT, a Ph.D. from Union Institute and a Masters of Social Work from Catholic University (Wadeson in Junge & Wadeson, 2006, p. 93).

While Wadeson has held many elected posts in the American Art Therapy Association, she refused Hanna Kwiatkowska's invitation from the first AATA meeting in Louisville to serve on the Executive Board as Financial Chair. And a few years later she said "no" to Bob Ault, Chair of the Nominating Committee when he asked her to run for President. She said: "I told him that I might be masochistic, but I wasn't totally crazy" (Wadeson in Junge & Wadeson, 2006, p. 97). Her favorite post was as Publications Chair and most recently, until 2006, she was Associate Editor of *Art Therapy, Journal of the American Art Therapy Association.*

A self-confessed "eclectic," Wadeson's approach to art psychotherapy integrates a number of theoretical concepts which characteristically drive her own clinical ideas. In this writer's opinion the word "eclectic" unfortunately means for many that there is no coherent theory or approach and the practitioner bounces around according to changing, current fads. This is often not the case and it certainly isn't for Wadeson. She wrote: "An eclectic approach respects the contributions of many theorists and enables the clinician to draw on many sources of knowledge. It places a great deal of responsibility on the therapist to form a functional synthesis" (Wadeson in Rubin, 1987, p. 299).

In her early years, babysitting and reading her psychiatrist uncle's books, she was most influenced by Freud, especially his dreamwork. But, she said: "I believe my most significant teachers were the patients with whom I worked. I came to "know" through the accumulation of experience" (Wadeson, 1980, p. 30). Working, learning and seeing patients, Wadeson became interested in phenomenology, the human potential movement (which began on the West Coast and moved East) and Humanistic psychology. She also incorporated parts of existentialism, behaviorism, Erik Erikson's developmental model, Gestalt Psychology and Carl Jung's Analytic Psychology into her conceptual framework. In her 1980 book, *Art Psychotherapy,* Wadeson calls herself humanistic, existential and phenomenological. She has clearly continued to learn, grow and to assemble a compendium of theories to enhance her art therapy practice with clients.

Wadeson, like Naumburg, proposes that the art therapist is a *psychotherapist*–playing down the formalized creation of an art product, encouraging the client to interpret their own work, paying attention to and maneuvering the relationship between therapist and client and using discussion, free association and verbal means to further the psychotherapy. She does not adhere to the medical model that was essential to much Northeastern art therapy. She does not aim to "heal" or free the client from disease: "I see psychotherapy as primarily an educational process to help people with problems in living rather than as a treatment for disease" (Wadeson, 1980, p. xi). She wrote:

> The client's creativity, as well as the therapist's, encompasses the entire art psychotherapeutic process. Such is the case in any form of therapy. In art therapy, however, the medium of expression is an art form, thereby encouraging a more focused creativity than otherwise. (Wadeson, 1980, p. 7)

Since her childhood in Washington D.C., Harriet Wadeson has traveled across the United States and to much of the larger world; she has lived in Texas and the Midwest. She is a creative person who uses her environment to learn about people and their cultures and she has continued to make artwork in many forms over the years. Using this "traveler" metaphor, Wadeson seems to have derived useful theoretical and practical information from many sources and integrated it into her practice evolving a unique form of art psychotherapy. Wadeson's books are: *Art Psychotherapy* (1980), *The Dynamics of Art Psychotherapy* (1987b), *Advances in Art Therapy* (edited with J. Durkin and D. Perach, 1989), and *Art Therapy Practice: Innovative Approaches with Diverse Populations* (2000). She was Co-Editor of *Architects of Art Therapy, Memoirs and Life Stories* (2006). She has recently written and published a new updated edition of *Art Psychotherapy.*

Important to the understanding of Wadeson's perspective is her chapter "An eclectic approach to art therapy" in *Approaches to Art Therapy* (Rubin, J. (Ed.), 1987b). In addition, she edited *A Guide to Conducting Art Therapy Research* (1992) which was the first book published by the American Art Therapy Association and certainly the first book to focus on art therapy research.

In the 1970s and 80s, art therapy courses and Masters-level training programs were springing up all over the United States. The lure of the new profession was considerable and gaining in importance and there seemed to be potential students across the country wanting art therapy education and training. Many of the original art therapy pioneers also became teachers and academics for the next generations of art therapists. Some, established programs in colleges and universities. Wadeson began teaching an art therapy course at Montgomery Community College, MD and for the education section of the National Institutes of Health in Betheseda, MD. In 1979, she moved to the University of Houston at Clear Lake to direct the art therapy training program. After a year and at the age of 49, she moved to Chicago to initiate a new program at the University of Illinois in Chicago, School of Art and Design. During this time, Wadeson also directed an "Annual Summer Institute" at Lake Geneva, WI which went on for 20 years, bringing well-known art therapists in to teach. In 2003, after 23 years, she retired from the University of Illinois, but "I missed working with students" so she established a post-graduate art therapy program at Northwestern University (Wadeson in Junge & Wadeson, 2006, p. 102).

To use a clichéd phrase: Harriet Wadeson could be called the "Johnny Appleseed" of art therapy. Her love of travel has taken her to many countries across the globe and in each she has presented workshops and spread the magic of art therapy. For the past ten years she has taught annually in Sweden. In 1995, she led a professional exchange group to China with delegations to Indonesia and Bali to study arts and healing. Throughout the years, she has continued making art, sometimes morphing into theater and street theater experiences. In 1992, she was awarded the highest award in art therapy, the Honorary Life Membership by the American Art Therapy Association. Accepting, she said that "art therapy was my professional home and that AATA was my professional family" (Wadeson in Junge & Wadeson, p. 98). In 2006, as she looked back, Wadeson wrote:

> Being a part of an emerging profession, growing up with it, co-mingling with the creative colleagues and students it attracts, feeling like one of its "architects," though at times a difficult path, always made my work an exciting adventure. This profound new territory we explore together has offered many creative opportunities that would not have been available to me on a more traditional professional path. I am grateful for every minute of it. . . . There have been moments when I have wished for a more peaceful life. It has been unpredictable. I never expected the rich opportunities I have been afforded, nor did I anticipate some of the painful difficulties. (Wadeson in Junge & Wadeson, 2006, p. 103)

Important Dates and Events

1949–Harriet Wadeson's art therapy career begins at St. Elizabeth's Hospital in Washington, D.C. She leads groups with art teacher Prentice Taylor.

1950s–Marries and raises three children.

1961-1974–Begins work at National Institute of Mental Health. Trains and works with Hanna Yaxa Kwiatkowska. Stays 13 years. Attends classes at the Washington School of Psychiatry.

1964–Her first publication "Communication Through Painting in a Therapy Group" is printed in the second edition of the *Bulletin of Art Therapy*.

1975–Receives her Master of Arts degree in Psychology and Art Therapy from Goddard College in Vermont.

1978–Receives her Masters in Social Welfare from Catholic University, Chicago, IL.

1978–Receives her Ph.D. from Union Institute.

1979–Age 47, teaches art therapy at the University of Houston-Clear Lake.

1980–*Art Psychotherapy* is published.

1981–Iniates a new art therapy program at the University of Illinois, Chicago Circle. Each summer, Wadeson also directs the Annual Summer Institute at Lake Geneva, WI which runs for 20 years.

1987–*The Dynamics of Art Psychotherapy* is published.

1988–Age 57, begins karate practice.

1989–With J. Durkin and D. Perach, Wadeson edits and publishes *Advances in Art Therapy.*

1992–Edits *A Guide to Conducting Art Therapy Research,* the first book published by the American Art Therapy Association. Receives the highest award in art therapy, the Honorary Life Membership from the American Art Therapy Association.

1995–Leads a delegation of art therapists to China, with side trips to Indonesia and Bali.

1998–Begins to teach annually in Sweden where she celebrates the Summer Solstice each year.

2000–Wadeson's *Art Therapy Practice: Innovative Approaches With Diverse Populations* is published.

2003–Retires from the University of Illinois art therapy program. Establishes a post-Masters art therapy program at Northwestern University.

2004-2006–Wadeson is Associate Editor of *Art Therapy, Journal of the American Art Therapy Association.*

2006–With Maxine Borowsky Junge, Wadeson edits and publishes her 6th book, *Architects of Art Therapy, Memoirs and Life Stories.*

2009–Living in Evanston, IL near Chicago, Wadeson continues to travel, teach, paint and write novels.

Study Questions

1. Describe Harriet Wadeson's early interest in art and people and how this "morphed" into art therapy.
2. Discuss Wadeson's "eclectic" approach to art therapy.
3. Discuss the importance of Wadeson's books to the art therapy

profession.

4. Describe and discuss the importance of travel to Wadeson's world view.

5. Create an image in the spirit of Harriet Wadeson.

HELEN LANDGARTEN[3] (b. 1921)
THE WEST COAST AND CLINICAL ART THERAPY

Figure 12-4. "Helen Landgarten Conducting Art Therapy."

---

3. A disclaimer is in order: I apprenticed with Helen Landgarten and learned to be an art therapist from her. In addition, I was a member of her faculty at Immaculate Heart College in Hollywood, CA beginning in 1974 and Chair of the art therapy graduate program at Loyola Marymount University. Much of Landgarten's work was done in the same years as Myra Levick's and the two collaborated a great deal.

Beginning in the mid 1960s in Southern California, Helen Landgarten's particular brand of art therapy became an important branch of the profession. For the most part in the Northeastern United States, art therapists practiced adjunctively as part of a psychiatric team and often in inpatient hospital settings. In outpatient agencies and clinics in parts of Southern California, mental health practice was less hierarchical and clinicians from many disciplines all did psychotherapy and saw a wide variety of client problems and populations. In addition, community mental health agencies were being built and gaining ground. Each discipline retained its particular focus–for example, only psychiatrists could prescribe medication and only psychologists could administer psychological tests–but generally, the art therapist of Landgarten's vision learned skills of assessing and treating the client and functioning as a primary care practitioner: They were trained to carry full case responsibility. If art therapists could function as primary therapists, they might also go into private practice.

The art therapist as primary care clinician is what Landgarten called "Clinical Art Therapy" and her training program, first at Immaculate Heart College in Hollywood, California and later at Loyola Marymount University in Los Angeles educated students to be art psychotherapists; in other words, they were trained as psychotherapists who used special tools–the art.

Helen Landgarten was born in Detroit and moved to California with her husband, Nate. In her forties, after raising two children, Landgarten returned to school at UCLA where she received her Bachelor of Fine Arts degree and worked in sculpting, painting and printmaking. Landgarten remembers: "Somewhere along the line I decided painting wasn't enough for me, that I wanted to work in the community. . . . [I] felt I had two talents, as an artist and as a therapist. I decided I wanted to combine the two. I did some work in a county hospital adolescent unit. They called it art therapy" (1975). Before that, Landgarten–as a psychologically-minded art teacher taught geriatric patients in a community center. Like many art therapists, Landgarten, working in isolation, thought she had invented art therapy by herself. Later she found the *Bulletin of Art Therapy:*

> One of the residents at the county hospital told me there was a Bulletin of Art Therapy. . . . I got the journal and found out there were people on the East Coast doing the same thing I was doing . . . [the journal] was

my lifeline. . . . I came to [the formation meeting in] Louisville and met other real live art therapists. (1975)

In 1968, Landgarten began work as a therapist in the Department of Psychiatry, Family, Child Division, Mt. Sinai Medical Center in Los Angeles. (Mt. Sinai Hospital later integrated with Cedars of Lebanon Hospital in Hollywood and in about 1974 became the Thalians Community Mental Health Center of Cedars-Sinai Hospital.)

In her art therapy oral history, Landgarten said: "I gave a presentation at Cedars-Sinai. . . . The agreement was that they would give me a group of adolescents and if, at the end of six weeks, they liked what I did, they would hire me and they did" (1975). Landgarten stayed at Thalians until her retirement in 1991 working as "Coordinator of Art Psychotherapy." There she developed a department with five art psychotherapists, functioning as primary clinicians in both inpatient and outpatient settings. She worked under Dr. Saul Brown, a psychiatrist who strongly believed in the value of art therapy.

Landing at Cedars-Sinai with Saul Brown, Landgarten became part of what was probably the premier family therapy setting and training arena in Southern California. She learned to integrate the personality theory and psychodynamic approach of Freud with the here-and-now stance of family theorists. Her insistence on seeing the whole family and her rich experience with the variety of families seeking treatment were unique in art therapy (and often in family therapy itself). When she began her Masters training program at Immaculate Heart College, it was the only one in the United States that focused on family therapy and had seasoned family art therapists as faculty. By today, most art therapy training programs in the United States have a *course* on family art therapy, but it is regarded as another art therapy "approach." Landgarten's program was unique in that it provided an integrated curriculum based in systems thinking about change, rather than in individual psychotherapeutic philosophy from Freud and Jung, which was typical historically and is still the case in most mental health education programs of all disciplines.

Landgarten's first family art therapy publication appeared in 1975 "Group art therapy for mothers and their daughters." It described a case in which Landgarten as the primary therapist practiced art psychotherapy in every session (1975b). Her second book, *Family Art Psychotherapy* (1987) contains descriptions of many of her family cases at Cedars-Sinai and is the only book of its kind. Her innovative art therapy protocol for evaluating a family's dynamics through a joint family mural is the first one after Kwiatkowska's and the first one to focus on a family's dynamics and communication styles as they work together on the mural. She reasoned that the way the family *behaved* as they went about the mural task and how they handled the structure was indicative of how the family *behaved with each other* outside the consulting room. Her proposal of this interaction was often an important insight for the family (Landgarten, 1987, Kerr & Hoshino, 2008).

In her clinical work, Landgarten was primarily a psychotherapist in an outpatient clinic, who used art as her way of approaching her clients' problems and challenges. Typically, people would not be referred specifically to art therapy and were often surprised and even resistant to using art. Landgarten's passion for the art process was infectious and very early on in treatment, most clients came to see art's tremendous value to them. Landgarten's approach required that the art therapist first assess or evaluate the client or family and make a plan for the treatment with structured, practical goals. Landgarten wrote: "The invading device is the art directive, which contains the appropriate media and is clinically sound. . . . [The directive is] dictated by the dynamics of each session with consideration to short and long-term goals" (Landgarten, 1987, p. 5).

Arguably, Landgarten "invented" the term and use of *directives*. Within her framework, the art therapist is an active "agent of change" whose perspective is to intrude on the family system's homeostasis and support a restructuring. "The family art therapist must be creative in two areas simultaneously; while being psychologically attuned to the participants, he or she must make an immediate decision about the appropriate art task which serves a therapeutic purpose" (Landgarten, 1987, p. 281). The art therapist, while aware of the overt and covert messages in the art, relies (as Naumburg proposed) on *the client's interpretation:* "The therapist provides insightful feedback, being cautious of the client's ability and readiness to receive such feedback" (Junge, 1994).

As in all psychotherapy, in Landgarten's art therapy, verbal exploration is encouraged to enhance an understanding of the unconscious, active in the artwork. Making art and then talking about it are done in each session, from the first one on. Resistance to doing art is considered appropriate and expected as a natural resistance to the sometimes uncomfortable entry into the unconscious. Landgarten believes it is more comfortable for the client to exhibit this resistance to the art process itself, than it is to express it toward the therapist and/or the therapy. As therapist and client process the session, the verbal interplay stays with the artwork as *evidence* and recorder of the messages. "The clinician's verbalized interactional assessment gains credibility through the visual proof of the [art] product itself. The artwork is always referred to as the source for the psychotherapist's insight. . . " (Landgarten, 1987, p. 16).

For Landgarten, the art product is the externalized illustration of an intrapsychic process, both conscious and unconscious, of the client or family. It also provides a permanent record of the "therapeutic process, and acts a catalyst for change" (Junge, 1994). "The value of the art task is threefold: the *process* as a diagnostic, interactional, and rehearsal tool; the *contents* as a means of portraying the unconscious and communication; and the *product* as lasting evidence of . . . dynamics" (Landgarten, 1987, p. 5, emphasis in the original).

Landgarten published a number of books in the wave of art therapy literature. They are *Clinical Art Therapy: Comprehensive Guide* (1981), *Family Art Psychotherapy: A Casebook and Clinical Guide* (1987), and *Magazine Photo Collage: A Multicultural Assessment and Technique* (1993). Landgarten, pioneered and expanded uses of collage in art therapy practice. She also co-edited *Adult Art Psychotherapy: Issues and Applications* with Darcy Lubbers (1991). In 1994, I wrote about her in *A History of Art Therapy in the United States:*

> [Landgarten] provides a model of practice that includes a wide age range and a variety of settings including outpatient clinics, psychiatric hospitals, and rehabilitation centers. . . . [*Clinical Art Therapy*] is also explicit in its definition of an art therapist as a psychotherapist with special tools and abilities capable of functioning as a primary care clinician. . . . (Junge, 1994)

Landgarten established a clinical art therapy Masters program at Immaculate Heart College in Hollywood, CA. Beginning in 1973 as a certificate program, it graduated its first Masters Degree class in 1974. The program moved to Loyola Marymount University in 1980 where it still remains. (I was the second faculty member hired by Landgarten–after the Hahnemann–trained and now-deceased Leslie Thompson–

and remained with the program as Professor and Director until 2001 when I retired.) Administratively, the program was a separate department—the first Department of Art Therapy in America.

Feeling that proficient clinicians could best show off art therapy to the community, Landgarten focused on educating first-class art psychotherapists. She encouraged her students to learn about assessing the client or family and then from the assessment to develop a set of specific short and long-term goals for therapy. These goals were intended to be both practical and realistic. Media were viewed as having their own inherent structuring properties and were thoughtfully applied to enhance therapeutic goals.

Throughout her teaching and clinical work, Landgarten's intention was to develop and promote the profession of art therapy. In order to achieve her goal, Landgarten used the students' internship to expand awareness of the power of art therapy into the mental health community: Students functioned as primary therapists and, in the early days, had two supervisors for their clinical work. One was the "clinical supervisor"—usually employed by the institution and the other an art therapy supervisor—often supplied by the educational program. In part, the intention of this dual supervision provided an agency employee with knowledge of art therapy and the art therapist's talents. This often resulted in employment for art therapists. Landgarten says "I was determined to make art therapy a known modality because I often witnessed my clients' gains. . . . I managed those difficult times because I was on a mission" (Landgarten in Junge & Wadeson, 2006, p. 152).

Helen Landgarten was a member of the first Executive Board of the American Art Therapy Association where she was Chair of Public Information. In 1969, with another art therapist (Christine Sharpes), she founded the Southern California Art Therapy Association. In 1975, she was awarded Honorary Life Membership by the American Art Therapy Association.

Now retired, Landgarten lives in Los Angeles where she paints, writes fiction, is a supportive mentor and colleague and pays close attention to the ebbs and flows of the art therapy profession. She is proud of the art therapy clinic named for her at Loyola Marymount University and acts as an art psychotherapist for it. The clinic, providing art therapy to the community, is the first in a university setting.

Important Dates and Events

1921–Helen Landgarten is born in Detroit, Michigan.

1964–Landgarten is a psychologically oriented art teacher with geriatric patients in a community center. She later becomes an art therapist on an inpatient unit at Los Angeles County/USC Hospital.

1968–Begins as art therapist at Mt. Sinai Hospital, Department of Psychiatry, Family and Child Division. This later becomes Cedars-Sinai Hospital, Thalians Community Mental Health Center. Its philosophy is family therapy and Landgarten trains art therapists as primary therapists who are knowledgeable enough to carry full case responsibility.

1969–Attends formation meeting for AATA and becomes Public Information Chair on AATA's first Executive Board. Co-founds the Southern California Art Therapy Association.

1973–Innovates a Clinical Art Therapy training program at Immaculate Heart College, Hollywood, CA. For its first year it is a Certificate program. This is the first separate department of art therapy in the country: It is not a sub-group of the art or psychology department nor of any other department.

1974–The Immaculate Heart art therapy program becomes a Masters program and graduates its first students.

1975–Landgarten's first publication "Group art therapy for mothers and daughters" based on casework at Cedars-Sinai Medical Center in Los Angeles appears in the *American Journal of Art Therapy.* She receives art therapy's highest award, the Honorary Life Membership, from the American Art Therapy Association.

1980–Landgarten's training program moves to Loyola Marymount University where it remains today, 30 years later.

1981–*Clinical Art Therapy: A Comprehensive Guide,* describing Landgarten's clinical art therapy approach is published.

1987–*Family Art Psychotherapy: A Clinical Guide and Casebook* is published. This book will remain the only book on family art therapy until 1994 when Riley & Malchiodi publish *Integrative Approaches to Family Art Therapy.* Riley trained in family art therapy with Landgarten and was a faculty member and Field Placement Coordinator in the Immaculate Heart College and Loyola Marymount programs and later at Phillips Graduate School in Encino, California. Riley was also a family art therapist at Didi

Hirsh Community Mental Health Center in Culver City, CA.

1987–Landgarten retires as Professor Emerita from Loyola Marymount University.

1991–*Adult Art Psychotherapy: Issues and Applications* (edited with Darcy Lubbers) is published. Landgarten retires from Thalians Community Mental Health Center.

1993–*Magazine Photo Collage: A Multicultural Assessment and Treatment Technique* is published.

2007–The Helen B. Landgarten Clinic is innagurated at Loyola Marymount University to provide art therapy to the community. It begins by offering a group led by Landgarten and Judy Flesh for pregnant teenagers at a continuation school in South Los Angeles.

Study Questions

1. Explain the concept of "Clinical Art Therapy."
2. Describe the basic ideas of Landgarten's family art therapy.
3. Describe Landgarten's notions of furthering the art therapy profession through well-trained art therapists.
4. Create an image in the spirit of Helen Landgarten.

JANIE RHYNE (1913–1995)
GESTALT ART THERAPY

Janie Rhyne was best known within the art therapy community for her fascination with and espousal of Gestalt art therapy. Like the typical story of other pioneers, she was interested in both art and psychology and pursued education in both. Intuitively, she also taught art in a psychological fashion to emotionally disturbed children, paraplegics at a Naval Hospital and to boys in Mexico where she lived from 1956 to 1960. Writing about her in *Architects of Art Therapy, Memoirs and Life Stories,* Vija Lusebrink, a colleague of Rhyne's at the University of Louisville stated: "[She] used art as expression and communication in the 1940s. . . . In her life Janie followed her own path; her life styles and professional development worked in tandem" (Lusebrink in Junge & Wadeson, 2006, p. 159). Janie Rhyne was a "liver" and an experimenter not a theorist; She lived in at least five

Figure 12-5. "Janie Rhyne."

countries and in a commune in British Columbia.[4]

Gestalt Psychology, as part of the Human Potential Movement of the 1960s was a Humanistically-oriented approach which aimed for the individual's personal growth, instead of "treating" an illness or dysfunction. According to this perspective, rather than a medical and/or "disease" model, human development is regarded as a natural human path based in continuing self awareness.[5] Pathology can occur through the impact of environmental stress and as a result, development stops. Within a Human Potential perspective, treatment concerns *removal of the blocks to self awareness.* Using a Humanistic philosophical framework, when blocks to self awareness are removed, innate positive development and growth can continue. The Gestalt therapist attempts to break through fear, to "open up" the person's awareness in the present. Any relevant individual history is thought to be played out in the "here and now" of the current personality and therefore, it is not important for the Gestalt therapist to hear or understand a client's past. Rhyne wrote: "Gestaltists offer ways to get through this wall of fear— we seek ways to recognize what we have hidden away and to integrate our disowned parts into our total personality (Rhyne, 1973, pp. 3-4).

In addition to Gestalt Psychology, Rhyne integrated Kurt Lewin's

---

4. Much of Janie Rhyne's history cited here is from Lusebrink in Junge & Wadeson, 2006.
5. Psychodynamic language uses the term "consciousness."

field theories and Goldstein's organismic theory which proposed a unity and consistency of the normal person. In her last decades, she adapted into her art therapy work, aspects of existential psychotherapy and developments in emotions. In a sense, like Wadeson and others she was eclectic. But her syntheses put her firmly within the philosophy of systems thinking.[6]

In the 1960s, Esalen Institute at Big Sur on the California Coast was the center of the Human Potential Movement in the United States and offered workshops and experiences to therapists and the public. Upon her return from Mexico, Rhyne moved to San Francisco to study with Fritz and Laura Perls, the most eminent Gestalt therapists at Esalen and later at the San Francisco Gestalt Institute which Rhyne founded in 1968 with two other therapists.

Rhyne's relationship to the profession of art therapy is a fascinating one. About discovering Gestalt Psychology and art therapy, she stated:

> I was intrigued and excited. For the first time academic theoretical psychology came together with what I was doing in art. . . . I had been using Gestalt psychological principles without even knowing it. . . . I realized I'd been doing art therapy but had never called myself an art therapist nor heard of Margaret Naumburg or Edith Kramer. . . . I didn't even know of it [art therapy] until long after it had started. Most of the people were originally psychoanalytical and [used the] medical model. However, I met a number of these people, specifically Elinor Ulman and Hanna Kwiatkowska, and found that though they claimed to be staunchly psychoanalytical and I claimed to be a staunch Gestaltist, we operate as therapists pretty much the same way. (Rhyne, 1975)

In San Francisco, Rhyne lived in the Haight Ashbury area of the city as the hippie movement was beginning there. She started a drop-in clinic, "The Off-Ramp," and began a private practice. She worked as a training therapist at the Gestalt Institute of San Francisco. Rhyne wrote: "I was using art with hippies and flower children. Art was a natural there . . . the way I used it was more for process than product oriented" (Rhyne, 1975).

---

6. In my opinion and although not acknowledged, much of art therapy practice, historically and in the present, is really a form of systems thinking in that a number of theoretical frameworks plus the art are integrated into a workable perspective.

With encouragement from the famous theorist of Humanistic Psychology, Abraham Maslow, Janie Rhyne, using the notes she had kept of her work, published *The Gestalt Art Experience* in 1973. In that year, Rhyne also began studies for her doctorate in Psychology at the University of California, Santa Cruz. She was 60 years old. After receiving her Ph.D., she taught at the University of Louisville, Vermont College of Norwich University and at many art therapy programs across the country.

For Rhyne, art within therapy is a fundamental and powerful integrating force for personality growth, development and expansion. Art allows the individual the experience of self awareness. The art product can be a metaphor for the whole of a person's life and its exploration provides a visual expression of the client's reality. The Gestalt art therapist believes with this unblocking of self-awareness, the client is able to make more effective choices about life. Rhyne wrote: "Let's put aside the categorizing that is not relevant to art as personal experience. Let's use art to make us more aware of ourselves as psychic and social beings" (Rhyne, 1973, pp. 98-99).

Janie Rhyne was active in the American Art Therapy Association. In particular, she made important contributions to thinking about research in art therapy. In 1980, she received the American Art Therapy Association's highest award, the Honorary Life Membership.

Important Dates and Events

1913–Janie Rhyne is born in Tallahassee, Fl.

1935–She receives her Bachelor of Arts degree from the Florida State University in art and social science. Before 1956-Teaches art to emotionally disturbed children and to paraplegics at a naval hospital.

1956-1960–Lives in Mexico and teaches art.

1960–Moves to San Francisco, CA. Studies Gestalt Therapy with Fritz and Laura Perls. Works with hippies and flower children. Founds a drop-in clinic "The Off-Ramp" and begins private practice.

1965-1967–Is Senior Training Therapist in Gestalt Therapy and at the Gestalt Therapy Institute of San Francisco.

1968–With two other therapists, founds the Gestalt Institute of San Francisco.

1973–Publishes her book, *The Gestalt Art Experience.* Age 60, begins doctoral work in the Psychology Department at the University of

California, Santa Cruz.

1978-1980–Teaches in art therapy program at the University of Louisville.

1979–Receives her Ph.D. in Psychology.

1979-1992–Teaches at Vermont College of Norwich University. Moves to Iowa City.

1995–Janie Rhyne dies.

Study Questions

1. Describe Rhyne's central beliefs about Gestalt Art Therapy.
2. What kind of person might be especially appropriate for Gestalt Art Therapy treatment?
3. What kind of person is not appropriate for Gestalt Art Therapy treatment?
4. Why is Gestalt Art Therapy not of particular importance in the art therapy community today?
5. Create an image in the spirit of Janie Rhyne.

JUDITH RUBIN (b. 1936)
PEACEMAKER, WRITER AND FILM MAKER

Figure 12-6. "Judith Rubin."

Judith Rubin is a self-confessed optimist—even a "Pollyanna" where art therapy and the American Art Therapy Association are concerned. For many years, she has been a conciliator and peacemaker in art therapy and her consistent attempts at consensus building in the face of vehement disagreements and "sides-taking" by many pioneers are legend. Rather than take a stand on one side or the other, Rubin's role within organized art therapy has been to act as a mediator, negotiator, peacemaker—and she is respected by all factions for this role. Perhaps, this stems from her early days of knowing both Naumburg and Kramer in Manhattan and being able to use and appreciate philosophies from those quite different theoreticians without getting mired in their differences. She seems to be a respecter of authority and of age. Or if we were calling forth the stereotypes of birth order, Rubin would be the middle child, who attempts to reconcile warring factions in her family.

I believe that Rubin's first priority is the development and forward progression of art therapy and to achieve her aim, she long ago decided on her peacemaker role. (Certainly, art therapy and the American Art Therapy Association have needed one.) She was involved from the early days in art and the art therapy profession and was the fifth president of AATA (1977-79). She calls AATA her "professional extended family" (Rubin in Junge & Wadeson, 2006, p. 117). She is a member of the current Executive Board of the American Art Therapy Association as she struggles to help free AATA from the quicksand it has gotten itself into; she has revived the long-gone Membership Committee. In 1981, Rubin was awarded the Honorary Life Membership by the American Art Therapy Association.

Rubin wrote that she saw herself as an "ugly duckling" finding the swans. "The swans" that Rubin refers to are art therapy, and in particular Margaret Naumburg and Edith Kramer whom she sought out to get "advice about becoming a 'real' art therapist" (Rubin in Junge & Wadeson, 2006, p. 111). According to Rubin, both Naumburg and Kramer were generous with their consultation; they advised Rubin to undertake personal psychotherapy to learn more about herself and to find a good clinician to supervise her work. She was employed as an art therapist in the Child Development & Child Care Program of the Department of Psychiatry at the University of Pittsburgh founded by Benjamin Spock and Erik Erikson, the great developmentalist (and artist.) After Rubin presented a case and its artwork, Erikson who was there as a consultant advised her to avoid further training, feeling it "might well ruin–or at least interfere with–something of value in the intuitive approach [she] was, by default, forced to follow" (Rubin in Junge & Wadeson, 2006, p. 112).

For Rubin, art making started early in her childhood, but at the age of 17, she recognized it as a coping mechanism when a close friend died. The painting she made in response to the death was not a portrait of her friend, but an expression of Rubin's grief, loss and rage:

> It was a new symbolic replacement for my friend who was lost, a mute tangible testament. Doing it afforded me tremendous relief. It did not take away the hurt and the ache, but it did help in releasing some of the anguished tangle of feelings that held me in their grip. (Rubin in Junge & Wadeson, 2006, p. 107)

Rubin received a Bachelors degree in art from Wellesley College, a Masters in education from the Harvard Graduate School of Education and a doctorate in counseling from the University of Pittsburgh. She discovered art in psychology in college in a Child Psychology course when she met a researcher who was studying preschool children's finger paintings to understand the effects of child-rearing practices. She focused on children in the Wellesley nursery school, assessing behavior and their use of art materials. In graduate school, taking a Human Development course, Rubin searched the library for the psychology of children's art, read Lowenfeld and Cane's work and a group of Margaret Naumburg's early papers. She remained fascinated with the combination of children and art and first, became a teacher about which, she says: "Sadly, my teaching experiences turned out to be less satisfying than I had hoped, though I could see that many children benefited from making art" (Rubin in Junge & Wadeson, 2006, p. 110).

To gain more understanding of herself and her patients in 1973, Rubin decided to undertake psychoanalytic training and her theoretical conceptualization of art therapy practice is as close to traditional Freudian psychoanalytic personality theories and therapeutic methods as they come. Unlike Wadeson and others, she would probably not call herself "eclectic." With Freud, Rubin emphasizes the importance of early history in the development of psychiatric problems:

> [Goals are] uncovering repressed material . . . and helping the patient

gain insight into the meaning of his [sic] behavior. . . . I find the use of art in an insight-oriented approach to be the most powerful and exciting kind of art therapy for myself, as well as for most of my patients. (Rubin, 1987b, p. 12)

And about her theoretical bent, Rubin writes:

I have read, studied, and worked with different theoretical perspectives, and have usually found in each one or more concepts relevant to the work I do. . . . I thought that the solution to my problem [of formulating a theoretical orientation] would be a kind of patchwork—a mosaic or collage of different ideas from different theories-which together would account for what seems to happen in art therapy. . . . What now seems more probable is that a theory about art therapy will have to emerge from art therapy itself. . . . (Rubin, 1978, p. 18)

Ironically in 1987, Rubin published *Approaches to Art Therapy* which she edited. With this book, in 21 chapters, by different art therapy authors and covering a wide range of perspectives, Rubin illuminates how the use of art can integrate with and expand an extensive variety of psychological theoretical orientations. The sections of the book are "Psychodynamic Approaches," "Analytic Therapy (Jungian)," "Humanistic Approaches," "Psycho-Educational Approaches," "Systemic Approaches," and "Integrative Approaches."

Judith Rubin has also been a teacher of art therapy and a mentor to many. In 1968, she established an art therapy program with her colleague and friend Ellie Irwin at the outpatient clinic of the Pittsburgh Child Guidance Center. Together, they ran Art-Drama Therapy groups and together they started a Creative and Expressive Arts Therapy program in a psychiatric hospital.

Early in her art therapy career, Judith Rubin discovered her love of writing. Her first journal article "A diagnostic art interview" was published in 1973 and Rubin's first book, *Child Art Therapy* was published in 1978. It is a classic in art therapy; in it she describes clinical work with families, individuals and groups and persuasively describes blind and multiply-disabled children and their enhancing uses of art:

The use of art materials like clay as fantasied replacements, additions, or perhaps protectors is also common with the blind. . . it seemed to be a way of compensating in fantasy for the missing body part or function and may also have served as protection against the ever-present threat of further injury. (Rubin, 1978, pp. 121-122)

One of the reasons Rubin wrote *Child Art Therapy* was because "I was distressed by the ignorance and confusion evident in some [art therapy] papers and presentations" (Rubin in Junge & Wadeson, 2006, p. 120). Judith Rubin has arguably written more books about art therapy than anyone else to date. Many of her books are attempts to show art therapy to others, such as social workers, counselors and other mental health professionals. Along with *Child Art Therapy*, Rubin's books are *The Art of Art Therapy* (1984), *Approaches to Art Therapy* (1987), *Art Therapy: An Introduction* (1998), *Art Therapy* (1999), *Artful Therapy* (2005), and a creative drawing book *My Mom & Dad Don't Live Together Anymore* for the American Psychological Association (2002). She says ". . . if I ever write another book, it might be one about using art and imagery in psychoanalysis" (Rubin in Junge & Wadeson, 2006, p. 118).

Rubin's affection for movie-making is unique in art therapy as far as I know. While others have made videos of art therapy in a specific project or an especially interesting population,[7] Rubin has expanded her work into film making almost from the beginning. She writes "Oddly, while I like the books, I love the films" (Rubin in Junge & Wadeson, 2006, p. 119). Her first film, "We'll Show You What We're Gonna Do!" (1972 in Rubin 2008d)[8] was about the blind and disabled population she wrote about in *Child Art Therapy*. For a third revision of *Child Art Therapy* and for *Artful Therapy,* she crafted DVDs to go with the books. "Beyond Words: Art Therapy with Older Adults" is a short film about working with seniors (Rubin, 2008b) and "Art Therapy Has Many Faces" is a 55-minute description of the profession and its clinical applications, including the work of many art therapists around the world. "The Green Creature Within: Art & Drama in Group Psychotherapy with Adolescents" (2008) which Rubin produced with drama therapist Ellie Irwin, also includes music, movement, poetry and filmmaking.

Retired, Rubin lives part-time in Pittsburgh and part-time on

---

7. An exception is Robert Ault's (1986) video "Art Therapy: A Healing Vision," produced by the Menninger Foundation which provides an overview of art therapy.
8. Rubin's films have been put on DVDs and are listed in "References" with 2008 dates. "The Green Creature Within" is under "Irwin & Rubin" (2008).

Sanibel Island, Florida. She continues to travel and present about art therapy and hopes to make a series of art therapy teaching films. She is studying tap dancing.

Important Dates and Events

1936–Judith Rubin is born in New York City. From early childhood she is interested in art.

Age 17–After the death of a close friend, Rubin recognizes that art can be used as a coping agent for trauma.

1954–At Wellesley College, discovers psychology of art and psychological art education. At Harvard Graduate School, intending to be an art teacher, in a Human Development seminar, Rubin reads works by Naumburg, Florence Cane, Viktor Lowenfeld and child psychotherapists.

1958–Is an art teacher in the Cambridge, MA public schools. Has a hard time "fitting in."

1963–Invited to do "art therapy" with schizophrenic children. Supervised by the woman who was mentor of Fred Rogers (of "Mister Rogers' neighborhood.")

1964 on–Consults with Naumburg and Kramer in New York. Wants to become a "real" art therapist.

1964–For Child Study Center Grand Rounds, Rubin presents an art therapy case and meets Erik Erikson who dissuades her from undertaking further clinical training fearing it will hinder her intuitive approach.

1966-1969–"Art Lady" for "Mister Rogers' Neighborhood" on public television.

1967–Establishes art program for physically-disabled children.

1968–Meets Marvin Shapiro and joins his Expressive Arts Study Group at the Pittsburgh Child Guidance Center.

1968–Establishes one-day a week pilot program in art therapy at Pittsburgh Child Guidance, Department of Psychiatry, University of Pittsburgh. Attends meeting of the American Society for Psychopathology of Expression in Boston and meets art therapists Hanna Kwiatkowska, Elinor Ulman and Carolyn Refsnes.

1972–Makes film about her art therapy with blind children: "We'll Show You What We're Gonna Do." Decides to undertake psychoanalytic training and psychoanalysis.

1973–"A Diagnostic Art Interview," Rubin's first art therapy piece is published. Makes a second film "Children and the Arts."

1976–Earns Ph.D at the Analytic Institute.

1977-1979–Is president of the American Art Therapy Association.

1978–Rubin's first book, *Child Art Therapy,* is published.

1981–Receives AATA's highest award, the Honorary Life Membership.

1984–*The Art of Art Therapy* is published.

1987–*Approaches to Art Therapy* is published. Edited by Rubin, it illustrates the uses of art therapy within a variety of theoretical perspectives.

1998–*Art Therapy: An Introduction* is published.

1999–*Artful Therapy* is published.

2001–Second edition of *Approaches to Art Therapy* is published.

2002–*My Mom & Dad Don't Live Together Anymore* (a drawing book) is published by the American Psychological Association.

2005–Third edition of *Child Art Therapy.*

2008–"Art Therapy Has Many Faces" a 55-minute film about art therapy is released. "Beyond Words," a film about older adults, is produced. All films are updated.

2009–Second edition of *Art Therapy: An Introduction* is published.

2010–Second edition of *Art of Art Therapy* is published.

Study Questions

1. Speculate about the importance of Judith Rubin's "peacemaker" role in the development of art therapy.

2. What is the importance of her "peacemaker" role within the American Art Therapy Association.

3. Describe the importance of Rubin's work as a writer and film maker. Read one of Rubin's books and write a brief "book review."

4. Create an image in the spirit of Judith Rubin.

Chapter 13

OTHER ART THERAPISTS
WHO BEGAN IN THE 1960s[1]

Apart from those art therapists mentioned in previous chapters, other prominent art therapists who began work in the 1960s are Gwen Gibson, Bernard Levy, Frances Anderson, Rawley Silver and Gladys Agell.

GWEN GIBSON (b. 1923)

Born in 1923, Gwen Gibson is a doctor's daughter from Pennsylvania. As a teenager, she toured small towns of Pennsylvania playing the saxophone as part of a marching band. She was an art therapist at the Baltimore City Psychiatric Day Treatment Center and Johns Hopkins University, primarily working with schizophrenic patients. Before becoming an art therapist, Gibson was a laboratory technician. She saw herself as a painter and a potter, but those were the times when artists were hired in many psychiatric hospitals. When Gibson was hired as an art therapist, she had to learn what that was and so she studied, in depth, the psychological side of the work. Gibson became President of the American Art Therapy Association in 1979 and received the Honorary Life Membership in 1993. Gibson writes: "In retirement, I have time to compose poetry and attend classes for senior citizens. . . . Each week, I take a piano player plus 10 men and women volunteer singers into a retirement home, lead sing-alongs

---

1. Many historical facts in this chapter are from the autobiographies in Junge & Wadeson (2006) *Architects of Art Therapy, Memoirs and Life Stories.*

and encourage the residents to exchange anecdotes from their lives. . ."
(Gibson in Junge & Wadeson, 2006, p. 172).

BERNARD LEVY (1924–1984)

Bernard Levy was born in 1924 and died in 1984. He was a passionate watercolor painter and studied ceramics at Pratt Institute. After
serving in World War II, he earned a Ph.D. in psychology and became
Chief Psychologist at D.C. General Hospital where he met Elinor
Ulman. Levy served as Chair of the Psychology Department at George
Washington University. With Elinor Ulman, he co-founded the art
therapy program there, one of the first in the nation. He received the
American Art Therapy Association's Honorary Life Membership in
1977. Of Levy, Wadeson wrote: "I remember Bernie best for his wry
wit, outspoken opinions and the strong leadership he provided AATA
as we were becoming a profession" (Wadeson in Junge & Wadeson,
2006, p. 176).

FRANCES ANDERSON (b. 1941)

Frances Anderson came to art therapy from art education. In the
early days of art therapy, she began her career as a teacher–grades
1-12–in southern Indiana. There she discovered children with "problems"–it was not yet called Special Education. She attended the founding meeting of the American Art Therapy Association at the University
of Louisville in 1969. In 1972, with Helen Landgarten, Anderson conducted a survey about the status of art therapy in mental health organizations across the country. Through this study and their followup studies, Anderson and Landgarten documented the need for art therapists
and through their efforts, many art therapists were able to gain work,
particularly in the West. They later published their data results in
Ulman's journal the *Bulletin of Art Therapy* (1974) and in *Art Education*
(1975). Anderson received her doctorate in Art Education and Curriculum and Instruction from Indiana University in the 1960s. She is
known, in part, as an important art therapy researcher.

Anderson taught ceramics in Australia in 1971 and established the
graduate art therapy program at Illinois State University in 1970. She

was Editor of *Art Therapy: Journal of the American Art Therapy Association* from 2000-2002. She resigned from the editorship of the journal to accept a Fulbright Award to Argentina and she later traveled on a Fulbright to Taiwan where she helped establish the first art therapy program there. She received the 1990 Honorary Life Membership from the American Art Therapy Association.

Anderson's clinical work has focused on children and children with special needs, within an art as therapy approach. Later she developed clay groups for adult survivors who were sexually molested as children. Like most of the early art therapists, she wrote books about her clinical work; her first, published in 1978, with a second edition in 1992, was *Art for All the Children: A Sourcebook for Impaired Children.* She has published seven books.

RAWLEY SILVER (b. 1917)

Rawley Silver is well-known as an art therapy researcher. (Her art therapy assessments are discussed more fully in Chapter 24, "The Question of Art Therapy Assessment and Assessment Procedures.") She was "the first person to develop the systematic use of art for a wide range of children and adults with cognitive deficits" (Honorary Life Membership Award Speech, quoted by Silver in Junge & Wadeson, 2006, p. 211). She established the Silver Drawing Test (SDT), one of the first and best known assessments in art therapy and one of the few that has been subjected to extensive research and validity and reliability studies. Using stimulus drawings, the SDT is a test of cognition and emotion. Silver first published her research in the early 1970s and has published many of her specific studies as journal articles. Her two books outlining the test are *Art as Language: Access to Thoughts and Feelings Through Stimulus Drawings* (2001) and *Three Art Assessments: Silver Drawing Test of Cognition and Emotion, Draw a Story, Screening for Depression and Stimulus Drawings and Techniques* (2002).

After a mid-life accident which deafened her, Silver grew interested in deaf children and their art. She was horrified at the low expectations for them and volunteered to teach them art. The deaf children in her class had been designated emotionally disturbed. She writes: "The deaf children's drawings awakened the therapist in me" (Silver in Junge & Wadeson, 2006, p. 204). During this time, she earned a

Masters and a doctorate in Fine Arts and Fine Arts Education, from Columbia University Teachers College. She also attended an art therapy course taught by Margaret Naumburg at New York University. Much of Silver's deafness healed, but she retains some today. The challenge of deafness for Silver is both a problem in her life and has provided her with a deep understanding of the difficulties of physically disabled people and encouraged her to be an advocate for them.

An artist since childhood, Silver said: "A career in fine arts was considered impossible for women in the 1930s" (in Junge & Wadeson, 2006, p. 204). She believed the tenth century Chinese painter, Ching Hao, who said "that the goal of an artist was to capture the essential qualities of the chosen subject" (Silver in Junge & Wadeson, 2006, p. 205) and states:

> Neuroscientists today seem to agree . . . the preeminent function of both art and the visual brain is to acquire knowledge about the world by selecting what is essential and discarding what is superfluous. Neurons in the brain's visual pathways search for constancies, just as artists search for the constant, essential features of objects and situations. (Silver in Junge & Wadeson, 2006, p. 206)

Silver presented a paper in 1970 at the first conference of the American Art Therapy Association, received AATA's research award in 1976, 1980 and 1992 and the Honorary Life Membership in 1983. About research, she says:

> I believe that research in art therapy should be objective as well as subjective, quantitative [as] well as qualitative. Unless we can combine art experiences and psychological insights with scientific evidence, we convince only ourselves of the contributions art therapy can make to knowledge about human intelligence, emotional needs, and behavior. . . . I believe that qualified art therapists can make contributions that artists and psychotherapists cannot provide. . . . (Silver in Junge & Wadeson, p. 213)

GLADYS AGELL

In high school, Gladys Agell discovered the French painter Honore Daumier and, like him, tried to capture human foibles in her art. Agell says that her artwork is the basis for her interest in people and her interest in people led her back to artwork. Agell, thus was fascinated by the combination of art and psychology, which has become a common and familiar story for early art therapists.

After completing a Bachelor's degree in art and psychology at New York University, Agell took classes with both Margaret Naumburg and Edith Kramer. She initiated the art therapy program at Goddard College in Vermont which eventually moved to Vermont College of Norwich in 1979.[2] When Ulman's journal (then the *American Journal of Art Therapy*) was not picked up by the American Art Therapy Association in 1983,[3] Agell convinced Norwich University to publish it–with Agell as Coordinator and later Editor, it remained there until 1986. Agell's clinical work was at Rockland County New York Community Mental Health, Vermont State Hospital, and Veterans' Association Medical Center on Long Island.

Gladys Agell attended the 1969 formation meeting of the American Art Therapy Association and, in alphabetical order, is at the top of the roster of "Members in Good Standing." She was President of the American Art Therapy Association 1983-85 and received the Honorary Life Membership in 1987. After a more than 40-year career in art therapy, Agell is a member of the current American Art Therapy Association Executive Board.

STUDY QUESTIONS

1. Describe the particular interests of the four pioneer art therapists of this chapter.
2. Discuss how art impacted each one.
3. Create an image in the spirit of *one* of these art therapists.

---

2. The art therapy program at Vermont College at Norwich University was structured so that students took classes in the summer and could have internships and remain in their hometowns and cities for the other months of the year. It was the first and for a long time, the only art therapy program, with this model. Unfortunately, it has closed.
3. With the *American Journal of Art Therapy's* move to Norwich University, the American Art Therapy Association established its own journal, *Art Therapy, Journal of the American Art Therapy Association*. Now there were two. In addition to *Art Therapy* there was the journal *Art Psychotherapy* founded by Ernest Harms in 1973 and including dance/movement, poetry, drama and music with visual arts. (In 1980, it changed its name to *The Arts in Psychotherapy*. Myra Levick has served as Editor-In-Chief. See Chapter 25, "Expansion of Literature.")

Chapter 14

QUALITIES AND PATTERNS IN THE
LIVES OF PIONEER ART THERAPISTS

There are stunning similarities in the defining interests, stories and career paths of pioneer art therapists. There was often trauma of some kind for them in the near and distant background. For example, World War II occurred during many of these people's childhood and some fled Europe and Nazi tyranny. In this section, I trace and discuss some of these distinctive patterns. Although, there was no such thing as art therapy or art therapy education then when most of the early art therapists began their work, the patterns may reflect what makes a good art therapist today and are therefore worth teasing out. I am an example: I loved drawing from an early age and I believe I was seriously interested in art therapy as a young adolescent from about the age of 13 on, but it would only be 20 years later, in about 1973 that I actually heard the words "art therapy" and began to know there was an evolving mental health profession that perfectly fit my passions. While pioneers' life stories may not contain all the themes and patterns discussed in this section, an amazing number of them do.

Today applicants for art therapy education and training must meet certain pre-requisite requirements in art and psychology established by the American Art Therapy Association. Having interviewed many applicants and observed the pathways of many art therapy students, graduates and art therapists over the years, I have concluded that many, if not all, apply to art therapy programs because they have come in close contact *in themselves* with the power of art to heal—sometimes completely by accident. *After* this awareness, many fulfill formal art courses needed for application—often in a short time. Thus the questions persist to continuously plague art therapy: What is the role of *art* in the creation of an art therapist? Does the art therapist need to be a trained artist of long-standing in order to become an art therapist? Does the study of art and the development of skills in art making enhance the abilities of the art therapist? Does the immersion in art need to be over a long period of time or can it be briefly acquired and understood? On the other hand, can a "talk" therapist learn to be an art therapist? Is there ever an "ideal" combination of art and psychology? The strikingly similar patterns in the lives of pioneer art therapists may provide answers to some of these questions and should be taken into serious consideration in art therapy training systems. On the other hand, perhaps the designs and characteristics underscored in these art therapists' lives may provide clues about what makes a "pioneer"–not what makes an art therapist.

Major patterns in the life of pioneer art therapists are:

1. Artist from early childhood.
2. Fascination with people and their development.
3. Pursuit of education and training in art and psychotherapy.
4. Important role models and–as we would call them now, "mentors."
5. Tolerance of "outsider" status.

ARTISTS FROM EARLY CHILDHOOD

Pioneering art therapists found creativity and the visual arts early on in childhood. They used art for themselves as an intense source of pleasure and exploration of feelings. For these potential art therapists, art making could provide a welcome space of isolation in a sometimes difficult environment. It could create a satisfying bubble around a child or adolescent and the doing of it could provide a "place apart" accepted and respected by family members and others. In their special space, the sensitive child found a safe place to explore an internal and exterior landscape through art. Making art could be a way of creating interest from family members in the artist and their work, and closeness as they moved further into the realm of the serious young artist. A "specialness" and the unique talents of the artist were often recognized in the child by the family.

Many pioneers came from artistic families, some where reproductions of great art were hung on the walls, and the child as artist was encouraged.[1] The following statements are from art therapy pioneers' memoirs in *Architects of Art Therapy*. Edith Kramer wrote: "Ever since I can remember, the center of my life was the making of art: drawing, painting and sculpting. . . . When I was ten years old, the noted artist and art teacher, Friedl Dicker saw my drawings and declared she would take me on as a student. . ." (p. 11). Harriet Wadeson's mother said, "Harriet made art before it was fashionable." Wadeson, herself, wrote: "I drew stories before I could write" (p. 84). In *Architects of Art Therapy, Memoirs and Life Stories,* there is a photo of Wadeson, age 7, lying on the floor intently drawing. Judith Rubin's chapter in the same book, contains a photograph "Judith A. Rubin [about age 4] drawing with Daddy watching." Don Jones: "I began drawing at age four . . . I used to save the white cards that divided the shredded wheat biscuits [to draw on]" (p. 38). Helen Landgarten stated:

> I remember that a number of artists and art therapists also were ill as children. Perhaps turning into an artist is in part due to our childhood when we had to spend a great deal of time in bed. It gave us a chance to make more intense observations, a chance to lay quietly to fantasize, visualize, and to draw. (Landgarten in Junge & Wadeson, 2006, p. 146)

Bernard Stone was an artist through adolescence and earned his Masters of Fine Arts (MFA) in his early 20s. Ault: "For many, it was a good time to grow up, but very tough if you were a young man in Texas in the '40s and '50s more interested in art than football. The girls preferred jocks not artists" (p. 65). Levick: "As far back as I can remember I was creating something. In fact, my mother often told the story that as a toddler she found me pulling corners of wallpaper, pulling out the plaster underneath and trying to mold it" (p. 127).

Pioneer art therapists recognized themselves as artists very early in their life. As they grew into adolescence, they pursued art training in high school and college often going to art school or earning a Bachelor of Fine Arts in college and even a Masters of Fine Arts in graduate

---

1. Robert Ault's family of origin is an exception. He wrote: ". . . both my parents had difficulty understanding what I did or why accumulation of wealth wasn't important to me. . . . From that day on [when Ault was appointed university professor, his father] referred to me . . . as his professor son, never his artist or art therapist son" (Ault in Junge & Wadeson, 2006, p. 68).

school. "In college I took more classes in art than in my major, psychology" (Wadeson in Junge & Wadeson, 2006, p. 84).

FASCINATION WITH PEOPLE AND THEIR DEVELOPMENT

As they looked outward as young children, pioneer art therapists were sometimes secret observers of human behavior. My guess is that they were especially sensitive to the varieties and vicissitudes of family life. "[At age 13] I was already a practiced, quiet observer in all my relationships and increasingly more and more psychologically free, 'open' to subjectively evaluate and critique circumstances" (Jones in Junge & Wadeson, 2006, p. 39). Wadeson writes:

> The sirloin steak my Mother served mapped the family power dynamics. She placed it before my father, who cut it up and took the heart of the steak for himself. Sonny [younger brother] and I were passed the platter of outside pieces. The outer edge and fat were left for my Mother, who was still in the kitchen. (Wadeson in Junge & Wadeson, 2006, p. 83)

I have written of myself as an early observer when I was a small child and sat at the top of the stairway watching and listening to the fascinating adult world spilling out of the living room party below.

PURSUIT OF EDUCATION IN ART AND IN PSYCHOTHERAPY

Pioneer art therapists became aware of their environment and also of their internal landscape. They were smart and often driven. Using their art as an enhancement to adolescent and young adult identity, many sought significant education specifically in art. Stone pursued a Masters of Fine Arts at the University of Kansas and very soon after graduation was hired by psychiatrist Pedro Corrons as an art therapist at Columbus State Hospital in Ohio. The following quotes are from memoirs in Junge & Wadeson, 2006. Levick stated: "As I was about to enter high school, we learned that one school in Philadelphia had made the decision to include art as a fifth major in the academic track for qualified students. I qualified and my parents arranged for me to attend. . . . I did well both academically and in art and was recommended for a scholarship to Moore College of Art in Philadelphia" (p. 127). Landgarten: "In high school I took all the art classes that were available. After graduation, I attended Wayne University as an art major, transferred to School Society of Arts and Crafts, then attended New York's Grand Central School of Art" (p. 146). Williams wrote of Elinor Ulman's ten years post Bachelors art education:

> She graduated Phi Beta Kappa from Wellesley (1930), studied oil painting in France (1932-34), brush painting in China (1934-36), and landscape architecture in the United States (1943). From 1934-1940 she painted and taught private pupils. Her paintings were exhibited at the Corcoran Biennial, the Phillips Gallery in Washington, the Baltimore Museum of Art, and at the 1939 New York World's Fair. (p. 52)

Recognizing the psychological side of their personal equation, Margaret Naumburg undertook both a Freudian and a Jungian analysis and Kramer began her psychoanalysis in Prague and continued it when she immigrated to New York City. Jones discovered the profound power and meaning of art within serious human duress: During World War II, A Conscientious Objector, Jones, writing of his work with mental patients at the Marlboro State Mental Hospital in New Jersey said "this experience became my 'university of psychiatry' . . . these abandoned, hopeless men and women were and are never still anonymous abstractions to me. I painted and drew them and their plight" (pp. 41-42). Wadeson:

> My interest in psychology began when I was about 14, babysitting for my cousin. After I put her to bed, I would peruse the study bookcase of my psychiatrist uncle. I was fascinated by Freud's interpretation of dreams. . . . I began taking courses at the Washington School of Psychiatry, American University, and Catholic University. (pp. 85-86)

Judith Rubin:

> Although Margaret [Naumburg] and Edith's [Kramer] ideas were quite different, their advice about what I should do was identical. Both suggested that I learn about myself through personal therapy and that I learn about being a therapist through supervised work under an experienced clinician. For therapy, I went for two years twice weekly to psychiatrist Naomi Ragins. (p. 111)

Ault: "In the '60s I was psychoanalyzed at Menningers'. . . . It was quite an experience and I feel I learned a great deal from it and benefited greatly" (p. 70). "Janie's [Rhyne] life and involvements changed after two years of psychoanalysis and divorce" (Lusebrink, p. 159).

Many pioneers were employed in psychiatric institutions as art teachers and art therapists and learned there what an art therapist was and did. Some of these were the great training institutions in the country. Kramer:

> [I was hired] at Wiltwyck's therapeutic treatment home for disadvantaged and delinquent boys, ages 8-13. . . . For the next seven years I commuted three days a week from Manhattan to upstate New York . . . It was at Wiltwyck that I began to develop my ideas that would later become Art as Therapy. (p. 15)

Wadeson, through a contact with Adele Wynne with whom she was in an art class, went to work for Wynne's husband Lyman at the National Institute of Mental Health. She met staff member Hanna Kwiatkowska and was trained in art therapy by her:

> NIH [National Institutes of Health] was eye-opening. It was exhilarating. I felt perched on the leading edge of psychiatric research. Each week I attended a research conference in which luminaries from all over the world presented their research followed by a lively discussion. (p. 86)

Through social worker Ellen Ruderman, Helen Landgarten met psychiatrist Saul Brown, Chief of Staff of the outpatient Family and Child Division of Psychiatry at Mt. Sinai Hospital in Los Angeles (later Cedars-Sinai, Thalians Community Mental Health Center):

> We agreed that I would volunteer my services during the summer, working with groups as an adjunct to their primary treatment. If the clinic was impressed with my performance then I would be hired in the fall. . . . Thus, in 1967 [I was hired as an art therapist]. . . . At the clinic I attended the many seminars given for the psychiatrists, psychologists, and social workers. I owe my knowledge and my skills to the Thalians [Cedars-Sinai] staff who taught me how to become the primary therapist. (p. 148)

Rubin:

> In 1967 I was asked to start an art program at an institution for physi-
> cally-handicapped youngsters. [I was] shocked by how few children
> were seen by the professionals. . . . In 1968, my therapist suggested that
> I meet with child psychiatrist Marvin Shapiro, who was interested in the
> arts in therapy. He invited me to join an Expressive Arts Study Group
> he had recently started at the Pittsburgh Child Guidance Center
> (PCGC), the outpatient clinic of Child Psychiatry. (p. 112)

ROLE MODELS AND MENTORS

Most early art therapists were lucky to have important advocates as
role models and mentors. Mentors recognized the unique talents of
these artists with a psychological bent, offered them employment,
supervised them and, sometimes encouraged them to seek further education and even to establish art therapy training programs. With Paul
Jay Fink's help, Myra Levick took the difficult and important steps to
form the American Art Therapy Association. Importantly, these role
models and mentors were willing to take a chance on the innovative
but largely unproven approach of art therapy.

Advocates tended to come from the two points of the theoretical
continuum later represented by Naumburg and Kramer: art psychotherapy and art as therapy. They were psychiatrists who were
mostly men—as was the cultural tradition at the time—and they were
psychologically-knowledgeable art teachers, who were mostly women
since women's roles were considerably limited and often concerned
what was supposed to be their innate maternal instinct.

Pioneers' role models and mentors had a special awareness and
respect for the uses of art with mental health clients and other marginalized populations—some having used it themselves. They recognized art as an exceptionally potent medium not only with children,
but with adults, families and groups; this significant recognition was
immensely important to the development of the profession. Parents,
mental health professionals and others knew of the value of drawing
and art for children, but up to this time, few had recognized the unique
opportunities which art and the creative process could offer through
the life span.

In 1941, Naumburg had Nolan D. C. Lewis, Director of the New

York State Psychiatric Institute. Kramer met Friedl Dicker as a young child:

> Later, I also assisted Friedl in her work with children of political refugees who lived in camps provided by the Czech government. It was during this work with uprooted children that I first experienced how art could help them regain their emotional equilibrium. . . . Friedl prompt-ly established art sessions [in Theresienstadt/Terezin Concentration Camp]. . . . Friedl sustained the quality of life and emotional health of innumerable children at Terezin. (pp. 12-13)

Jones had Karl and Will Menninger at the Menninger Foundation Clinic. Psychiatrists Curt Boenheim and Pedro Corrons mentored Bernard Stone and, in reality, began art psychotherapy in Ohio. Boenheim attended the formation meeting of AATA at Hahnemann Medical College. Bernie Stone calls Irene Jakab, founder of the International and American Societies for the Pathology of Expression, his first mentor. Ault had Don Jones and Karl and Will Menninger. Hanna Kwiatkowska had Murray Bowen and Lyman Wynne. Harriet Wadeson had Lyman Wynne and Kwiatkowska. Rubin wrote: "In col-lege, I had taken Child Psychology from a woman named Thelma Alper. While I was in her class, she was collecting data for a study about the effect of child-rearing practices on finger paintings by pre-school children" (Rubin in Junge & Wadeson, 2006, p. 109). Then Rubin was the "Art Lady" for Mr. Rogers of public television where she had Fred Rogers' support: "I used my ad-libbed segment to com-municate the therapeutic value of art to parents and children" (Rubin in Junge & Wadeson, p. 112). Felice Cohen had Irving Kraft, Chief of Child Psychiatry at Houston State Psychiatric Hospital. Helen Landgarten had Saul Brown who championed her career at Thalians Community Mental Health Center (Cedars-Sinai Hospital) and Myra Levick had Paul Jay Fink and Morris J. Goldman:

> The four years that I was at Albert Einstein Medical Center were some-thing like the first five years of life. . . . For me those first . . . years sym-bolized major giant steps in my professional career. I went from being a painter and thinking medium and product, to thinking, medium, art making and process. And most of all, I learned about the psychological implications in that creative process. (Levick in Junge & Wadeson, 2006, p. 129)

As a young artist, I was contacted by well-known Los Angeles psychoanalyst Ralph Greenson to teach art to some of his patients.

When art therapy formed itself as a separate mental health discipline, many of its founders believed it must be controlled by art therapists, not psychiatrists or other supporters; therefore, names of these early essential mentors are not generally included in histories of the profession. Placing control in the hands of art therapists was undoubtedly tremendously politically important to drive art therapy forward. In reality, however, without the support from a variety of other mental health professionals who profoundly loved the arts, were sometimes practicing artists themselves, and who often were in positions of power in clinics and institutions, art therapy as a profession would probably not exist. These mentors had the foresight to hire art therapists, teach them, encourage their clinical work, give them opportunities for important research and presentations at mental health conferences and they sometimes helped them start whole graduate educational programs and clinical departments. They offered support and opportunities to art therapists which were an immeasurable benefit to the evolving profession. Most important, perhaps, is the fact that because of their own professional status within the medical hierarchy and within institutions, they provided visible credibility and legitimacy to the evolution of this new profession.

Different today, but perhaps no less necessary, the encouragement of colleagues is still of great importance and plays a role as art therapy continues to move forward. This collaborative relationship has its tacit echoes every year in that the keynote speaker for the annual art therapy conference put on by the American Art Therapy Association is often a psychiatrist interested in the arts. Many have said that the profession has matured enough so that a major art therapist ought to headline the conference. But the practice of art therapists learning through honoring and collaboration with mental health colleagues and artists continues even although its origins are probably forgotten.

TOLERANCE OF OUTSIDER STATUS

That few have heard of art therapy is a common joke in training programs and students are taught what to say when somebody asks "what is that?" Fifty years ago and more, *nobody* knew what art thera-

py was except the few pioneering art therapists who thought they single-handedly had invented the spectacular integration of art and psychology. To be an art therapist then, almost by definition, was to be a
sometimes unwelcome upstart in the traditional mental health disciplines which, after World War II, were struggling themselves to become
established as professionals.

Artists are historically known as outsiders to the establishment.
Even some traditional court painters and those supported by powerful
patronage needed to find their own way through the labyrinths of the
creative process to profound expressive excellence; the painter Goya
is an example. I speculate that early art therapists' identities as artists
helped them conquer the risks and fears of being an outlier in a
strange land, but that this was an extraordinarily difficult feat cannot
be denied. To be an outsider is to stand alone—sometimes isolated and
lonely; it took energy, intelligence, stamina, passion, courage and a
profound belief in the "rightness" of the cause. Perhaps, most importantly, it took the willingness to stand up, be seen and forcefully and
persuasively speak out.

Although we know little of her struggles, we can assume that Mary
Huntoon had plenty of them at Menningers'. Rubin writes of
Naumburg's "courageous and energetic efforts . . . like all pioneers, she
had to fight hard for her creation" (Rubin in Junge & Wadeson, 2006,
p. 8). Because of his pacifist beliefs during World War II, Don Jones
became a Conscientious Objector. Williams in her description of
Ulman writes: "Elinor's reputation for fierceness was not unfounded.
She did not suffer fools and could ignite instantly when one of her passions was challenged . . . even though her forcefulness and passion did
create enemies, they also fueled the pursuit of excellence that marked
everything she did" (Williams in Junge & Wadeson, 2006, pp. 51 &
52). Landgarten describes a number of difficult experiences in her section in *Architects of Art Therapy, Memoirs and Life Stories,* called "A Rough
Terrain." She states: "I managed those difficult times because I was on
a mission." And: "Even after 35 years, it still pains me when I think
about the humiliation that I experienced so long ago" (pp. 152-153).
Wadeson wrote "The Last Lesson," a poem about her mentor Hanna
Yaxa Kwiatkowska. She said, "The wind roars the name of that last lesson: Courage" (p. 59).

Chapter 15

DEFINING ART THERAPY

It has been the broad, inclusive definitions of art therapy, I believe, that have enabled the profession and the American Art Therapy Association to thrive and move forward. Nevertheless, the fierce fights along the way have been loud and ongoing and the war scars sometimes enduring. Never dull, many of the battles in the American Art Therapy Association have centered on the definition of art therapy, itself.

Generally speaking, art therapy is the use of art with human beings toward the goal of helping, healing and growth. But the theoretical tenets of the profession spring from very different milieus and orientations—that of psychoanalytic psychotherapy and that of psychologically informed art education. With its two major theoreticians—Margaret Naumburg and Edith Kramer—promoting these differing views. Rather than achieving an integrated wholistic perspective, there have been ongoing vehement and reductionistic arguments as to which is a better focus for the field; education and training programs tend to hew to one or other philosophy.[1]

ART AS THERAPY VERSUS ART PSYCHOTHERAPY

Perceived as a political division by many, originally the argument was over where the "cure" was in treatment and what role the art played. Naumburg's vision was of a psychotherapeutic process which, through spontaneous art tasks, uncovered unconscious mechanisms.

---

1. In the chapter "Reconsidering the Wars Between Art and Therapy" in my book *Mourning, Memory and Life Itself, Essays by an Art Therapist,* I propose a synthesis between these two factions.

Thus her use of art in psychotherapy as a means to uncover and plum the depths of the person's *unconscious* and, through projecting unconscious material concretely through art, to bring it into consciousness. With this process, growth and change could occur. For Naumburg, art as aesthetic is unimportant because whatever "art" evolves in psychotherapy is not regarded as an aesthetic product, but a form of *communication* between the client and therapist which then needs to be verbally explored.

Kramer contends that it is *the creative process in the making of the art product itself* that is healing and thus clients are encouraged to immerse themselves in creativity. Ego integration and synthesis—not opening up unconscious processes—are Kramer's goals. Kramer claims *successful sublimation is the signature indicator of growth and healing.* Sublimation as understood by Kramer is key in her theory. "Sublimation" is a defense mechanism defined by Freud whereby antisocial desires and drives are transformed into socially acceptable ones.[2] Kramer maintains that the more complete *aesthetically* the art product is, the better sublimation has occurred—e.g., the aesthetic quality of the art product is a visual indicator of the success of art therapy. For Kramer, the art product then is the focus of the work and the client is helped to make a complete and technically competent work of art.

Unlike Naumburg's art psychotherapy patient, Kramer's client usually doesn't explore the art verbally. Kramer maintains she is not a psychotherapist and eschews psychotherapeutic training for art therapists; according to Kramer, making the art is enough. As is often the case, later generations of art therapists strongly hold to one side of the argument or the other as the "right" way, whereas it does not *seem* so important for the originators. Edith Kramer recently wrote about the "Historic Rift" between herself and Naumburg:

> The difference between Art as Therapy and Art Psychotherapy perhaps has more to do with the age group and social environment of the individuals under our care. It is significant that early in her career, Naumburg worked with disturbed children . . . and our approaches were very similar. It is unfortunate that few art therapists seem to read Naumburg's early material. . . . It was only after she began her work with middle-class adults, many of whom found art making daunting, did

---

2. Anna Freud and the Ego Psychologists later determined that sublimation was not a defense mechanism at all but a normal function of the ego.

Naumburg evolve and change her methods. Her technique of Dynamically Oriented Art Therapy then became more aligned with the talking-based free associative techniques of classical psychoanalysis. (Kramer in Junge & Wadeson, 2006, p. 20)

ART THERAPY WITHIN A MEDICAL MODEL

Fink, Levick[3] and Goldman (1967) defined art therapy within a medical model as "that discipline which combines elements of psychotherapy with untapped sources of creativity and expression in the patient" (p. 2). Using the medical model, art therapists work in psychiatric hospitals and outpatient clinics, with "patients" (not "clients") who have mental dysfunctions. Words like "treatment" and "cure" are used. Patients are given a diagnosis and, in the early days, a psychiatrist's referral for treatment by the art therapist was necessary. Bernard Stone, who was on the first American Art Therapy Association Executive Board and worked in the Ohio state psychiatric hospitals said: "Art therapy means No. 1 a clinical setting, No. 2 a physician's referral and diagnosis, No. 3 an identified patient, No. 4 art therapy coordinated with [a] physician, nursing, social work, psychology, patient rights" (B. Stone, personal communication, 2009).[4] Obviously, art psychotherapy usually falls within this definition.

In art therapy the medical model tended to be dominant in the northeastern sections of the United States and in the Midwest. The west coast during the 1960s and later was less hierarchical. But then and now art therapists often gain training internships in psychiatric settings and do their important learning with mentally dysfunctional individuals.

In 1970, standards for art therapy registration (ATR) were established by the American Art Therapy Association (AATA.) It was voted to grandparent in all those who had worked for five years in a psychiatric setting. Many art therapists saw this requirement as a "premature narrowing of the field" (Robbins quoted in Junge, 1994). Some who were eligible for grandparenting, including Kramer, originally did not

---

3. Myra Levick, with Paul Jay Fink's help, established the American Art Therapy Association and was its first President. (See Chapter 11.)
4. See "Helen Landgarten" in Chapter 12. Landgarten, in California, innovated a system where art therapy training taught the student knowledge necessary to be the primary therapist which included diagnosing the patient/client if necessary.

want to be certified in this way. In a letter to the AATA Newsletter, Kramer said:

> It seems to me that any ill-prepared moves in this direction would be likely to jeopardize our ultimate goal . . . I therefore see no other reason to rush to certification than the desire to quickly establish standards of excellence amongst art therapists. Certification, however seems to me to be apt to induce premature rigidity within a field that must remain flexible and open to experimentation if it is to grow and prove its work. (Kramer, 1970)

Felice Cohen, Secretary of the American Art Therapy Association, responded to Kramer's letter saying:

> The rationale behind certification and registration was precisely to remove rigidity within the field. Up to this time, art therapy has been quite rigid. There have been so few who were included into what was a rather small group of art therapists. Those art therapists were mostly located in the East . . . there is now diversification in the field . . . more people can be heard. Since the formation of AATA, we have qualified art therapists from practically every state in the country and Canada. This can be construed as flexibility. (Junge, 1994, p. 128)

Rubin remembers the battle over what kinds of standards for registration to have:

> There were no villains or heroes, but everyone was very passionate and wanted to insure the survival of the profession to which they had given their life's blood. But they had different ideas of how to get there. . . . [Later] Sandra Graves [Alcorn, nee Kagin] came up with a wonderful compromise which made it possible for people pursuing alternative avenues in art therapy education and experience to be considered to meet standards for registration and the argument was resolved. (J. Rubin, personal communication, 1994)[5]

---

5. Graves' proposal was to award Professional Quality Credits (PQCs) for different kinds of education and experiences for applicants for Registration. The applicant had to have a total of 12 PQCs to qualify for Registration.

VISUAL ART VERSUS EXPRESSIVE ARTS

The American Art Therapy Association has struggled to define art therapy as focusing deeply and solely on the visual arts. Nonetheless, within the profession a few art therapists–such as Arthur Robbins[6] and Shaun McNiff–and some training programs, have included the possibilities of the therapist using a variety of arts interventions with clients. Along with the visual arts, dance and movement, poetry, drama and music might be used. This approach lends itself to the breadth versus depth argument. Those in art therapy who argue for an expressive arts approach say that different arts are therapeutic and effective for different people and therapists should be able to find the right combination for their client. Those who argue against it worry that it is difficult, perhaps impossible to train a therapist well in the necessary variety of arts media and to attempt to do so will result in a therapist who can only approach the surface of a number of different arts mediums. Focusing on the visual arts boundary in therapy, they say, is to learn to work deeply. Some art therapy training programs have a specialization in a number of therapeutic arts, but the student specializes in one art form. Hahnemann Medical College (now Drexel) and Lesley College (now University) are examples. Doctoral education at Lesley is listed as a Ph.D. degree in Expressive Therapies.

The National Coalition of Creative Arts Therapies (NCATA) founded in 1979 to further the arts in therapy is a collective organization of *arts therapies associations.* NCATA does not have individual members, it has only *professional organizations* as members–the American Art Therapy Association, for example is a member. The International Expressive Arts Therapies Association which was not established until 1994, is a group for "artists, educators, consultants and therapists . . . using multimodal expressive arts [within psychology] for personal and community transformation."[7]

---

6. There *was* no "Expressive Arts Therapies Association" until 1994 when it was founded. Therefore, people like Robbins and McNiff were and remain members of AATA, and yet developed their own multimodal approaches to art therapy.
7. Information about the National Coalition of Creative Arts Therapies and the International Expressive Arts Therapies Association is from their websites on the internet.

COMMUNITY ARTS IN ART THERAPY

Although there is no formal community arts section of the art therapy profession, using the arts to help communities build, bond and thrive has been important for many years. Published writing about community arts has only appeared in the last 15 years or so and the Expressive Arts Therapies Association's focus on community arts as transformation is fairly recent. However, the arts in social action have been a strong part of the art therapy field for a long time. For decades, the power of the arts has made it possible for artists and art therapists to make a strong impact in community work and with implied or intentional social change.[8]

Years ago, before I knew that there was such a thing as "art therapy," I worked in the barrios of East Los Angeles using the arts as alternative education. My belief was that, through the arts, children could learn anything. Before that, I collaborated with a dancer to teach art and movement to young children in San Diego. Another example is Los Angeles artist Judy Baca's citywide mural project intended to bring together culturally and racially diverse groups for social change. Over a three-year period, Baca initiated 40 murals including "The Great Wall" along the Los Angeles River.[9] International and nationwide examples of community arts projects are many: Maya Lynn's Vietnam Memorial Wall in Washington, D.C. and the AIDS Quilt are both important uses of art which promote grieving and healing in participants and in observers.[10]

In 1975, a group of therapists from Thalians Community Mental Health Center including Helen Landgarten and me went into a South Los Angeles public school to use art to help children who had been traumatized by the burning of human beings in their neighborhood. The L. A. Police Department set fire to a series of small houses and burned to death most of the human remnants of the Symbionese Liberation Army (SLA)[11] (Landgarten, Tasem, Junge & Watson, 1978). Not long after, in 1981, an art therapist Suzanne Silverstein (with two

8. A community arts "coming of age" book, by Frances Kaplan, *Art Therapy and Social Action* was published in 2007.
9. For more on Baca, see my book *Creative Realities, The Search for Meanings.*
10. In my book *Mourning, Memory and Life Itself, Essays by an Art Therapist,* the title chapter is a discussion of the Vietnam Wall and the AIDS Quilt.
11. Known for its infamous kidnapping of heiress Patty Hearst.

mental health professionals) founded the Psychological Trauma Center at Cedars Sinai Hospital, Thalians Community Mental Health Center; the trauma center's mission is to help children coping with violence. It has existed for more than 25 years.

Art therapists have used art's power to help for years. As they ventured out of their clinic offices and into the community to work with marginalized, disenfranchised groups and individuals and specific problem populations such as *the homeless*[12] (Wadeson, Durkin & Perach (Eds.), 1989, Feen, 2008); *trauma* (Gantt, 1979); and *AIDS* (Kaufman, 1996); *political refugees* (Junge, Alvarez, Kellogg & Volker, 1993); *domestic violence* (Malchiodi, 1990 and 2008); and *Nazi holocaust survivors and their children* (Landgarten, 1981). In addition, art therapists have worked with cancer patients, survivors of incest, psychosomatic clients and incarcerated clients. During the 1970s, presentations and panels were given at the annual art therapy conferences about gender orientation, homosexuality and homophobia. According to Malchiodi (2008), art can heal and bear witness when words are useless or when words are likely to result in rewounding.

The Studio Arts Movement which is at least 17 years old was started by art therapist Patricia Allen (1992) as an alternative approach to what Allen felt was the over "clinification" of the field (see Chapter 24, "The Centrality of Art in Art Therapy"). According to Allen, the pendulum had moved too far away from art-making toward psychotherapy and art was all-too-often being left out of the art therapy equation. The Studio Arts movement attempts to place art and the creative process in art therapy in a centrist position, by making the art therapist *an artist in residence,* inviting people into the artist's studio and encouraging them to make art through a focus on the creative process. While some of the writing about this approach is transpersonal and verges quite directly on spirituality, it proposes a push-back from Naumburg's art as communication within psychotherapy to Kramer's art as therapy ideas.

---

12. Art therapist Jean Durkin was the first to work with the homeless in Chicago in the early '80s (H. Wadeson, personal communication, 2009).

HUMANISTIC PSYCHOLOGY DEFINITIONS

The person's ability to gain self-awareness in order to find the "authentic self" is the primary goal of Humanistic Psychology approaches. Within this perspective, definitions of art therapy postulate that it is *the art experience* which provides the wellspring and the source of self awareness. Mala Betensky's phenomenological philosophy functions from this framework. Within a Gestalt psychological typology, Janie Rhyne believes the created artwork posits alternative ways of being for "creating yourself as you would like to be" (Rhyne, 1973, p. 9).

DEFINITIONS BY THE AMERICAN
ART THERAPY ASSOCIATION

One of the earliest definitions by the American Art Therapy Association was that the goal of art therapy was to "help . . . the individual child or adult to find a more compatible relationship between his [sic] inner and outer worlds" (originally within a pamphlet and restated by Levick, 1983, p. 3). It will be noticed that the process and content of the artwork are not mentioned within this definition. In the late 1970s, the American Art Therapy Association expressed a more extensive viewpoint, but defined art therapy as *nonverbal.*

Art therapy provides the opportunity for nonverbal expression and communication. Within the field there are two major approaches. The use of art as therapy implies that the creative process can be a means both of reconciling emotional conflicts and of fostering self-awareness and personal growth. When using art as a vehicle for psychotherapy, both the product and the associative references may be used in an effort to help the individual find a more compatible relationship between his [sic] inner and outer worlds. . . . The art therapist is concerned with the individual's inner experience. (American Art Therapy Association pamphlet, 1977)

In 1987, in a Model Job Description, the art therapist was defined as treating:

Individuals, couples, families and groups through therapeutic art tasks.

While the art therapy process utilizes art making as a means of nonverbal communication and expression, the art therapist will typically make use of verbal explorations and interventions as well. The art therapist may act as a primary therapist or as adjunctive within the treatment team, depending upon the needs of the institution and treatment objectives of the patient. He/she provides a range of services, diagnostic evaluation, assessment and treatment using art therapy techniques and process. (Junge, 1994, pp. 313-314)

Although both more inclusive and more specific, the use of the words "treatment" and "patient" establishes this definition as within the medical model.

Part III

ART THERAPY EXPANDING

Chapter 16

EVENTS OF THE 1970s AND 1980s

DECADE OF THE 1970s

In April 1970, the first Earth Day was held, launching the environmental movement in the United States. In May, four Kent State University students were killed by the Ohio National Guard as they demonstrated against the Vietnam War. In June, the first Gay Pride Parade was held in New York City. In 1972, the Watergate burglars were at work at Democratic National Headquarters in Washington, D.C. which would lead to the impeachment and resignation of President Richard Nixon. Mandatory busing was occurring to achieve racial school integration, igniting the rage underlying forced change.[1] A pamphlet was published by the Parent Teachers Association (PTA) titled "How to Tell if Your Child is a Potential Hippie" (Himelstein, 1970).

In 1970, when I was looking into social work masters programs, I went to see an Admissions Coordinator at a local university in Los Angeles. He tried to discourage me from applying by saying "We don't take any white, middle-class, middle-age Jewish women." Despite his now actionable and objectionable statement, I understood–and to some extent agreed with–what he meant. Spurred on by the events of the 1960s, and in particular the insights of the Civil Rights Movement, by the 1970s university programs, along with others across the country were trying to give affirmative action preference in admittance to people of color. In addition, with the nationwide awareness and acknowledgment of institutional racism, faculty everywhere were tak-

---

1. From "American History–1970–1979." kclibrary.lonestar.edu/decade70.html-84k

ing a long overdue look at curriculum; with this new awareness, revisions were in order. Previously, social work training and the profession nationally had been dominated by the demographic of the "we don't take . . ." statement. But change had come (and the UCLA Admissions coordinator was not happy about it).

For many years, interns in art therapy education, had people of color as clients. Art therapy students are predominantly Caucasian, as are supervisors. I believe this difference which is so important in doing effective therapy, is seldom confronted directly in a student's training nor in the therapy they do—and it should be. In the 1970s, as people with good intentions, the art therapy community attempted to embrace people of color as part of their national organization—the American Art Therapy Association. There are many examples, of white art therapists mentoring and helping art therapists of color. But, unfortunately achieving racial parity was an uphill battle, at least in part because of American tacit racism. Despite the generally good intentions of the art therapy community, racism was an ugly reality.

About 1990 when I searched the Archives of the American Art Therapy Association for my 1994 *A History of Art Therapy in the United States* (my first history relied heavily on those Archives), Georgette Powell was the only person of color there. Ironically for a visual medium such as art therapy, words and communication had become the essential medium; if an art therapist did not present consistently at conferences, participate in the American Art Therapy Organization (with writings kept in the Archives) and/or write and publish articles and books, they may be rendered invisible. Although many were early promoters of the arts in communities and with the poor and worked as art therapists in the trenches, art therapists of color often felt uncomfortable and overlooked within the formal art therapy profession and that the American Art Therapy Association organization "consists mostly of privileged, white women" (Hoshino & Junge, 2006, p. 141). Art therapists and the influence of the Civil Rights Movement are described in Chapter 18.

DECADE OF THE 1980s

Jimmy Carter was President and in 1980 Medicare was authored by Senator Ted Kennedy. But the 1980s[2] in the United States was also the narcissistic decade of the "Me" generation. Binge buying and credit were pervasive and "shop 'til you drop" the motto of the day. Ronald Reagan was elected President in 1981 and ended his term in 1989. By 1982 the most serious recession since the Great Depression occurred and in 1987 the 2nd largest stock market crash in U.S. history happened. Despite these, it was an optimistic time. Reagan ran as a conservative who promised to end big government and cap taxes. He declared war on drugs, but in the last five years of the decade, cocaine addiction was up 35 percent. Unemployment rose and at the end of the 80s the Berlin Wall came down. Taxes were increased and the national deficit went up.

A 1980 study by UCLA and the American Council on Education found that college freshman were more interested in status, power and money than at any time in the past 15 years. Business was the most popular major.

There were major advances in genetics and many were lost to AIDS (movie star Rock Hudson died of AIDS in 1985). George H. W. Bush was elected President in 1989 and called for a "kinder, gentler nation."

Families changed drastically: There were more divorces, more unmarrieds living together and more single parent families. During the 1980s, black single parent families went from 48.70 percent to 58 percent; most were headed by single mothers and all-too-often fathers were not present in their children's life. Cable and MTV were born and TV included many anti-family sitcoms. The two-earner family became common. Women earned college and advanced degrees and had fewer children.

Some artists of the era were Jasper Johns, Wilhem De Kooning, Robert Rauschenberg and Andy Warhol. Poet Adrienne Rich wrote:

> In those years
> In those years people will say, we lost track
> of the meaning of *we* and *you*

---

2. From "American History–1980–1989." kclibrary.lonestar.edu/decade80/html-26k

we found ourselves
reduced to I
and the whole thing
became silly, ironic, terrible . . .
                    "In Those Years"

ART THERAPY IN THE 1970s AND 1980s: INTRODUCTION

In following chapters, I present art therapists and influencing issues and movements which began in the 1970s, moved into the 80s, and impacted the development of professional art therapy. The 1970s was a decade of particular innovation and creativity in the United States. Published writings by art therapists of the period were predominantly case histories integrating the visual arts (and in some cases other expressive art forms) illuminating the dimensions of art therapy and expanding its use for art therapists and other mental health clinicians as it became more public. Art therapy flourished as art therapists defined practice spheres which included many theoretical philosophies and populations.

The 1970s was the decade when many of the first art therapy Masters training programs began. Each program tended to have its own theoretical orientation, depending on the philosophy of its founder. The development of art therapy education is discussed in Chapter 17 of this section.

Chapter 17

DEVELOPMENT OF MASTERS-LEVEL ART THERAPY EDUCATION

Soon after the establishment of the American Art Therapy Association and even a few years before, many art therapy pioneers founded art therapy training programs in institutions and colleges across the country. Programs usually reflected the beliefs of its founder, and many still do today. As mentioned in Chapter 11, the program at the University of Louisville was the first. It had been initiated in 1959, but after graduating two students, it closed for 10 years and reopened with the founding of the American Art Therapy Association in 1969; Sandra Kagin Graves-Alcorn was Director. (In 1973, the name was changed to the Institute for Expressive Therapies.) Currently, it is a Masters degree program in Counseling and Personnel Services with a specialization in expressive therapies (C. Malchiodi, personal communication, 2009). Myra Levick helped found the Masters graduate program at Hahnemann Hospital and Medical College in Philadelphia in 1967.[1] First, Levick invited well-known art therapists to lecture at Hahnemann; attendance was good which indicated that there was enough public interest in the arts in therapy for art therapists to draw a crowd. Then with Paul Jay Fink, she provided a hospitable forum for art therapists nationwide and the impetus and energy to form a national organization–the American Art Therapy Association–through which art therapists could form a credible mental health discipline. The profession of art therapy as we know it and

---

1. Levick's co-founder at Hahnemann was psychoanalyst Morris J. Goldman. A few months after the program began, Goldman suddenly died suddenly at the age of 39 and Paul Jay Fink took over (M. Levick, personal communication, 2009).

art therapy graduate education both began with Myra Levick. At the time there were few formal opportunities to train as an art therapist before this.

SELF-TAUGHT PIONEERS

Pioneer art therapists generally taught themselves because of their passionate commitment to art and their intrigue with people and their problems. For early art therapists, to integrate these two interests seemed a natural fit. They pursued art training in art schools, colleges and universities and psychological and psychiatric training in a variety of training programs and sometimes with psychiatrists and psychologists they knew. They also learned from their clients as they practiced as clinicians in a variety of institutions. Naumburg presented art therapy to many professional groups and in 1958 instigated what she called "the first course introducing principles and methods of art therapy in a university setting to graduate students at New York University (Naumburg, 1966, p. 32).

HISTORICAL IMPETUS FOR ART THERAPY EDUCATION

The 1970s was a decade of tremendous experimentation and innovation in America and it was the decade in which much of art therapy education began. The burgeoning interest in the arts and therapy, the Human Potential Movement promoting values of self-awareness and self understanding along with a nationwide focus on a philosophy of education relevant to life and identity all combined to drive the development of art therapy Masters programs.

Another essential element was John F. Kennedy's legislation, enacted in 1963 to remove the mentally ill from distant psychiatric hospitals and treat them in their home communities as outpatients.[2] Large amounts of money and expertise were expended to the cities to set up the required outpatient resources. A series of Community Mental

2. JFK's act was intended to provide a more humane treatment than "warehousing" patients, but over the years as most psychiatric hospitals were closed by President Ronald Reagan and others, or at best, were drastically reduced, enough effective community outpatient services never appeared and the numbers of mentally ill homeless and incarcerated patients vastly increased.

Health Centers were built which housed a large collection of therapies and pioneered brief treatment interventions; they were designed to serve a specific geographical area. The impetus of the bill and the installation of civil rights laws for the mentally ill were intended to provide a much more humane environment for treatment and to release patients who had been warehoused because of political or family issues—sometimes wrongly—in psychiatric hospitals for years. Most unfortunately, much of this goal was never fulfilled.

GRADUATE-LEVEL ART THERAPY EDUCATION

With the establishment of art therapy Masters-level education, a sea change in the field had occurred. No longer were most people discovering art "accidentally" and putting together their own learnings from practical experience, needing to be strong, courageous and often politically savvy to make a success of it. I believe the newly formed education tended to attract a different kind of person from the early art therapists. From now on, adolescents could dream about art therapy as a career-path and plan for their graduate education sometimes as early as high school. Art requirements for admission to graduate art therapy programs were at the "competency" level and while there were always intensely interested and well trained artists entering the field, as the years went by, many who undertook art therapy education had come to it because they discovered their art was healing for their own issues and traumas and wanted to learn to help others. Although entry level to the field was known as a Masters degree, there were even undergraduate art therapy programs springing up across the country.

This new educational path provided a more protected and predictable journey for students and possibly a more professional graduate. This was very different from the old fits and starts and necessary integrations that many art therapy pioneers encountered: They had needed to be "adults," not students and had to find their own way—even if they were in their twenties. The new education had its advantages, of course. What it may have done was adequately test new generations in the realities of the mental health system. But some felt a huge shock upon graduation into the larger world of increasingly difficult employment.

ART THERAPY REGISTRATION AND EDUCATION

As the American Art Therapy Association designed standards for Registration (ATR) in 1970, it rightfully recognized that Registration for art therapists would be intrinsically tied to education. However, there was a problem: although there was a great deal of interest in establishing future training programs across the country, at the beginning few formal opportunities for education existed. Thus at the time, there were few trained art therapists to teach in the new programs. AATA tackled this problem initially by accepting a diversity of educational approaches for Registration—such as self-education, apprenticeships, in-service hospital training and a variety of university courses. The first five Masters education in art therapy programs were initiated at Hahnemann Medical College and Hospital, Philadelphia (Myra Levick, Director, 1967), University of Louisville (Director Sandra Kagin Graves-Alcorn, reopened in 1969), Pratt Institute, New York City (Josef Garai, Director, 1970), George Washington University, Washington D.C. (Elinor Ulman and Bernard Levy, Directors, 1971), and Immaculate Heart College/Loyola Marymount University, Los Angeles (Helen Landgarten, Director, 1973). The program at New York University also came in 1973 (Laurie Wilson, Director).

GUIDELINES FOR EDUCATION AND TRAINING

In 1973, specific curricular Guidelines for Education and Training were developed by Gladys Agell for the American Art Therapy Association. By this time, a requirement for art therapy Registration was specific education in art therapy. In 1975, the Education and Training Board (ETB)[3] was formed by AATA to assess art therapy educational programs and to award "Approval"[3] to programs meeting the requirements of the Guidelines[4] The first graduate programs to receive

---

3. AATA's Education and Training Board later changed its name to Educational Program Approval Board (EPAB). It continues to assess and award "Approval."
4. "Approval" is the highest standard given by the American Art Therapy Association for educational programs. The program submits a self-study describing its resources and curriculum in depth. AATA's process does not require that the program undergo a *site visit* which could lead to the term "Accreditation" rather than "Approval."

"Approval" by the American Art Therapy Association in 1979 were Hahnemann Medical College and Hospital, Loyola Marymount University, George Washington University and New York University. By 1977, there were twenty-one art therapy training programs across the United States. In 1985, there were a total of 32 Master's degree programs and numerous undergraduate and graduate courses. Of these, 14 were AATA-"Approved" programs. By 1992, the number of "Approved" programs was 24. Unfortunately, due to financial exigencies a few of the university degree programs have closed, while others have opened. Currently, the AATA website lists 33 "Approved programs" in the United States. (See Chapter 25, "Education, Licensing and Employment," for Levick's views about the current state of art therapy education.)

THE ARGUMENT ABOUT ACADEMIC DEGREE EDUCATION AND INTRINSIC CREATIVITY

Some art therapists–Edith Kramer was one–worried that the academic formalization of education would create "academic mills." She argued for "alternative possibilities of entering the profession . . . to supplement the academic one" (Kramer in Junge, 1994, p. 137). Kramer feared that standardization of education might crowd out the

> intuitive artistic individual who can function exquisitely with people and with art materials but has no aptitude for book learning. . . . How to find a way of implementing a broader definition of art therapy and make it acceptable on the labor market is, I admit, a difficult question. . . . On the whole, I am distressed by the tendency in our profession to define the field of art therapy exclusively by academic standards. . . . I know that I should never have entered the field of art therapy had I been required to follow a conventional course of academic training. (Kramer, 1971b)

Myra Levick, first president of the American Art Therapy Association responded:

> . . . I agree with you, there is much to be said against the acquiring of degrees. Nevertheless, this is the system, and until we can come up with a better one, we have no choice. . . . Art therapists cannot experiment

and learn unless there are environments for them to learn in . . . we must start somewhere. (Levick, 1971)

A consistent argument over the years which continues today is about art therapy's need to increase its standardization to prove credibility and to be accepted as a respected mental health discipline versus continuing its unfettered, intuitive, unstandardized creativity.[5]

For many years, Kramer taught at graduate programs at Hahnemann, George Washington University, New York University and numerous other institutions in the United States–in particular the northeastern part.

YEARS OF EDUCATION TOWARD PROFESSIONALISM

In the years since the first establishment of the American Art Therapy Association's Guidelines for Education and Training, art therapy education has steadily progressed towards more standardized curricular and internship requirements. As other mental health disciplines have advanced in their educational professionalism, so too the art therapy profession–as it needed to–has used education as a means to solidify itself as a credible member of the tribe. The education of excellent and skilled art therapists brings to the mental health community and the larger public both the awareness of art therapy as a profession and the acknowledgement of art therapists as well-trained professionals with something extra to offer–the art.

Nationwide, clinical licensing has become an important tool toward the ability of art therapists to find post-graduate employment and gain professional credibility and many educational programs offer a curriculum that is applicable for post-graduate licensing as well as art therapy registration and certification. While this integration enables post-graduate art therapists to find work, there may be problems now and to come: Generally, the license attached to art therapy training is not uniquely an art therapy license. To date, as far as I know, there is not yet a specific license for art therapists anywhere in the United

---

5. Kramer has often spoken out publically against the disappearance and quality of the art in art therapy. Recently, she criticized the articles in *Art Therapy* because they had plenty of charts and statistics but little art. The "other faction" maintains that careful outcome research is necessary to prove that art therapy "works."

States.[6] Of course, the art therapist must be able to work once they graduate and making a living wage is always of the essence, but the danger of this necessary practice is that there may be problems with the development of the student's *identity as an art therapist* and once they are graduated and are working with difficult clients, they may "meld" their professional stance into their licensing discipline.

As I see it, learning to be an art therapist is more difficult than learning to be another kind of therapist, because the necessity is that the student really learn two practices: psychotherapy and art therapy. As learning more and more clinical information becomes essential in the usual two years of Masters education, I foresee the potential of a major dilemma for art therapy educators that needs to be grappled with and resolved now. The real answer to the dilemma would, of course, be a unique state license for art therapists. Such a license would mandate a specific art therapy curriculum and post-graduate skills and experience (as do the ATR registration and the BC certification). Unfortunately, this is not likely to happen for the foreseeable future because of financial constraints, mental health hierarchical and political struggles and the fact that the organized art therapy profession will always remain relatively small.

IMPORTANT DATES AND EVENTS

1950s on—Art therapists teach courses to professional groups and in mental health training institutions.

1958—Margaret Naumburg teaches what she calls "the first course introducing principles and methods of art therapy in a university setting" to graduate students at New York University.

1957-1959—Roger White opens a graduate program in art therapy at the University of Lousiville, based in both the art and the psychology departments. After graduating two students, it closes.

1967—Myra Levick founds the art therapy educational program at

---

6. New Mexico was the first state to gain art therapy licensing, but after many political maneuverings, when it was finally signed by Governor Bruce King in March 1993, it was called the "Counselors and Therapists Practice Act." There *are* some states in which art therapists can gain licensing under a general "Counselors," mental health or "Creative Arts" license, but there is nowhere that there is a *specifically named* art therapy license. Since the process to gain licensing is largely political and such there are relatively, very few art therapists, in my opinion, specific licensing for art therapists is unlikely to happen in the coming years.

Hahnemann Medical College and Hospital. This is the first graduate art therapy program in the country.

1969–*University of Louisville* art therapy program reopens after a hiatus of ten years, the same day that the American Art Therapy Association is founded in Louisville. Sandra Kagin Graves-Alcorn is hired as the new Director.

1970–The American Art Therapy Association designs standards for art therapy registration (ATR). At first, qualifying experience is diverse. As the years go on, Registration becomes more closely tied to academic art therapy education.

1970s–The 1970s were a time of innovation in education giving impetus to art therapy education. Another driving force of the times is JFK's Community Mental Health Centers act of 1963 which provides federal funding for new buildings and resources. The intent of the bill is to return in-patient psychiatric hospital patients to their home community where they can be treated as outpatients.

1970–*Pratt Institute* in New York City, graduate art therapy program established. Josef Garai is Director.

1971–*George Washington University,* Washington, D.C. graduate art therapy program is established. Elinor Ulman and psychologist Bernard Levy are Directors.

1973–*Immaculate Heart College,* Los Angeles, graduate art therapy program is established. Helen Landgarten is Director. This program moves to Loyola Marymount University in 1980. It remains there today.

1973–The American Art Therapy Association develops standards for education called "Guidelines for Education and Training" (written by Gladys Agell).

1975–Education and Training Board (ETB) is formed by AATA. This board assesses educational programs and awards "Approval" to those meeting its curricular and internship standards. Later, its name is changed to Education Program Approval Board (EPAB).

1977–There are 21 art therapy training programs across the United States.

1979–The first programs to gain "Approval" by AATA's Education and Training Board are at Hahnemann, Loyola Marymount University, George Washington University and New York University.

1970s, 1980s on–State clinical licensing becomes increasingly important for art therapy employment.

1985–There are 32 art therapy graduate programs. Of these, 14 are "Approved" by the American Art Therapy Association.

2009–Thirty-three art therapy graduate programs are "Approved" by the American Art Therapy Association.

STUDY QUESTIONS

1. Describe the argument about "the restrictions" of academic educational programs versus the self-educated creative personality. Name advantages and disadvantages of each. What is *your* opinion?

2. Describe the *historical milieu* which encouraged the growth of academic art therapy education.

3. Discuss the events ***within*** *the American Art Therapy Association and the art therapy profession* which drove the development of academic art therapy education.

4. Why was the establishment of art therapy education within accredited academic settings an advantage for the developing profession?

Chapter 18

ART THERAPISTS OF
COLOR AND INFLUENCE

LUCILLE VENTURE (1919–2006)

Lucille Venture was the first person in the country to earn a Ph.D. with a dissertation focused on art therapy–*The Black Beat in Art Therapy Experiences* (1977). Venture received her Ph.D. at the age of 58. That Venture earned the first art therapy Ph.D. in the country was a major step for the profession and provided a significant role model for many art therapists seeking further education.

According to Potash (2005), Venture found Naumburg's conceptualization of art psychotherapy close to Freud, to be an elite practice which excluded the poor and communities of color because of its emphasis on the client who has extensive time and money to pursue it. Venture believed Kramer's notion of the focus on the creative process itself to be potentially more inclusive of a wide variety of people. In reality, Venture's approach sounds more like the personal growth enhancing process encompassed within Humanistic Psychology. In fact, Venture embraced the establishment of Pratt's Humanistic Psychology program and found its focus on the *whole person* to "allow art therapists to serve a new, and not just entitled, population" (Potash, 2005, p. 187). She believed that the many training programs based in Freudian psychodynamics were "grim for minority students" (Venture, 1977, p. 56).

Having experienced institutional racism, many people of color in the American Art Therapy Association formed their own committees to better focus on multicultural issues and make their voices heard in the field. But, unfortunately, many people of color discontinued membership in the American Art Therapy Association[1] and so many voices were not heard there at all. Venture noted:

> In 1973, the ad-hoc committee To Investigate Encouraging Minority Groups to Enter and Study in the Field of Art Therapy[2] was formed. It was composed of four Black ATRs [Registered art therapists] and four Black master's degree students. The resulting monograph from the committee was titled *Art Therapy and the Third World.* (Venture, 1977, p. 78)[3]

In the mid-1970s the particular nature of education for art therapists grew increasingly important in order to enhance the legitimacy of the field. But as education standards for the American Art Therapy Association's Registration (ATR, Registered Art Therapist) became more formalized toward a requirement of specific art therapy curriculum and experience in a psychiatric setting, many saw these new standards as restrictive and exclusive. Edith Kramer, among others, was against the narrowing of requirements for academic training and the Masters as entry level to the profession, because she felt it would exclude "the intellectually gifted, self-directed person . . . and the intuitive person" (Junge, 1994, p. 138). In her dissertation, Venture supported Kramer and worried "that practicing art therapists of color, many of whom were involved in community arts rather than mental health settings might not meet the new criteria. . . . She [Kramer] feels that the masters degree requirement of AATA is 'shutting the door' to minority individuals interested in art therapy" (Potash, 2005, p. 186, Venture, 1977, p. 37). Venture, with Kramer's help, presented an alternate plan for education at the 1977 American Art Therapy Association Executive Board meeting. She noted her disappointment at the result:

> The writer feels that institutions and organizations arbitrarily create entry requirements that only certain segments of the population can

---

1. By 1993–4 only one art therapist of color was mentioned in the AATA archives: Georgette Powell and thus she was the only one mentioned in my first history of art therapy in the United States (Junge, 1994).
2. Author's note: Doby-Copeland (2006) lists the following early members of the committee: Georgette Powell, Lucille Venture, Charles Anderson, Cliff Joseph, Lemuel Joyner, Dimitra Risueno, and Gwendolyn McPhaul.
3. In 1974, this monograph was presented as a panel led by Cliff Joseph at AATA's 5th Annual Conference. This panel is discussed more fully in the section on Joseph in this chapter.

attain. . . . The American Art Therapy Association had the opportunity to make tremendous inroads into the exclusionary status of the field when it began to formalize and articulate standards of requirements for the Registered Art Therapist. . . . Instead, the AATA followed the conventional path of the institutions and organizations, and created entry requirements which can be met by only a certain segment of the population. (Venture, 1977, pp. 193-94)

According to Potash, Lucille Venture "sees a great role for art therapists of color and their allies to be charged with the role of 'constantly bringing to the larger body's attention the needs and concerns of and for minorities'" (2005, p. 188). Lucille Venture died in 2006 at the age of 87.

GEORGETTE SEABROOK POWELL (b. 1916)

Georgette Powell stated in an interview in 1994[4] that she believed her contributions to the development of the profession of art therapy had been overlooked. Powell is now 93 years old. She was born in Charleston, South Carolina and grew up in New York City. She has been a practicing artist since the 1930s when she began exhibiting her work and has a long and illustrious career as an artist. Under WPA,[5] she was involved in the Harlem Arts Workshop and the Harlem Hospital Art Project. In 1966, she established "Art in the Park" as an annual event in Washington, D.C. and in 1970, "Tomorrow's World Art Center" where art therapy was provided for children, adolescents and the elderly.

In 1958, caring for her mother who had dementia, Powell read about art therapy and began her art therapy education with Edith Kramer. Through Kramer, she met Elinor Ulman. In the early 1960s, Powell moved to Washington D.C. where she worked as an art therapist with the Health and Welfare Council, at St. Elizabeth's Hospital and at D.C. General Hospital in the Acute Psychiatry building. She became a clinical supervisor for students of the George Washington University art therapy program and, in particular, was a significant

---

4. By Boston & Short, (2006). *Art Therapy: Journal of the American Art Therapy Association*, p. 89.
5. "WPA" or "Works Project Administration was begun by President Franklin Roosevelt during the Great Depression to give work to artists, writers and others.

mentor to students of color. She received her BFA (Bachelor of Fine Arts) degree from Howard University in 1973 at the age of 57.

While she was involved with art therapy in the early days and was a part of the discussions about education and the formation of the American Art Therapy Association, it is difficult to tease out Georgette Powell's exact contributions–there were many unsung supportive and encouraging people who helped along the development of the profession. But it is easy to describe Powell's considerable contributions as a mentor to students of color at the George Washington University art therapy masters program. Phoebe Farris (2006), art therapist and now Professor at Purdue University, discusses the racism she felt in her Masters program and how she was helped to stick it out and to thrive:

> Through Georgia Mills-Jessup, I met Georgette Powell, an African-American art therapist, artist and founder of "Tomorrow's World Art Center" located on 14th Street in the northwest section of New York City. Ms. Powell offered me supervision as needed and also the opportunity to meet other minority art therapists. . . . (Farris, 2006, p. 87)

CLIFF JOSEPH (b. 1927)

In the diverse culture of New York City, there was another art therapist who was important in the early years of the profession. Within the art therapy community, Cliff Joseph acted as a strong voice for the oppressed in society: "My work has been primarily in communities of racial and economic oppression. . . . Even with patients from a more economically privileged context, I have observed that alienation and insecurity contribute to mental health problems" (Joseph, 2006, p. 30). Born in Panama and defining himself as Afro-Caribbean, Joseph came with his parents to Harlem in Manhattan when he was 18 months old.

Joseph cites his entry year into art therapy as 1963 when, with the encouragement of the national Civil Rights Movement, he abandoned commercial art in favor of using art for "personal and corporate change" (Joseph, 2006, p. 31). He began work at Abraham Jacobi Hospital in the north Bronx where he met Edith Kramer who invited him to attend the formation meeting[6] at Hahnemann Medical College

---

6. For more information on the formation of the American Art Therapy Association, the reader is directed to Chapter 11.

for a professional art therapy association in the late 1960s. Joseph described his sense of this meeting:

> I remember attending my first meeting when the A.A.T.A. was begin-
> ning to form and being to the best of my knowledge the only black art
> therapist present. It was of course disturbing to me to see this almost all-
> white assemblage, particularly since I knew that a large number of those
> in attendance worked with Third World patients. Nor was there any evi-
> dence to indicate that in spite of their white middle-class background,
> they were in touch with the feelings and specific needs of Third World
> people. On the contrary, I sensed that many were having difficulty
> relating to me because of my blackness. (Joseph, 1973, no page num-
> ber)

Later, Joseph worked as an art therapist and Director of Art Therapy at Albert Einstein College of Medicine Hospital (Yeshiva University) and at Lincoln Community Mental Health Center in the south Bronx–both in New York.

For the 1973 conference of the American Art Therapy Association, Cliff Joseph organized a panel of art therapists and prominent people from New York's mental health world to tackle and discuss the immense challenge of racism and the Third World. "Art Therapy and the Third World" included art therapists Lemuel Joyner, Barbara Maciag, Georgette Seabrook Powell and Vera Zilzer along with Joseph. Panelist Dorothy Knox addressed the audience: "I think that as art therapists you can help a great deal if you are willing to reach out and risk becoming involved with some real and disturbing issues" (Joseph, 1973, p. 8).

Recognizing the tremendously damaging impact of racism as a root cause of mental health problems, panelists discussed whether thera-pists of color were more effective because they understood the cultur-al specificities of therapy with patients of color and Joseph concluded that "Third World art therapists . . . can more appropriately respond to the mental health requirements of Third World people." Panelists presented an alternative proposal for art therapy training for Third World People (Joseph, 1973, p. 15).

Perhaps Joseph's most important and dramatic concern, however, was the internal threat he felt within the art therapy profession, itself. "My reference is to racism," said Joseph, "institutional, organizational and individual racism" (Joseph, 1973, p. 3). In his 2006 life story, Joseph says that this observation of racism in art therapy, made more than thirty years is still relevant today: "I continue to address this concern from the point of view of my racial and ethnic identity. . . . Centuries of lessons and yet so little learned" (Joseph, 2006, pp. 32-33).

For 11 years, Cliff Joseph was a faculty member at the Pratt Institute: "During this time, I met psychologist Dr. Josef E. Garai, who asked me to join him and Dr. Arthur Robbins to establish, at Pratt Institute in Brooklyn, the first college program in New York for art therapy and creativity development" (Joseph, 2006, p. 31). Joseph's book, co-authored with Harris, *Murals of the Mind,* is a portrait of art and mural-making in group work. A contemporary art therapist of color, Cheryl Doby-Copeland writes: "To this day, I value the instruction I received from Cliff Joseph . . . his book . . . is responsible for my enduring use of murals as a part of my art therapy approach" (Doby-Copeland, 2006, p. 82).

Writing of the importance to her of Cliff Joseph as a mentor, Farris (2006) describes:

> While I was a graduate student at Pratt Institute, Cliff Joseph was one of my professors and my thesis advisor. He helped me immensely to deal with the racism that I and the only other minority student . . . were facing from one of the major professors in the program. . . . [Students were required to undergo psychotherapy treatment] I had to choose from a list of therapists that included [only] White people, predominantly men. . . . I protested and . . . was threatened with expulsion. . . . Despite risks to his own job, Cliff supported my position and found an African-American licensed psychotherapist who offered therapeutic services on a sliding scale. (Farris, 2006, p. 86)

IMPORTANT DATES AND EVENTS

1916–Georgette Seabrook Powell is born in Charleston, South Carolina.

1919–Lucille Venture is born.

1920s–Cliff Joseph is born in Panama. Comes to Harlem with his parents at 18 months old.

1930s–Georgette Powell begins exhibiting her artwork.

1958–While taking care of her ill mother, Powell reads about art therapy.

Early 1960s–Powell goes to Washington, D.C. where she works as an art therapist at St. Elizabeth's Hospital and D.C. General Hospital.

1963–Cliff Joseph leaves commercial art to devote himself to art therapy. He begins protest paintings about racism and later the Vietnam War.

1969–Invited by Edith Kramer, Joseph attends the formation meeting of the American Art Therapy Association.

1966–Powell establishes "Art in the Park" an annual event in Washington, D.C.

1970–Powell establishes "Tomorrow's World Art Center" in New York City.

1970–Joseph is Director of Art Therapy at Albert Einstein College of Medicine Hospital and at Lincoln Community Mental Health Center in the south Bronx, New York City.

Early 1970s–Venture is co-founder and, in 1976, 3rd President of the Maryland Art Therapy Association.

1973–Venture helps form the Ad-Hoc Committee to Investigate Encouraging Minority Groups to Enter and Study in the Field of Art Therapy for the American Art Therapy Association. In 1977, the committee's report *Art Therapy and the Third World* is presented as a monograph.

1973–*Murals of the Mind* is published by J. Harris and Joseph.

1973–Joseph organizes a panel "Art Therapy and the Third World" at the annual conference of the American Art Therapy Association, in New York.

1970s–Powell teaches at Pratt Institute, NYC.

1970s–Joseph teaches at Pratt Institute for 11 years.

1973–Powell receives her Bachelor of Fine Arts from Howard University. She is age 57.

1977–Venture receives her Ph.D. Her dissertation is the first in the country focusing on art therapy: "The Black Beat in Art Therapy Experiences." She is 58 years old.

1977–Opposing academic education as the only option, with Edith Kramer's help, Venture presents an alternative educational plan to the Executive Board of the American Art Therapy Association. Her plan is not accepted.

1981–Joseph is President of the New York Art Therapy Association
2006–Lucille Venture dies at the age of 87.

STUDY QUESTIONS

1. Describe the contributions of Venture, Powell and Joseph to the history of art therapy.
2. Discuss the problems of institutional racism in AATA and other professional mental health organizations.
3. What are the cultural constraints contributing to racism today?
4. What do you think a Caucasian art therapist must know in order to be able to work with a person of a different race or ethnicity?
5. How has your education helped you with No. 4 and how has it not?

Chapter 19

HUMANISTIC PSYCHOLOGY
AND ART THERAPY[1]

HISTORY AND DEFINITION

Humanistic psychology flourished in the 1970s, its primary form then often being groups. Despite art therapists and the American Art Therapy Association historically and primarily embracing Freudian psychoanalytic and psychodynamic theory, the philosophy of humanism and the Humanistic Psychology movement made its way, into psychotherapy and with some difficulty, into the formal art therapy profession. Ironically, today, many training programs for art therapists nationally and counseling programs in general espouse Humanistic theory along with Jungian ideas; while there continue to be many psychodynamically-based programs in art therapy, strict Freudianism is all but gone as is the psychoanalytic approach. Behaviorism and Humanistic Psychology are at the top of the heap.

Humanistic Psychology emerged after World War II in the late 1950s when Abraham Maslow, Carl Rogers and Clark Moustakas met to form a professional association. As a reaction against behaviorism and psychoanalysis, Humanistic Psychology is a philosophy concerned with the nature of human experience and uses the human context for the development of psychological theory. It eschews the medical model and as non-pathologizing, is a more optimistic philosophy than either behaviorism or Freudian theory and psychoanalytic thinking. It fits well with the emphasis on positive thinking in the United

---

1. This description of Humanistic Psychology is from en.Wikipedia.org/wiki/Humanistic_ Psychology

States in the last 20 years or so.

The goal of Humanistic Psychology is that the person gains a more healthy sense of self, leading to–as Maslow termed it–"self-actualization." With focus on the human being as an holistic creature, Maslow named Humanistic Psychology, the "third force" of psychotherapy with behaviorism and psychoanalysis as the first two.

Having roots in the existential thought of European philosophers Kierkegaard, Nietzsche, Heidigger and Sartre, major American theorists of Humanistic Psychology are Abraham Maslow, Carl Rogers and Rollo May. Maslow, considered the founder of Humanistic Psychology, developed his personality theory–a structure of human needs leading to self actualization. Carl Rogers believed in the client's intrinsic good, capacity for self-direction and innate motivation for self-actualization. Rollo May studied human choice and the tragic parts of human experience. Fritz Perls (who trained Janie Rhyne) and Gestalt Therapy are within this perspective as is the self-help movement.

Its proponents say that Humanistic Psychology is a philosophy and an outlook on life, not an empirical science. It is based in the personal, individual experience of life and focuses on uniquely human issues. Criticisms of Humanistic Psychology center on the issue that the goal of personal growth and self actualization, sometimes intentionally overlooks serious pathology and is not right for everybody. Francis & Kritsonis (2006) state "There is an ongoing tension [in Maslow's work] that focuses on the collective action versus individuality" (p. 5). A central criticism questions Humanistic Psychology's adherence to social change because of its affirmation of societal and political status quo. Yet Maslow referred to himself as "a psychologist for the peace table." His goal was "one day uniting the entire world in acts of continuous peace through individual understanding" (p. 6).

JOSEF E. GARAI (1914–1995)

Josef Garai presented a paper on Humanistic art therapy at the second annual conference of the American Art Therapy Association in 1971. The paper was called "The Humanistic Approach to Art Therapy and Creativity Development." Garai discussed his work, in Carl Rogers' terms, as client centered and client oriented. At a panel discussion in 1985 "Meet the ole timers: Perspectives on the American Art Therapy Association," Garai described the reception to his 1971 paper:

> The younger members of the Association were showing by their enthusiastic applause how much they favored this new and unconventional approach. But in the ensuing discussion, I saw myself confronted by attacks orchestrated by the "Old Guard" who regarded this theory as heresy and insisted on the traditional psychoanalytic approach. . . . Soon afterwards I was denounced as a "troublemaker, rebel and crazy person." (1985, p. 28)

About his Humanistic approach, Gantt stated: "I think that Garai was trying to set himself apart from those he thought were interpreting art in a mechanistic unvarying fashion" (Junge, 1994, p. 153). Garai *was* attempting to set a more expansive tone for art therapy than that provided by the limits of Freud's psychodynamics. Included with Humanistic ideas, Garai found Carl Jung's appreciation for and understanding of imagery amenable to the practice of art therapy.

Previous to his presentation at the 1971 American Art Therapy Association conference, in 1970 Garai had started an art therapy training program at Pratt Institute, a free-standing art school in New York City. The new program was first called "Creativity Development." Finding work for his art therapy graduates was important to Garai: Each year he invited to Pratt community people who might offer employment to meet the students and see their work.

Innovativeness and new approaches to old problems were pervasive at the time. Garai, a photographer and poet and the Chair of Pratt's psychology program was contacted by Arthur Robbins, a sculptor interested in psychoanalysis and, according to Robbins, they later became "partners" to combine the arts and psychology (Robbins in Junge & Wadeson, 2006, p. 261). At that time psychology and psychiatry were not very well accepted in the arts community, and therapy itself was viewed with a good deal of suspicion.[2] Artists often hewed to the Freudian notion that artistic creativity was next to madness in the personality and believed that psychotherapy might "cure" them of personality difficulties, but in the process would eliminate any need to

---

2. I believe this statement is still true.

create.[3] Many artists stayed away from psychotherapy, and still stay away because of this flawed notion. That two practicing professional artists, Garai and Robbins, saw a way to integrate the arts and psychology helped art therapy gain credibility within the arts and therapeutic communities.

Arthur Robbins: "We thought that the title "Creativity Development" was much more palatable and politically acceptable to the faculty" (Robbins in Junge & Wadeson, 2006, p. 261). Pratt accepted the program and the name was later changed to "Creativity Development and Art Therapy." Robbins saw in Garai a close friend and colleague: "In many quarters our program was viewed as wild and unorthodox. . ." (Robbins in Junge & Wadeson, 2006, p. 262).

Josef Garai was born in Germany and came of age during Hitler's holocaust. As a 12-year-old, he discovered Freud's ideas and gave lectures on them to anyone who would listen. He avoided the Nazi concentration camps and escaped to Switzerland with 100 people; then he went to France and finally to Israel before he came to the United States. He started a language school in Israel where people came to study on bicycle. Shortly after he came to the United States, Garai earned his Ph.D. in Psychology from New York University (S. Garai, personal communication, 2009).

MALA GITLIN BETENSKY (1910–1999)

Born in Lodz, Poland, Mala Gitlin Betensky was a Phenomenologist. In 1973, she published *Self-Discovery Through Self- Expression,* a compelling collection of cases for which the author, also a psychologist, was art therapist. In 1987, Betensky contributed a chapter to Rubin's *Approaches to Art Therapy* on "Phenomenological Art Therapy." In 1995, she published her second book, *What Do You See? The Phenomenology of Therapeutic Art Expression* which describes in specific detail her perspective on art therapy as phenomenology.

What is Phenomenology?

Phenomenology is an eighteenth century philosophy and culture of inquiry for contemporary qualitative research. It is attributed to

---

3. Many artists today believe this mistaken but prevalent notion.

European philosopher Husserl (1913/1976) who defined it as "the Science of Consciousness." Phenomenology is defined as a *Human Science*. Betensky wrote: "[It is] a study of phenomena (things, objects) as they present themselves in consciousness as immediate experience. Phenomenologists attempt to discover the *essence of a phenomenon*. Phenomenology influenced philosophy, psychology and psychotherapies.

It was particularly influential in Humanistic therapies because it eschewed behaviorism or reductionist psychodynamic ideas and emphasized the *lived subjective experience* separate from theories about them or already-held notions.[4] As much as possible, Phenomenology requires a fresh approach to the visible or textual lived experience. Today it is one of the qualitative researcher's most important perspectives and is usually known as the most objective of the qualitative cultures of inquiry.

Betensky's Approach

Betensky considers the art product created by a client to be the outward "text" of the inner-lived experience. As client and therapist carefully look at the work together and talk about it, feelings come to the fore and the client as "co-researcher" can begin to consciously understand their behavior; thus the client may encounter the "authentic self." Rather than focus on symbols or content, phenomenological art therapy discovers *structure:*

> While trait theory of personality assigns the individual into a diagnostic category and predicts his[5] future behavior, and the psychodynamic personality model leans on the unconscious, both theories neglect the rich and illuminating variety of states of the conscious quite potent in relation to the human ability to change. . . . When an individual experiences himself through art, he sometimes manages to restore his stream of awareness. This is an act of self discovery. . . . This therapy was present oriented . . . [and] was also change oriented. (Betensky, 1973, pp. xi & 336)

---

5. The sexist language of the original quote is retained.

Betensky's first book *Self-Discovery and Self-Expression* was published in 1973, four years after the founding of the American Art Therapy Association, and the same year that another Humanistic art therapist, Janie Rhyne's book *The Gestalt Art Experience* came out.

Betensky's book was welcomed in the art therapy community because it contained solid case histories of art and therapy—and at the time, it was one of the very few. Casebooks which illuminated the integration of art and psychology in art therapy were just beginning to appear in the 1970s. They would help provide an important window into the developing art therapy profession for other mental health professionals and the general public. But the fact that Betensky's work did not stem from psychoanalytic theory, but from an alternative theory—Phenomenology—tended to be overlooked. What moderated against her perspective was the then dominant sway of the psychoanalytical/psychodynamic theory base of the formal art therapy profession as manifested by the American Art Therapy Association. I also speculate that Betensky's theoretical model may not have been accepted, in part, because of her lack of a permanent base in an academic training program in the United States which could have provided Betensky and her philosophy consistent contact with new generations of art therapists. She was a visiting professor of art therapy at the University of Delaware in Newark, NJ, and at Haifa University in Israel, and a consultant to the Peace Corps. For the most part, Betensky lived in Washington D.C. where the Ulman and Levy-Masters program at George Washington University was focused on an art as therapy viewpoint. In addition, she was a doctorate-level psychologist at a time when few art therapists had doctoral degrees of any kind. She never received the award of the Honorary Life Membership of the American Art Therapy Association. Mala Gitlin Betensky died at the age of 88 in 1999 in Pittsburgh, PA of Alzheimer's disease.

Ironically today, 40 years after the publication of Betensky's first book, many training programs use Humanistic philosophies, sometimes combined with Jungian ideas, as their expressed theoretical base and many contemporary art therapists find these methods extremely valuable. Humanistic Psychology proposes a more optimistic vision of human beings and their potential for growth than does traditional psychodynamic theory and its descendents, and therefore is more appealing as a theory to contemporary art therapists within the current hopeful cultural milieu. Betensky's second *book* was published in 1995. In

What Do You See?: Phenomenology of Therapeutic Art Experience she describes a four-step phenomenological procedure using art that a therapist can lead a client through.

IMPORTANT DATES AND EVENTS

18th Century–The term "Phenomenology" is known in Europe.

1910–Mala Gitlin Betensky is born in Lodz, Poland.

1913–Husserl calls Phenomenology "The Science of Consciousness."

1914–Joseph Garai is born in Germany.

1926–As a 12-year-old, Garai discovers Freud's writings.

Late 1950s–Abraham Maslow, Carl Rogers and Clark Moustakas form the Humanistic Psychology Association.

1959–Garai earns his doctorate in Social Psychology and Personality from New York University.

1970s–Humanistic Psychology flourishes in the United States–particularly in the West.

1970–Garai founds the art therapy graduate program at Pratt Institute in New York City. According to Arthur Robbins, they later become "partners" to develop the program.

1971–Garai presents a paper at the second American Art Therapy Association conference: "The Humanistic Approach to Art Therapy and Creativity Development." Because of the dominance of psychoanalytic theory in art therapy, it is not well received and Garai is called crazy, a rebel and a troublemaker, according to him.

1978–Garai founds dance and movement therapy programs at Pratt.

1980–Garai retires from Pratt and becomes "Professor Emeritus."

1995–Joseph Garai dies in New York City.

1999–Mala Gitlin Betensky dies in a nursing home in Pittsburgh, PA. She has Alzheimer's disease.

STUDY QUESTIONS

1. Describe the basic tenets of Humanistic Psychology. How does it fit with your own philosophy of art therapy?

2. Describe Joseph Garai's contributions to the art therapy profession.

3. What is the basic idea of Phenomenology? How does it differ from psychoanalytic/psychodynamic theory?
4. Discuss Mala Betensky's integration of art and phenomenology.
5. How does Humanistic Psychology's basic optimism about human beings fit with the cultural optimism of the last 20 years or so in the United States?
6. Create an image in the spirit of one of the pioneers in this chapter.

Chapter 20

EXPRESSIVE ARTS THERAPY[1]

Expressive Arts Therapy–the use of the various arts together in therapy–has gained a great deal of momentum and many advocates in current years. Lesley University is perhaps the best-known Masters level training institution which offers this integration of the arts. The expressive arts therapists described in this chapter–Shaun McNiff, Arthur Robbins and Natalie Rogers–are those I consider to be the most influential in the art therapy profession. It is interesting that the three hold different theoretical assumptions–McNiff and Jung, Robbins and neo-Freudian Object Relations Theory, and Rogers and a Humanistic Psychology Rogerian approach–but I have grouped them together in their common intent to integrate the arts in therapy.

SHAUN MCNIFF (b. 1946)
The Art Therapist as Shaman

While it is true that Shaun McNiff is an "expressive therapist" using many varieties of arts approaches, his theoretical conceptualization of the art therapist as shaman is a unique and compelling notion in the

---

1. "Expressive Arts Therapy" is the potential use of drama, movement, dance, music, journal writing, poetry, imagery, meditation and the visual arts in therapy, whereas art therapy is usually, although not always, the visual arts alone. An expressive arts therapist may use some or all of the arts listed above depending on the needs of the client. Arthur Robbins calls his work a "multi-modal approach." Expressive arts therapy is often Humanistic in philosophy and contains aspects of Jungian theory and practice. A professional organization for the expressive arts called the International Expressive Arts Therapy Association, was formed in 1994. Students at the Union Graduate University can earn a doctorate in "Expressive Arts" and Saybrook has had a certificate program, led by Natalie Rogers. But as far as I know it is questionable whether it will continue after Rogers' retirement.

history of art therapy. Like many other expressive therapists, he focuses on "socially relevant applications" and places himself outside the medical model and within Humanistic and Transpersonal frames: "I have always believed that the work of art therapy applies as much to healthy people as it does to those afflicted by severe emotional disturbances. I approach art therapy as a mode of public health (McNiff in Junge & Wadeson, 2006, p. 231). His focus lies within Carl Jung's depth psychology philosophy.

McNiff argues that the artist is the descendent of the shaman; his cross-cultural and anthropological perspective is in contrast to most art therapy pioneers who believed that expressive arts therapy practice evolved from twentieth century psychiatry and psychology:

> The ancient predecessor of the expressive arts therapist can be found in every region of the world in the person anthropologists call the shaman. . . . The shaman's work is a response to communal needs. . . . Shamanism is characterized by a belief in the power of human beings to participate in a direct and personal relationship with the supernatural dynamic of life. (McNiff, 1981, p. 3)

McNiff believes that art therapy in clinical settings is too limiting. His work intentionally blurs boundaries. He does workshops in various places in the United States and internationally:

> People come with many different goals that shape what we do together—training, healing, artistic renewal, the need to revitalize therapeutic practice. . . . I believe we can be more creative and less literal-minded in encouraging a wider range of applications. (McNiff in Junge & Wadeson, 2006, p. 232)

McNiff's work centers on "the primacy of the artistic work of the therapist and is opposed to narrow specialization" (McNiff, 1985, p. 30). His vision includes an emphasis on spirituality and he argues that the more Freudian-based art therapists who struggle with making the unconscious conscious in their clients, still believe "in the will and the life of the spirit inside of and between people" (McNiff, 1981, p. v):

> Throughout time, art has shown that it can change, renew, and revalue the existing order. If art cannot physically eliminate the struggles of our

lives, it can give significance and new meaning and a sense of action participation in the life process. (McNiff, 1981, pp. v & vi)

The art therapist as shaman offers a healing ritual using the expressive arts. Clients enact the drama of their conflicts through symbols, myths and rituals. Emotional catharsis of the dramatized conflict provides exorcism and healing. McNiff writes: "Art therapy is a manifestation of an old and often suppressed religious tradition based upon creativity, imagination and participation in the artistic process" (1989, p. 5).

McNiff states: "I had [an] . . . abrupt, totally unplanned and almost magical start, becoming an art therapist completely by accident in March of 1970" (McNiff in Junge & Wadeson, 2006, p. 232).[2] Shaun McNiff was born November 29, 1946 in Peabody Massachusetts and grew up in Salem. He planned to be a lawyer like his father and even went to law school. His undergraduate years at Fordham University in New York were the time when Martin Luther King and Bobby Kennedy were assassinated. Although he was a history major, he studied painting with Abstract-Expressionist Theodore Stamos and at the Art Students League of New York. After dropping out of law school, McNiff worked as a welder intending to make large welded sculptures. To earn more money, he applied for a job at the Massachusetts State Mental Hospital (Danvers):

> [The personnel director said:] "The art therapist just moved to Hawaii. Are you interested in the position?" I had never heard of art therapy, but I walked out of the hospital as an art therapist. The idea of using art to help people fascinated me, and that incident became my life's most defining moment. The primary decision that I made was one of choosing art over the more traditional professions for men. . . . The work was in sync with my vision of art being something much more important than what I do alone in my studio. (McNiff in Junge & Wadeson, 2006, p. 234)

The 1970s was a decade when the arts began to be extensively used in community sites, jails and mental health institutions giving visual expression to the individual's personality and desires. Although the notion of "healing" was not necessarily always in the forefront with

---

2. Some of Shaun McNiff's history is from his memoir in Junge & Wadeson's *Architects of Art Therapy*, 2006.

these programs, the belief that the arts could be used to help positive growth and change and enhance identity for troubled people was increasingly central. Throughout his four years at Danvers (Massachusetts State Mental Hospital), McNiff connected his art therapy work to fine arts institutions. He collaborated with Christopher Cook of the Addison Gallery of American Art, Andover, MA and coordinated the art and video therapy program at the museum. McNiff's first publications represent this bonding of art therapy and fine art. They were "A New Perspective in Group Art Therapy," and *Art Therapy at Danvers–Addison Gallery of American Art,* catalog to the exhibition first presented in 1972.

During his years as a student in the Masters program at Goddard College in Vermont, McNiff contacted Rudolph Arnheim who became his mentor. Arnheim was and is probably the most eminent person in the country in the field of psychology of art. During his doctoral work at Union Institute, McNiff focused on cross-cultural art, healing practices and "began to see the indigenous shaman as the archetype of the artist healing":

> I knew that the art and healing were connected to an historical pattern of creativity, spirituality, physical medicine, and community well-being, and should not be understood solely as an adjunctive aspect of contemporary mental health systems. . . . As I examine my work over the past three decades, I see that everything I do grows from my first years of art therapy practice and my original vision of what art therapy can be. . . . I realize . . . how fortunate I have been to have fallen into a life work that gathers together all of my interests and continuously presents new areas of challenge and opportunity. . . . The work of art therapy is itself a deep mainstream of human experience that has flowed throughout history in different ways. (McNiff in Junge & Wadeson, 2006, pp. 235-236)

Shaun McNiff founded the arts therapies program at Lesley College (now Lesley University) in Cambridge, MA in 1973 when he was 26 years old. From its inception, this program has been a multimodal and multidisciplinary expressive arts[3] program. McNiff writes: "We called

---

3. McNiff writes that he first encountered the term "expressive therapy" in 1973, from Dr. William Goldman on the Massachusetts Mental Health Advisory Committee. Goldman, from San Francisco was brought in to reform the mental health system by a Republican governor. The state adopted the term "expressive therapy" (McNiff in Junge & Wadeson, 2006, p. 238).

our place the Arts Institute because it was more than a collection of programs. It was a community within Lesley with a unifying philosophy of the arts" (McNiff in Junge & Wadeson, 2006, p. 237).

After his years at Lesley College, McNiff moved into other arenas including international teaching and training. He is now back at Lesley as a Dean of Lesley College and University Professor. In recent years, Julia Byers at Lesley established the first accredited expressive arts therapies doctoral program in the country. It enrolled its first class in 2001.

Shaun McNiff is well known as a prolific writer in the art therapy field.[4] Since 1981, he has published nine books, the first being *The Arts and Psychotherapy* and the last *Integrating the Arts in Therapy: History, Theory and Practice* (2009). This last book, 25 years after the first, is a reworking of the ideas of his first. He says: "My view of expressive arts therapies is constantly recreating itself" (McNiff, 2009, p. vii). Because McNiff is a "crossover" writer in that his books incorporate all the arts in therapy, and because he virtually defined the expressive arts therapies field as different from visual art therapy, his writings have had broad appeal. He is arguably the most well-known author in art therapy and expressive therapies today: "When I was an aspiring painter in the 1970s," he said, "I never imagined that my primary connection to the world would be through books" (S. McNiff, personal communication, 2009).

One of McNiff's most influential books is *Art-Based Research* in which he proposes the possibilities and advantages of the uses of the arts as methodology in research inquiries. As far as I know, this is the first book that has proposed this notion. He is a compelling, fluid and talented writer who has also had an ongoing career as an exhibiting painter. In his books, McNiff explores the nature of expressive arts therapies in different settings—many of them community and educational settings, Jungian art therapy and, in recent years, spirituality and art therapy. His books often contain art therapy case material, but they are not casebooks nor case histories. McNiff is vastly knowledgeable about the arts, creativity and consciousness throughout history and his writings are thoughtful and sometimes profound examinations of the arts and therapy.

McNiff's refusal to specialize and compartmentalize, his intentional

---

4. Shaun McNiff's books are listed in References.

blurring of boundaries and his refusal to draw the limits of his work within the formal medical/clinical mental health system have caused him to become something of a controversial figure. He writes:

> Although I am an art therapist, I am not doing conventional "therapy" in my studios, yet every aspect of the work is permeated by therapeutic values, sensitivities and goals for more creative and enhanced living. I focus on the person together with the image and the process of creation. This is what I learned through my formative art therapy experience. . . . My work has taken me to diverse places and settings where the soul is in need. (McNiff in Junge & Wadeson, 2006, p. 242)

Despite his career as an expressive therapist, or perhaps because of it, McNiff has remained close to the American Art Therapy Association. He was awarded AATA's HLM (Honorary Life Membership) in 1997 and was elected president of the American Art Therapy Association 2001-2003.

ARTHUR ROBBINS (b. 1928)
Object Relations Art Therapy

Arthur Robbins was born in Brooklyn, New York in 1928 and received the highest honor from the American Art Therapy Association for his contributions to art therapy in 1998. He earned a doctorate in psychology from Columbia Teachers College at the age of 24: "I was cynical about such theory, but I knew this was my meal ticket out of the morass and jungle I lived in. I therefore played ball" (Robbins in Junge & Wadeson, 2006, p. 255). During a stint as a psychologist in the army during the Korean War, he learned about short-term psychotherapy "by the seat of my pants. . . . Little did I know that I had begun my training as an art therapist" (p. 257).

Beginning in 1958, Robbins trained as a psychoanalyst. During this period he learned sculpture "as another way of putting my father and mother together. . . . Much to my surprise, I did not encounter any criticism or shame, but indeed, a celebration of my creativity and my ability to see the world in a different and nonconventional way" (Robbins in Junge & Wadeson, 2006, p. 259). Robbins has explored sculpture ever since and has become a creator of welded sculptures.

After teaching psychology to artists at Pratt Institute, Robbins became a co-founder[5] and faculty member in the new Creativity Development (and later Art Therapy) program at Pratt. Of Joe Garai, Director of the program, he said: "[He] had a vision that matched my own, and we became close and creative buddies, sharing the same values of anti-conformity and speaking out one's mind and not being frightened of the consequences" (Robbins in Junge & Wadeson, 2006, p. 260).

Robbins thought deeply about clinical work, and settled in object relations theory, self psychology and ego psychology which were revitalizing Freudian theory in the 1970s and 1980s. Intended as a textbook for his program, in 1976 *Creative Art Therapy* was published and in it Robbins (with Sibley) described his approach to art therapy: "Our emphasis was on creativity and the artistic utilization of the therapist's abilities in making contact with patients. Yes, we believed in the importance of art, but there was equal emphasis on the creative interventions" (Robbins, in Junge & Wadeson, 2006, p. 262). Typical of early art therapists, Robbins' perspective grew from direct experience with patients and with graduate students. Since the publication of *Creative Art Therapy,* Robbins has written six books outlining his evolving ideas about art therapy.[6]

Object Relations Theory and Multi-Modal Art Therapy

Despite the Humanistic Psychology philosophy of the Pratt Institute art therapy program, where Robbins taught for many years, Robbins' view of art therapy is strongly based in neo-Freudian Object Relations theory and psychoanalytic practices. He believes that the infant's early internalized relationships with those around them, particularly the primary caretaker, play out in the client's current-day reality. He adapts Winnicott's idea of a "holding environment" defined as "that space between patient and therapist in which we complement or mirror our patient's representational world" (Winnicott, 1971; Robbins, 1987a, p. 61). According to Robbins, art media can be used to establish and "promote an ever adapting holding environment sensitive to the

---

5. There is some confusion over the establishment of the art therapy program at Pratt. Arthur Robbins says he co-founded the program with Josef Garai (Robbins in Junge & Wadeson, 2006, p. 261). Others say Garai founded the program and Robbins came after.
6. These books are listed in References.

patient's changing levels of ego integration, defenses, resistances, object representations, and the like" (Robbins, 1987a, p. 104).

Margaret Mahler's stages of psychological separation and individuation also form part of Robbins' theory. His assumption is that patients come to therapy because they have unsuccessfully managed these developmental crises. In Mahler's system, the therapist becomes the patient's "lost object" and in part, helps through their organizing ego. Rather than uncovering unconscious material, Robbins' approach is to *build* on what went before. The goal of therapy, he says, is to find true creativity. "Patients and therapist alike are engaged in finding the artists within themselves" (Robbins, 1987a, p. 21).

For Robbins, the human developmental process forms and connects with personal creativity. A patient's inner and outer landscapes are recreated through the creative process. Artwork itself helps the patient outwardly reflect the world of their internal objects which leads to organizing the felt chaos. Art "can be a container or organizer that mirrors internal object relations as well as associated defenses and developmental problems" (Robbins in Rubin, 2001, p. 59). Robbins writes:

> Art therapy, then, strives to promote new levels of perceptual organization that involves shifts in energy patterns. The art form offers an added means for working with splits and polarities and integrating them into new wholes. The representations from our past are expressed through image and expand the boundaries of objective reality. (Robbins, 1987b, p. 68)

Robbins believes in a multimodal approach in that all the arts may be used, depending upon the specific needs of the patient. In this way, he can be defined as an Expressive Arts therapist. He says: "Changing art expression into poetic metaphor serves as a transition to the world of words and helps make sense of the truism that although verbal material is strongly connected to reality, not all of reality is encompassed by words" (Robbins, 1987a, p. 36).

According to Robbins, therapeutic artwork approaches aesthetics when it integrates symbolic forms and the communication of meanings. He believes when aesthetic expression is combined with personality development, it becomes therapeutic: "As art therapists, our skills in integrating all this offer a special and powerful dimension. . . . Our challenge will be one of utilizing these concepts from psychiatry and psychoanalysis, while maintaining the visions and perceptions we have as artists" (1987a, p. 74).

When Arthur Robbins received the Honorary Life Membership, art therapy's highest award in 1998 from the American Art Therapy Association. He stated:

> I am proud to be a member of an association that offers me this highest award, one that respects individualism and honors someone who needs to go his own way. I am grateful to the association and all my students and colleagues for providing so many enlightening experiences that have contributed to a broader vision of what art therapy can potentially offer our patients as well as ourselves. (Robbins in Junge & Wadeson, 2006, p. 271)

NATALIE ROGERS (b. 1928)
Person-Centered Expressive Arts Therapy

Natalie Rogers calls her perspective "Person-Centered Expressive Arts Therapy." On her internet website, she says:

> I am a psychologist, group facilitator, mother of three daughters and grandmother of four. My mission for the past 30 years has been to bring creativity, soul and spirit into our lives, to empower ourselves as artists in this troubled world. As an expressive arts therapist, the foundation of my work is based on Carl Rogers' (my father's) philosophy. (Retrieved from www.nrogers.com, July 13, 2009)

Rogers worked with her father Carl, summers from 1974-79 co-leading Person-Centered groups.

Rogers believes that therapy and creativity overlap. Her aim is to "awaken the creative life-force energy" (Rogers in Rubin, 2001, p. 163). According to Rogers, the arousal of creativity within the human being offers a healing experience. In Rogers' practice, expressive therapy is often group therapy and its intention is to integrate the arts to help the client *act out* deep inner conflicts which lead to resolution and healing. Rogers' art therapy is different from a medical model or analytic art therapy in that it does not "diagnose, analyze and treat people." She says ". . . we believe in the ability of individuals to find appropriate self-direction" (Rogers in Rubin, 2001, p. 164).

Unlike Edith Kramer's idea of Freudian sublimation through art, Rogers' expressive therapy does not emphasize the creation of a unique and integrated art product to provide the "real world" manifestation of psychological healing. Rather than focus on the product, Rogers' therapy is process-oriented. The various integrated arts are used as other means of expression than verbal. Through coming in touch with the creative spirit, the client is able to let go and to heal, but the aesthetic value of the art product itself is irrelevant to the process. Rogers writes:

> I base my approach to expressive arts therapy on this very deep faith in the innate ability of each person to reach toward full potential. Just as Carl [Rogers] veered away from psychoanalysis and interpretation, so, too, have I rejected analytic and interpretive forms of art and movement therapy. In terms of methodology, this means I follow the client's lead as he [sic] discusses his art, movement, or writing. (Rogers in Rubin, 2001, p. 164)

In 1984, Natalie Rogers founded the Person-Centered-Expressive Therapy Institute in Cotati, California. Her book outlining her philosophy and methods *The Creative Connection: Expressive Arts as Healing* was published in 1993. She received a Lifetime Achievement Award from the International Expressive Arts Therapy Association in 1998 and is a licensed Psychologist in Massachusetts. She is currently a faculty member at Saybrook Graduate School and Research Center in San Francisco, California where she co-founded a certificate program in Expressive Therapies. While Saybrook has many programs and curriculums, it is known to embrace a Humanistic and Transpersonal philosophy. It was founded in 1971 as the Humanistic Psychology Institute, a part of Sonoma State University.[7]

IMPORTANT DATES AND EVENT

1928–Arthur Robbins is born in Brooklyn, New York.
1928–Natalie Rogers is born.
1946–Shaun McNiff is born in Peabody, MA.

---

7. History of Saybrook Graduate School and Research Center is from www.Saybrook.edu

1950-1953–These are the dates of the Korean War in which Arthur Robbins served.

1952–Age 24, Robbins receives his Doctorate in Psychology from Columbia Teachers College.

1958–Robbins begins analytic training and discovers sculpture.

1970–Age 23, McNiff becomes an art therapist "by accident" at Massachusetts State Mental Hospital (Danvers) where he works for four years.

1971–Robbins begins teaching at Pratt Institute in New York.

1972–McNiff collaborates with the Addison Gallery of American Art in Andover, MA. He coordinates art and video therapy, writes "A New Perspective in Group Art Therapy," creates an exhibit and writes the exhibit catalog *Art Therapy at Danvers–Addison Gallery of Art.*

1973–At age 26, McNiff founds Lesley College Arts and Therapy Program. (Later Lesley University.)

1974-1979–In the summers, Rogers co-leads Person-Centered groups with her father, Carl Rogers.

1976–Intended as a textbook for his Pratt classes, Robbins' first book is published–*Creative Art Therapy* (with Linda Sibley.)

1980–Rogers publishes her book *Emerging Woman, A Decade of Midlife Transitions.*

1981–McNiff's first book is published–*The Arts in Psychotherapy.*

1984–Rogers founds the Person-Centered Expressive Therapies Institute in Cotati, CA.

1984–Rogers is Professor and co-founder of the certificate program in Expressive Therapies, Saybrook Graduate School and Research Center in San Francisco, CA.

1993–Age 65, Rogers receives her Ph.D. in Psychology from Summit University. Her book about her approach to expressive therapy is published: *Creative Connection: Expressive Arts as Healing.*

1997–Shaun McNiff receives the highest award in art therapy from the American Art Therapy Association.

1998–Arthur Robbins receives the highest award in art therapy from the American Art Therapy Association. Natalie Rogers receives the Lifetime Achievement Award from the International Expressive Arts Therapy Association.

2001-2003–McNiff is President of the American Art Therapy Association.

STUDY QUESTIONS

1. Define "expressive arts therapies."
2. Compare expressive arts therapies to art therapy. What are the differences?
3. Discuss Rogers, Robbins and McNiff–their similarities and differences.
4. Create an image of one of the pioneers listed in this chapter.

Chapter 21

JUNGIAN ART THERAPY

CARL JUNG'S IDEAS PRIMARILY TAKE HOLD IN ENGLAND AND CANADA

Despite Margaret Naumburg and her sister Florence Cane having undergone Jungian analyses, the origins and early development of the art therapy profession were dominated by Freudian thought and methods of psychoanalytic thinking. In the early days, Jung's ideas connected more readily with art therapy in England rather than in the United States. According to Edwards (1987), Margaret Naumburg discusses British Jungian, H. G. Baynes' *Mythology of the Soul* (1940) in her 1950 volume *Schizophrenic Art*. Baynes[1] worked closely with C. G. Jung and gained his emphasis on the arts in therapy directly from him. Baynes was a great influence on Irene Champernowne who founded Withymead during World War II in the 1940s in Great Britain; Withymead was defined as the first therapeutic arts community in England and was based on the notion that the community milieu itself is healing. Along with shared tasks and group work, many of the therapeutic methods at Withymead were from Carl Jung's analytic psychology. Champernowne went on to become one of the founders of the British Art Therapy Association. (See Chapter 9.)

Michael Edwards, a well-known Jungian art therapist contributed a chapter called "Jungian Analytic Art Therapy" to Rubin's *Approaches to Art Therapy*. Edwards' roots are in England and he made many contributions to the evolution of art therapy there. He founded the Graduate Art Therapy Program at Concordia University, Montreal, Canada and

---

1. Information on art therapy in Great Britain is from Hogan (2001).

Birmingham, England is currently in private practice as a Jungian analyst and art therapist in Cornwall, Great Britain (Hogan, 2001).[2]

JUNG (1875–1961) AND ART IMAGERY

From his early childhood, Jung was interested in imagery and dreams. Edwards (1987) writes: "At age 10, at a time of stress and personal alienation, he [Jung] discovered relief in making a secret totemic figure" (p. 81). Art maintained a central position in Jung's life. He believed it to be the outward projection of inner experiences and used it at times of personal difficulty to gain insight and healing; in this way, he anticipated much of art therapy: "No other major psychologist attended to his own inner life through imagery in this way"[3] (Edwards, 1987, p. 82).

Jung's awareness of the psychological importance of spontaneous imagery from his unconscious caused him to often ask his patients to use visual means to represent their dreams and fantasies. Jung's theoretical concept of "Active Imagination" relies on artwork to illuminate the unconscious. As early as 1917, he began to ask patients to draw and in a 1931 paper wrote:

> But why do I encourage patients to express themselves at a certain stage of development by means of brush, pencil or pen? . . . At first [the patient] puts on paper what has come to him [sic] in fantasy, and thereby gives it the status of a deliberate act. He [sic] not only talks about it, but he [sic] is actually *doing* something about it . . . the effort to give visible form to the image enforces a study of it in all its parts, so that in this way its effects can be completely experienced . . . the mere execution of the pictures is not all that is required. . . . They must be consciously integrated, made intelligible, and morally assimilated. We must subject them to a process of interpretation. (Jung, 1954)

Jung's idea of the "Collective Unconscious" links imagery to religion, fairy tales, mythology, alchemy and the arts. In his theory, he describes archetypal and universal symbolism and events connected to a

---

2. Michael Edwards died March 2010 in Falmouth, England.
3. Jung's The Red Book in December 2009 has been published for the first time. It contains his journal in calligraphy and personal artwork which he ostensibly used to reintegrate his personality after a break (Shamdasani, 2009).

collective origin. According to Jung, the collective unconscious is expressed through the personal unconscious and the personal unconscious is expressed through imagery. But Jung believed that universal archetypes are cross-cultural, underlie all important life events and are passed on symbolically and perhaps genetically through generations. In the individual, real figures, such as a child's parents also contain parental archetypal projections. The depths of the collective unconscious, structured by archetypes, are manifested through the individual and lead to a profound spiritual significance[4] After years of controversy, Jung's *Red Book* which includes his own art work, was published for the first time in late 2009.

Mandala

Jung's fascination with the mandala form of artwork has significantly carried into art therapy; many art therapists use its completion as a containing technique without adhering at all to Jungian thought. The word "mandala" means "magic or sacred circle" in Sanskrit. With its origins in ancient spiritual practices and in particular, Buddhism, Jung drew and painted many personal mandalas (cf. Shamdasani, 2009, among others). He considered the mandala to be a representation of the unconscious self and believed that emotional disorders could be identified through it. By making a mandala, a circle shape, according to Jung, the individual could work toward personality wholeness.

In art therapy, the circle of the mandala provides a literal frame and a border for creativity with no beginning and no end. It is connected to the past and to the future. Thereby, its inherent archetypal underpinnings and structure can point toward personality wholeness, transpersonal thought and spirituality. Jung's cross-cultural leanings are an early form of multicultural diversity and are very attractive to many contemporary art therapists.

In 1974, a book by, a Jungian therapist Margaret Frings Keyes was published. Called *The Inward Journey: Art as Therapy for You*, Keyes' book, written from a Jungian perspective, contains directives and art therapy clinical vignettes so the reader can understand how Jung's

---

4. Author's note: Unfortunately, Jung had little artistry with words and his ideas were difficult to understand from his writings. In my opinion, if Jung had been as great a writer as Freud, his ideas might have been more dominant in psychology rather than usually referred to as "alternative."

ideas unfold in psychotherapy. Keyes also includes a section on mandalas with appropriate directives. Several authors of this period published on the power of the mandala in art therapy (Brekke & Ireland, 1980, Slegelis, 1987).

Joan Kellogg (1922-2004) became fascinated with Jung's concepts, especially the mandala and designed a therapeutic and projective test–the Mandala Assessment Research Instrument and MARI card test (Cox, in Malchiodi, 2002). Kellogg was an artist in residence at psychiatric hospitals in New Jersey who since 1969 worked to understand the relationship between art therapy and the mandala. She met Stanislov Groff[5] who was researching the effects of LSD on the psyche at Maryland Psychiatric Hospital. Groff invited her to be a consultant to his project. Through her cross-cultural studies, Kellogg theorized an underlying life cycle theory based on Jung, called "The Archetypal Stages of the Great Round of Mandala" (Kellogg, MacRae, Bonny, & DiLeo, 1977).

JUNGIAN ART THERAPISTS IN AMERICA AND EDITH WALLACE (1909–2004)

Because of Jung's focus on art imagery and the creative process, for many, his ideas have been a natural fit with art therapy. In addition, in the early 1970s, neo-Jungian, James Hillman recast many of Jung's notions calling his version Archetypal Psychology (1975, 2004). Hillman avoided classical interpretation in favor of exploration of the image as metaphor. This idea is currently ubiquitous in art therapy. In 1994, I wrote: "Many of Jung's ideas have been absorbed naturally into general art therapy theory without attribution" (p. 251).

Jungian oriented art therapists sought analytic training in Jungian Institutes. They tended to be Jungian analysts first who sometimes practiced art therapy, not art therapists within a Jungian theoretical focus. For them, the art integration often was one interest of many; they were expansively compelled by other of Jung's ideas as well, used them in their clinical work without art and published papers about them. Keyes is an example. She calls herself a "Jungian psychothera-

---

5. Stanislov Grof was a founder of Transpersonal Psychology and a researcher into altered states of consciousness. He has also been connected to Psychosynthesis.

pist and writer." Along with *The Inward Journey: Art as Therapy for You,* Keyes' other books are *Staying Married, Out of the Shadows, Emotions and the Enneagram,*[6] and *The Enneagram Relationship Workbook.* Given the dominance of Freudian psychoanalytical thought in art therapy, it is no wonder that Jung's ideas which could be confusing and which were connected to spirituality took a backseat in the development of art therapy.

Edith Wallace (1909–2004)[7]

A prize-winning painter, Edith Wallace was a psychiatrist and Jungian analyst. She received her analytic training in New York and Zurich with C. G. Jung. She began practicing Jungian analysis in New York in 1951. Her later years were spent in Santa Fe, New Mexico. After founder of the journal *The Arts in Psychotherapy,* Ernest Harms died in 1974, with Myra Levick and Paul Jay Fink (of Hahnemann Medical College and Hospital) she became Editor. In 1975, Wallace published *Creativity and Jungian Thought* and in 1987 she contributed a chapter to *Rubin's Approaches to Art Therapy* called "Healing Through the Visual Arts" about Jung's concept of *active imagination.* Wallace relied on Jung's idea of imagery as a message from the unconscious. She said: "It can become a dialogue between conscious and unconscious . . . the image may be explained in . . . words, which represent articulation necessary for conscious understanding–a message received" (Wallace in Rubin, 1987, p. 115).

Wallace regularly presented her work at the annual conference of the American Art Therapy Association and received the Creative Edge Award from AATA. A major innovation was her Tissue Paper Collage method (1990). The intention of this approach was to enhance access to the unconscious, propel understanding and insight and promote psychic healing and wholeness. The four steps of the collage method are (1) make the collage, (2) view the collage, (3) write a story in the form of a fairy tale or myth, and (4) perform a dance about it.

---

6. The enneagram is a personality type index derived from a hexagon within a circle symbol. It is rooted in traditional teachings; more modern names applied to its development are George Gurdjieff, Oscar Ichazo and Claudio Narango. It purports to display a psychospiritual topology of the individual.

7. Much of the information for Edith Wallace comes from her website, www.duversity.org/people/edith_wallace.html, retrieved 10/29/09.

The artwork is work done individually but is shared in a group. Wallace wrote:

> I have chosen one method–that of active imagination–which deals with images and is based on the fact that we must trust such images, which arise from the depth of the psyche. This method presupposes that truth resides in the unconscious, not only on a personal, ego level, but as a profound historical truth, and is manifested in archetypal images arising from the collective unconscious. (Wallace in Rubin, 1987, p. 95)

IMPORTANT DATES AND EVENTS

1875–Carl Jung is born in Kessewil, Switzerland.

1885–Age 10, under stress, Jung creates a totem figure and discovers a sense of relief from his problems.

1909–Jungian art therapist Edith Wallace is born.

1917–Jung asks his analytic patients to draw spontaneous images which he considers messages from the unconscious.

1940s–During World War II in Great Britain, Irene Champernowne founds Withymead. This is the first therapeutic arts community in England and uses many methods based on C. G. Jung's Analytic Psychology.

1951–Wallace begins practice as a Jungian analyst in New York City.

Early 1970s–Humanistic psychologist James Hillman recasts Jung's ideas. He calls this "Archetypal Psychology." Moving away from Jung's notion of *interpretation* of imagery, he establishes the concept of *metaphor* in imagery.

1974–Edith Wallace co-edits *The Arts in Psychotherapy* journal.

1974-Margaret Frings Keyes' *The Inward Journey: Art as Therapy* for You is published.

1975–Wallace's *Creativity and Jungian Thought* is published.

1977–Joan Kellogg creates the Mandala Assessment Research Instrument and MARI card test, a tool for assessment and therapy.

1990–Wallace's technique of Tissue Paper Collage is established. It refers to Jung's concept of *active imagination.*

1995 on–Jungian thought finds its way into many art therapy training programs because of Jung's interest in and emphasis on spontaneous imagery from the unconscious.

2004–Edith Wallace dies at age 85.

STUDY QUESTIONS

1. Describe Carl Jung's ideas about spontaneous imagery.
2. Why are Jung's concepts about imagery important to art therapy?
3. Describe Jung's notion of *active imagination* and state how Edith Wallace's Tissue Paper Collage method uses it.

Chapter 22

OTHER ART THERAPISTS
WHO BEGAN IN THE 1970s[1]

In this section, I briefly describe other art therapists who began in the 1970s and who received the Honorary Life Membership–the highest award of the American Art Therapy Association–for their contributions to the field. Through their integration of the arts and psychology, these women enriched art therapy in many ways, some through university teaching, some through their art, some through writing and publishing and some through leadership roles in the American Art Therapy Association. Many combined all these talents.

MILDRED LACHMAN CHAPIN (b. 1922)

Mildred Lachman Chapin has been a practicing artist for many years and still is. She took classes with Ulman, Kramer, Kwiatkowska, Rhyne and Wallace. She said that Ulman and her colleague, psychologist Bernard Levy were her art therapy mentors. Chapin attended the first conference of the American Art Therapy Association at Airlie House near Washington, D.C. and, after earning a Masters in Special Education, beginning in 1972, was a Professor in the art therapy program at George Washington University. Her clinical work was primarily with children.

Chapin held a number of board positions with the American Art Therapy Association and was the first Associate Editor of *Art Therapy,*

---

1. More complete autobiographies for these art therapists can be found in *Architects of Art Therapy, Memoirs and Life Stories,* Junge & Wadeson, 2006.

Journal of the American Art Therapy Association when it was initiated in 1983. She moved to Arizona in 1993 and since then has been a poet and exhibiting painter of "Visual Haikus" and primarily nonobjective art work. During these later years Chapin led a movement to put the "art back into art therapy" (see Chapter 24) and with others has succeeded in refocusing the profession on the nuances and importance of the profound uses of the arts. She received the highest award in art therapy, the Honorary Life Membership from AATA in 2001.

VIJA LUSEBRINK (b. 1924)

Born in Latvia, Vija Lusebrink fled to the West during the German occupation of World War II. She writes:

> My parents escaped deportation by seeking refuge under a false name in an insane asylum . . . [by 1944] my father had died . . . and our car had been confiscated. My mother organized a horse, buggy and a cow . . . we joined the long lines of refugees fleeing to the west from the approaching armies. . . . Our opportunity came when the Allied forces bombed the camp . . . in the ensuing melee at the train station, we were able to escape the transport. We melted into German everyday life. . . . Eventually, in 1950, I ended up on a Sunday morning in June at the Sandusky, Ohio train station with $5 in my pocket and nowhere to go. (Lusebrink in Junge & Wadeson, 2006, p. 275)

In Latvia, Lusebrink trained as a medical technician and after coming to the United States, she received a Bachelors of Science in chemistry from the University of Nevada. She married, raised three daughters and lived in the San Francisco Bay area where she was able to return to her "first love, art." In 1964, she received a Masters of Fine Arts degree in painting from the University of California at Berkeley. Lusebrink exhibited her artwork and taught art in junior college but was looking for something more challenging. Like most early art therapists, she discovered art therapy by accident and found work on a National Institutes of Health research project with schizophrenics and psychotics at Agnews State Psychiatric Hospital:

> Living in the San Francisco Bay Area in the early 1970s gave me many opportunities to explore and participate in the Human Potential

Movement. I explored workshops dealing with guided imagery, Sufi stories, dance/movement therapy, Jungian symbolism, psychodrama and sand-tray therapy, among others. . . . I was able to participate in Gestalt therapy workshops at the Esalen Center in Big Sur, California. I also joined two groups of women therapists, one of which was interested in using art in therapy, the other in transpersonal psychology as therapy. (Lusebrink in Junge & Wadeson, 2006, p. 278)

Lusebrink taught in the University of Louisville graduate art therapy program and formulated her ideas about information processing in art therapy activated through different art media. She says: "This insight became the basis for the concept later defined as the "Expressive Therapies Continuum" (Lusebrink in Junge & Wadeson, 2006, p. 281). In 1984, she received a doctorate in Interdisciplinary Studies from the University of Louisville, concentrating on psychology and psychiatry. Investigating the psycho-physiological aspects of imagery, Lusebrink's work "illustrates how many important ideas have developed in art therapy and related fields since Naumburg wrote her first work" (Junge, 1994, p. 252). Her book, published in 1990 and based on her doctoral studies is *Imagery and Visual Expression in Therapy*. Vija Lusebrink received the American Art Therapy Association's highest award–the Honorary Life Membership in 1995.

LINDA GANTT (b. 1944)

Linda Gantt, from Texas, studied in Washington, D.C. with Elinor Ulman and Hanna Kwiatkowska. Gantt earned a Masters degree in art therapy from George Washington University. She taught at Vermont College and received her doctorate from the University of Pittsburgh in Interdisciplinary Studies. She was president of the American Art Therapy Association 1989-1991 during which time her primary focus was promoting art therapy in governmental matters to potentially propel the profession into the national political limelight. At the time, there were many art therapists who did not agree with this approach although it has proven itself to be incredibly essential to the development of the profession.

Stemming from her dissertation research, Gantt developed FEATS–Formal Elements Art Therapy Scale. Using the "Draw a Person Picking an Apple From a Tree" drawing, developed by Viktor

Lowenfeld (1990, 2001), Gantt's research (with Carmello Tabone), focuses on the *observation* of the art, *not its interpretation* and attempts to connect specific variables in artwork to the classification system of the diagnoses of the *Diagnostic and Statistical Manual (DSM-III)* published by the American Psychiatric Association. However, rather than diagnose particular psychological states, the FEATS approach attempts to assess *changes* in psychological states while the patient engages in psychotherapy (Gantt & Tabone, 2003).

Another interest and focus for Gantt has been trauma survivors. Psychiatrist Louis Tinnin, in 1996, set up the Trauma Recovery Center as an outpatient treatment center in Morgantown, West Virginia. Gantt worked closely with him, developed techniques using art and is now Executive Director. Her first publication on trauma was in 1979. Gantt received the American Art Therapy Association's Honorary Life Membership award in 1994.

MAXINE BOROWSKY JUNGE (b. 1937)

My career in art therapy began formally in the early 1970s when I apprenticed with Helen Landgarten and began to teach in her art therapy Masters program at Immaculate Heart College, Hollywood, California. But it had really begun in childhood before I had ever heard of "art therapy" from my passion for art making and my interest in understanding and helping people. I became fascinated with family art therapy when I had my own children and later learned to do family psychotherapy. Along with clinical practice since 1971 and teaching (at Immaculate Heart, Loyola Marymount University, Goddard College in Vermont and Antioch University-Seattle), I grew up in a liberal, activist family in Los Angeles and came of age in the civil rights era and the Hollywood Blacklist period, thus a major passion and thrust of my life and work has been social justice and action.

I have been a serious artist since my early teens and because I am interested in ideas and history, write a great deal and have published journal articles and books. My last book, *Mourning, Memory and Life Itself, Essays by An Art Therapist* (2008), contains most of my favorite published essays reworked and this book–*The Modern History of Art Therapy in the United States*–is my fifth. For a number of years, I was Director of the Marital and Family/Clinical Art Therapy program at Loyola

Marymount. I received the highest award in art therapy—the Honorary Life Membership—in 1995 from the American Art Therapy Association.

BOBBI STOLL (b. 1932)

Bobbi Stoll and Shirley Riley were in the first graduating class I taught at Immaculate Heart College. Stoll became president of AATA 1993-95 and virtually, single handedly, promoted and propelled international art therapy into a global force. (See Chapter 24.) Stoll was the first art therapist to receive the Marriage and Family Counseling License in 1979 in the state of California. She writes: "I insisted then and still do, that a license grants permission and legitimizes a practice. Once the door to my practice was legally open, I could do what I was trained to do" (Stoll in Junge & Wadeson, 2006, p. 357). Stoll received the Honorary Life Membership in 1999.

SHIRLEY RILEY (1921–2004)

After her retirement as a faculty member and Field Placement Coordinator from Loyola Marymount University, Shirley Riley, a family art therapist who called herself a "post-modernist" taught at Phillips Graduate Institute in Encino, California focusing on neuroscience and art therapy. She held a number of positions with the American Art Therapy Association and wrote books based on her long clinical practice at Didi Hirsh Community Mental Health Center in Culver City, California (Malchiodi & Riley, 1996, Riley, 1999, 2000). Riley was awarded the Clinician of the Year award in 1990 and in 2000, the Honorary Life Membership award by the American Art Therapy Association. Riley died suddenly in 2004 at the age of 83.

CAY DRACHNIK (b. 1924)

With Don Uhlin and psychiatrist Tarmo Pasto after settling in California, Cay Drachnik was instrumental in establishing the art therapy program at the University of California at Sacramento. She founded the Northern California Art Therapy Association and was a driving force in the state political battle which occurred in the early 1980s which attempted to disallow the Marriage and Family Therapy License legally earned by some art therapists. Drachnik was president of the American Art Therapy Association 1987-1989 and received the Honorary Life Membership in 1991. She had a clinical practice, taught art therapy at Sacramento State and Notre Dame de Namur in Belmont, California and continued painting. After her retirement, she continues to paint and exhibit.

VIRGINIA MINAR (b. 1923)

Virginia Minar was president of the American Art Therapy Association 1995-1997 and received the Honorary Life Membership from AATA in 2004. During Minar's presidency, the Art Therapy Credentials Board was formed and art therapy Board Certification (BC) initiated. Minar first received an education certificate in art and special education. She is from Wisconsin and as a child gave dance performances throughout the Midwest as part of a Danish folk dancing troupe. Particular clinical interests have been special education, children, and cancer patients where she integrates visual arts and poetry. She is a poet herself and retired, lives in Las Vegas, Nevada.

STUDY QUESTION

1. Describe the impact of art on the practice of each art therapist of this chapter.

Part IV

ART THERAPY IN THE LAST YEARS

Chapter 23

CULTURE OF THE TIMES[1]

During most of this period, the United States acted as a "world policeman." The decades saw three wars in which America played a major part: In 1990, the Gulf War was a response to the Iraqui invasion of Kuwait. In 1991, the Iraqui government surrendered. After George W. Bush's election by 537 votes in 2000 and after the terrorist attacks September 11, 2001 on the World Trade Center buildings in New York, the Pentagon and on a field in Shanksville, Pennsylvania, in 2002, the United States invaded Afghanistan with "Operation Enduring Freedom." In 2003, the invasion and occupation of Iraq began with "Operation Iraqui Freedom." America also participated in wars in Somalia, Haiti, Bosnia and Yugoslavia.

During the 1990s, the electronic age emerged. Created in 1992, the internet drastically changed our methods of communications. How we spend money and do business was also transformed. Steve Jobs and Bill Gates became household names.

In 1993, Bill Clinton was elected 42nd President of the United States. In 1996, he was re-elected and in 1999 acquitted in an impeachment trial by the United States senate. Clinton had a sexual relationship with a White House intern in the Oval Office and lied about it.

During Clinton's administration, there was a booming American economy with stock markets reaching all-time highs. There was also record low unemployment. The North American Free Trade Agreement (NAFTA) went into effect, the "Don't Ask, Don't Tell" policy for the armed forces was established in which homosexuals were allowed

---

1. Much of this information is culled from en.wikipedia.org/...timeline_of United_States_History and kclibrary.lonestar.edu/decade90.html

to serve, but not if they "came out of the closet." Health care reform was a central issue, but was not passed and welfare reform, which had begun in 1988, moved forward.

With all the plenty, it was an increasingly violent period. In 1995, the bombing of the Murrah Building in Oklahoma which killed 168 and wounded 800 occurred. The O.J. Simpson trial was held, in which Simpson allegedly murdered his ex-wife and her friend. (He was found "not guilty.") The bombing at Centennial Park in Atlanta in 1996 during the summer Olympics killed one and injured 111. TWA Flight 800 exploded over Long Island and 230 passengers and crew were killed. Between 1996 and 1999, there were 14 school shootings with Columbine High School in Littleton, Colorado being the most deadly. Gun control was hotly debated as the National Rifle Association asserted that legal ownership of a gun was a constitutional right. Currently, as guns and violence proliferate, gun control ironically seems to be a non-issue: In 2007, the massacre at Virginia Polytechnic Institute and State University (Virginia Tech) occurred in which a student, known to be seriously mentally ill was allowed to buy a gun, shot and killed 32 people and wounded many more.

While the new crop of antipsychotics and anti-depressants began to be used earlier, by the late twentieth century[2] almost everyone who saw a psychiatrist (and other doctors as well) came away with a prescription and seldom a recommendation for any form of psychotherapy. The nature/nurture pendulum has increasingly swung to nature as the cause of most psychiatric problems and the treatment of choice was medication.

In the 1960s and '70s, there had been an influential critique of psychiatry by disillusioned psychiatrists Thomas Szasz, R. D. Laing and David Cooper and French sociologist, philosopher and historian, Michel Foucault. They criticized the *Diagnostic and Statistical Manual* of the American Psychiatric Association and maintained that the fundamental assumptions and practices of psychiatry were little but examples of social control and human rights violations. By the 1990s, the continuum with environment on one end and genetics on the other had swung to biology as the root cause of mental disorder. New technology in brain research contributed to an emphasis on genetic and biological foci.

---

2. Prozac was approved by the FDA in the United States in December 1987.

Although research is decidedly unconvincing, the mass prescribing of medication which continues today closed the debate about the meaning of symptoms and behavior and affirmed the genetic nature of mental problems. Unhappiness had become taboo and positivity and "affirmations" increasingly became the philosophy of the time. There are those that argue that the widespread uses of medications established psychiatry as an important medical specialty akin to medicine. Psychiatric medications are also widely believed to be a form of social control of deviance. With the expansive practice of medication and the belief in biological causes for disease, the practice of psychotherapy tended to be left out in the cold. Psychotherapy that did flourish was behaviorally and cognitively focused. Ironically, health, nutrition and exercise were widely popular. At the same time obesity was at an all-time high.

More and more school children were diagnosed with Attention Deficit Disorder (ADD) or Attention Deficit Hyperactivity Disorder (ADHD) only newly in the *Diagnostic and Statistical Manual* of the American Psychiatric Association. Despite little research to support the use of medication, they were and are treated with Ritalin or another sedative (those diagnosed were primarily boys). Medication was widely viewed as an important and positive method to keep children focused in school and doing well. In 1999, 83 percent of students completed high school versus 41 percent in 1960.

Tattoos, body piercing and video games were ubiquitous with adolescents and young adults. Ninety-eight percent of households had TV and average viewer watching was seven hours per day. Restaurants proliferated and casinos emerged on the coasts. Green design products, houses and recycling became popular. Feng Shui as a philosophy of design prevailed while Martha Stewart became a name as a guru of homemaking and design.

Audio books, CDs and DVDs and in the twenty-first century, kindles, were widespread. On-line book stores like Amazon became popular and huge bookstores like Borders and Barnes and Noble pretty much obliterated small, independently-owned bookstores. Self-help books sold well. Oprah Winfrey became the most admired woman of the times and her "Oprah's Book Club" promoted reading, or at least book sales.

In the early twenty-first century, there was a series of bombings in the Middle East, killing numbers of people. In 2002, the Department of Homeland Security was created and in 2003 the space shuttle Columbia disaster occurred in which all seven astronauts were killed. George W. Bush was re-elected in 2004 and in 2005 there was Hurricane Katrina which decimated New Orleans and other cities in the Gulf Coast regions.

The global financial crisis began in 2008 as the stock market crashed. Also in 2008, Barack Obama was elected. He was the first African-American President. Joe Biden was elected Vice President. Unemployment rose precipitously as many businesses closed or went into bankruptcy and many workers were laid off. Swimmer Michael Phelps won eight gold medals at the Olympics surpassing Mark Spitz's previous record of seven. In 2009, President Obama presented a $787 billion stimulus package which was approved by Congress. As this book goes to press, President Obama is promoting a universal health care program which he hopes will be passed by Congress in early 2010. This would be a major step forward for health care in this country. Singer Michael Jackson, the "King of Pop," died in 2009. In late 2009, a psychiatrist treating returning military for Post Traumatic Stress Disorder at Fort Hood, Texas killed 13 people and wounded many more. Five of the dead were therapists (Carey, Cave & Alvarez, November 8, 2009).

On Christmas Day 2009, a terrorist with a bomb in his underwear attempted, but failed, to blow up an international airliner about to land in Detroit. March 2010, the Health Care Bill was passed in the United States Congress and signed into law by President Barack Obama. This bill provides for a major overhaul of the healthcare system—the first in 50 years.

Chapter 24

CONTEMPORARY ISSUES IN ART THERAPY

THE QUESTION OF ART THERAPY ASSESSMENT AND ASSESSMENT PROCEDURES

Frances F. Kaplan, D.A., ATR-BC

Introduction

S ome decades ago when I began my art therapy studies, the field of art therapy was too new to have developed much in the way of art therapy assessments. There were, however, a number of drawing tests developed by psychologists based largely on psychoanalytic theory (e.g., Buck, 1970), and I found myself fascinated by them. Could we really tell all the things about a person that the manuals for these instruments seemed to suggest? I was excited about the class I took in projective drawing techniques and tried my best to believe in their validity. Later, as I used these techniques in my work, I developed an increasingly uncomfortable feeling that I was making up my evaluations based on very slender evidence (Kaplan, 2003). Eventually, I reviewed studies done by psychologists who had similar doubts and discovered that these projective drawing tests did not stand up well to scientific scrutiny (Kahill, 1984; Smith & Dumont, 1995; Swensen, 1968; Wanderer, 1997).

Nonetheless, art therapists continue to use assessments designed by psychologists while at the same time developing more and more of their own. Feder and Feder (1998) have noted that these assessments comprise three main types: (a) the projective drawing tests developed by psychologists, (b) phenomenological approaches that involve observing the art, the art-making process, and the client's comments about both process and product, and (c) diagnostic rating scales that assess the art product largely on its formal elements and on global indicators of content. Is this whole enterprise futile? Setting aside the projective drawing techniques, which have largely proven invalid over the years, examining the other two types of art assessments currently in use should provide at least a partial answer.

Art-based assessments designed by art therapists can be considered the progeny of the original projective drawing techniques. Nonetheless, they are different in that they are generally either more phenomenological in approach or more focused on diagnosis, problem and strength detection than on attempting to do a psychoanalytical-style personality test. As to the phenomenological approach, suffice it to say that it is not so much an explicit technique as it is an interviewing and observational procedure with art making as the stimulus (Betensky, 1995; Groth-Marnat, 1997).

Within the phenomenological approach a wide variety of directives can be used including ones attached to projective drawings (e.g., "Draw a house, a tree, and a person," "Draw a family doing something"), or no directive at all. Traditional interpretations are either ignored or viewed as secondary to information obtained from the client. Considerable information can be gathered in this manner—including realistic art therapy treatment goals for working with the client. The usefulness of this approach, if sensitively applied, is evident. It is the approach that was frequently employed by art therapy pioneers (Kwiatkowska, 1978; Landgarten, 1981; Kramer, 2000) who used clinical experience, theory, and specific drawing tasks to assess their clients.

The diagnostic approach, in my opinion, deserves more attention. Beginning in the early 1980s, certain art therapists (Gantt & Tabone, 2003; Levick, 2009a; Mills, 2003; Silver, 2007) worked on developing diagnostic assessments using objective rating scales. Interestingly, this process has been largely a U.S. phenomenon. British art therapy, the other major model for art therapy worldwide, embraces the more subjective psychoanalytic and phenomenological approaches (Gilroy, 2006).

Undoubtedly, there are a number of reasons for this difference. A primary reason is that psychoanalysis does not continue to hold as much sway in the United States as it does in England, the final home of both Sigmund Freud and his daughter Anna. In addition, the strong emphasis on psychological research brought about by the behavior movement in this country, in conjunction with an increasing interest in cognitive studies and neuroscience, has called into question many of Freud's ideas (e.g., Holt, 1989).

I will set aside then, the first two types of art therapy assessments—the psychoanalytic because it appears to be outdated and the phenomenological because it seems to be reasonably useful—and concentrate on the better known art-based diagnostic techniques developed by American art therapists. The originators have employed scientific principles to develop and validate their assessments and most of them can be considered works in progress. A brief overview of these techniques, a comparison of the different assessment methods, and a discussion of their collective effectiveness follows.

Art Therapy Diagnostic Assessments

The Diagnostic Drawing Series (DDS)

Created in the early 1980s by Barry Cohen and colleagues (1983, 1986), the DDS has a somewhat different aim than the other tests described below (Feder & Feder, 1998; Mills, 2003). Instead of predicting what diagnostic category (depression, schizophrenia, bipolar disorder, and so on) might apply to a person, the DDS investigators focused on collecting standardized drawings by groups of individuals with diverse psychiatric diagnoses. Their goal was to concentrate on finding patterns of formal drawing elements that correlate with different diagnostic categories, and as a consequence, they have established a growing database of drawings with matching diagnoses that other researchers can use. Ideas about "form as content" developed by Gestalt art therapist Janie Rhyne provide the core philosophy for this particular assessment (Mills, 2003).

The DDS uses three drawings—a free drawing, a tree drawing, and an abstract feelings drawing. These three types of drawings provide an unstructured task, a structured task, and a semi-structured task to determine how the test-taker responds to different degrees of structure. After the artwork is finished, the drawings are discussed to gain information about the client's related thoughts and associations. Scoring of the drawings is subsequently done on the presence, absence, or type of 36 drawing elements (Feder & Feder, 1998). Because the DDS has been in use for more than 20 years, a number of studies of have been done that offer graphic profiles for both major clinical syndromes and personality disorders (Cohen, 1983 & 1986; Kessler, 1994; Mills, 2003; Morris, 1995).

As to the reliability and validity of these profiles and of the assessment overall, interrater reliability has been found to be quite good but validity is more complicated. As Mills, Cohen, and Meneses (1993) have stated, "Degree of success in prediction has not been fully tested to investigate validity of the DDS" (p. 85). They do report, however, that a computerized study was able to differentiate among four diagnostic categories with 77 percent accuracy using a small sample of DDS drawings.

The Formal Elements Art Therapy Scale (FEATS)

The FEATS was inspired by the work of pioneer art therapists Elinor Ulman and Bernard Levy (1975) who discovered that the structure of art was a better source of diagnostic information than its content. Developed by Linda Gantt and Carmello Tabone (1998, 2003) beginning in the late 1980s, it is a single-picture standardized assessment with the aim of discriminating among various diagnostic groups. The directive for the picture, one previously used by Lowenfeld (1964), is "Draw a person picking an apple from a tree" (PPAT), and the product is rated on 14 scales of 0-5 points each having to do with formal drawing elements. Initially, the FEATS was shown to differentiate among four major clinical syndromes: depression, hypomania, schizophrenia, and organic brain syndrome (Gantt & Tabone, 1998). However, Gantt and Tabone (2003) have continued to research their assessment and postulate that their scale can be used as a method for differentiating less severely afflicted individuals from the normally functioning. There have been some recent studies (Rockwell & Dunham, 2006; White, Wallace, & Huffman, 2004) that would seem to support this notion—but with some qualifications in order (see Discussion section below).

When it comes to the reliability and validity of the FEATS, Gantt and Tabone (2003) assert that their instrument is sensitive to change in psychological state, and therefore, test-retest reliability does not apply. Interrater reliability, however, is important and they have demonstrated that most of the FEATS's 14 scales have very good reliability of this type. With regard to validity, they have been working on repeating on a larger scale the original validity study done by Gantt (1990). Nonetheless, because the researchers view the FEATS as measuring psychological states rather then traits, they point out that they will need to conduct validity studies using an established measure of clinical condition for comparison.

The Levick Emotional and Cognitive Art Therapy Assessment (LECATA)

This assessment is the most complex and, in some ways, the most similar to the original drawing tests developed by psychologists. Myra Levick,[1] the originator of the LECATA, began work on it in 1986 with the assistance of other art therapists working in the Miami-Dade County, Florida School District (Levick, 2009). The portion of the assessment revealing emotions is based on the hierarchy of ego defensives devised by Anna Freud, and the cognition portion relies on the cognitive stages outlined by Jean Piaget (Feder & Feder, 1998).

The LECATA is focused primarily on children and uses five drawing tasks (Levick, 2009a, Appendix, p. 3):

1. A free art task and story about the complete image.
2. A drawing of the self.
3. A scribble with one color and a picture created from the scribble.
4. A place you would like to be (for 3-5 years old.) A place that is important to you (for 6-11+ years old.)
5. A family.

Checklists for each task are employed to determine mental age for both cognitive and emotional domains. Age categories start at 2 1/2 to 31/2 years and conclude at $10^{1/2}$ to 11+ years. The scores for the five art tasks are averaged and compared to the child's chronological age.

Levick (2009a) has recently completed a normative study involving 330 school children that provides partial support for the validity of her assessment. Moreover, as a result of this study, she has conjectured that a "new norm" for children today has to do with a slowing down

---

1. Levick was the first president of the American Art Therapy Association and is credited with being central in its formation. See Chapter 11.

of development. She attributes this to the fact that so many children spend time alone during the day due to an increase in divorce, parental separation, both parents working, and the prevalence of electronic media and devices.

Silver Drawing Test of Cognition and Emotion (SDT) and Draw a Story Test (DAS)

Rawley Silver's[2] (2003) first drawing tests were initially published in 1983 and have undergone consistent revision and expansion over the years. The major support for these tests comes from the work of Arnheim (1969) and others who espoused the belief that thinking is visual as well as verbal. The unfortunately named SDT includes three subtests: Predictive Drawing, Drawing from Observation, and Drawing from Imagination. The first two subtests are highly structured and involve adding lines to printed drawings (Predictive Drawing) and sketching a standardized arrangement of objects (Drawing from Observation). The third subtest (Drawing from Imagination) asks the test-taker to choose at least two stimulus drawing images (e.g., mouse, castle, tree, sitting man with sad expression) and to depict these images interacting. The person is then requested to add a title or story to the drawing. Each of these three subtests is rated on short scales that are meant, *in toto,* to provide information about cognitive, creative, and emotional functioning.

It is probably safe to say that the Draw a Story Test (Silver, 2007), which evolved from the Drawing from Imagination subtest of the SDT, is among the most frequently used of the Silver battery. It is easy to administer, easy to score, flexible in its applications, and works especially well with children. Art therapists use it to gather general information about the clients they are working with as well as to assess their depressive and aggressive tendencies. They may also use it on occasion to evaluate if art therapy treatment has resulted in improvement, based on positive changes in scale scores. The scales generally used for scoring are the Emotional Content Scale and the Self-Image Scale, both of which are rated 1-5 with a score of 5 representing the positive end of the scale.

It should be noted that the Draw a Story Test is scored primarily on

---

2. For more on Rawley Silver and her career, see Chapter 13.

content. Form (or structure) is not a major focus here as it is in some of the other assessments. Further, Silver (1999) has collected considerable evidence supporting her claim that her tests are reliable and valid. Indeed, the SDT appears to be among the most thoroughly researched of the art-based assessments developed by art therapists. It should be kept in mind, however, that the scales Silver uses amount to global ratings. That is: the whole drawing is taken into account along with the accompanying story.

Comparison of the Different Assessments and Overall Critique

The four assessments described above have a number of similarities and differences. These are summarized in Table 24.1. Although these assessments are built on different theories and use quite different procedures, they hold in common a course of development that relies on scientific methods and that their originators trust and hope will lead to well constructed standardized art therapy instruments. As an aside, it is interesting to note that the initial work on these four assessments took place during the 1980s—a time when art therapists were awakening to the fact that science has its place in art therapy (Kaplan, 2000).

There is an underlying similarity in the discussed assessments that is not so obvious when looking at their individual details. A case is made in the section below that this similarity involves a limitation in art-based assessments in general that will allow them to go only so far.

In the early days of art therapy research, it was found that judges were able to assign paintings to patient and nonpatient categories to a statistically significant degree (Ulman & Levy, 1975). It is not surprising, then, that more carefully developed assessments are generally able to separate the disturbed from the normal and thus can claim at least this measure of validity. Further, objective processes used in creating rating scales have ensured reasonably good interrater reliability for these measures. Such results would seem to justify the existence of these assessments—and to some extent, they do.

There are also some fairly serious limitations in art therapy assessments. First, let's look at the success of discriminating among various diagnoses. Based on previous psychological research, Smith and Dumont (1995) have stated, "Only the relationship between global measures (i.e., rating schemes that consider the drawing as a whole or a set of specific features in the drawing) and diagnoses of gross mal-

TABLE 24-1. COMPARISON OF STANDARDIZED
ASSESSMENTS DEVELOPED BY ART THERAPISTS

Assessments	DDS	FEATS	LECATA	SDT/DAS
Initial research population	adults	adults	children	children
Art tasks used	3 drawings	single drawing	5 drawings	drawing completions, from observation, based on stimulus images
Aim	differential diagnosis	differential diagnosis	determining mental age	detecting cognitive deficits, creativity, depression, and aggression
Scoring system	records patterns of formal art elements using checklist	records patterns of formal art elements using 14, 0-5 pt. scales	averages scores based on both form and content from 5 checklists	uses simple scales that vary depending upon construct assessed; content emphasized
Theory/ philosophy	Gestalt art therapy	Ulman & Levy's emphasis on structure rather than content of art	Anna Freud's ego defenses & Piaget's stages of cognitive development	visual thinking as espoused by Arnheim, others

adjustment has reached levels of statistical significance with some consistency" (p. 299). Here is a case in point: In 2006, Rockwell and
Dunham conducted a validity study using the FEATS. They sought to
differentiate a substance-use disordered population from those without
substance-use problems. Three scales on the FEATS (Realism,
Developmental Level, and Person) did show statistically significant dif-

ferences between the two populations. However, it takes more than one study to be sure a researcher has findings that generalize. Another study by Sand (2008) attempted to replicate the Rockwell and Dunham study and found only one scale (Line Quality) that discriminated between a substance-abuse disordered population and one without substance-abuse problems. In Sand's inquiry, the discriminatory scale was not only different from the three that produced significance in the previous study but also may have been an artifact of the likelihood of obtaining at least one significant result when utilizing a relatively large number of scales.

Other studies of less profound types of pathology–for example, adjustment disorders, eating disorders, thought impairment–have also found differences between the art of those so afflicted and normal youngsters (Kaiser & Deaver, 2009; Kessler, 1994; White, Wallace & Huffman, 2004). However, what is the most striking feature of this art, based on the illustrations that accompany the research reports, is that all those with the specified problems *draw less developed drawings than those lacking these problems.* This commonality hinders the ability to separate individuals with different types of maladjustment from each other. It suggests that many of the features of art rated by assessments, particularly those having to do with drawing development, correlate indirectly rather than directly with various aspects of psychopathology.

Although it does not deal with psychopathology *per se,* an anecdote from my long history as an art therapy educator should help clarify my last statement: A student designed a study to compare people-drawings done by deaf school children and those done by hearing students of the same age. She developed a simple rating scale that looked for indicators in the deaf children's drawings such as large hands–due to the importance of communicating by signing–and diminished or exaggerated emphasis on ears–for obvious reasons. She also used a global rating of drawing development. On the basis of this rating scheme, she hoped to be able to separate the deaf students' drawings from the hearing students' drawings. To her surprise, and mine, *the only thing that differentiated the two groups was the level of drawing development.* The deaf students' art was consistently at a lower stage of development than the art of the hearing students. From this study, it appears that developmental lag was the true correlate that separated the deaf students from the hearing. The condition of deafness was secondary. And because other attempts to separate psychologically impaired populations from normal populations have found similar differences in drawing development, it seems reasonable to assume that the impairment is responsible for causing either a developmental lag or a regression. The effect of the particular impairment, however, is often not evident in the drawing.

Now let's look at two additional limitations in art therapy assessments. First, there is a continuing tendency to look for individual pathogenic characteristics. Second, there is a general lack of recognition of the difference between clinical and statistical significance. Concerning the former, other authors beside Smith and Dumont (1995) have pointed to the improved validity of global ratings as opposed to looking for telltale drawing signs. For instance, Madigan, Ladd, and Goldberg (2003) who conducted a study of attachment category indicators in family drawings came to a similar conclusion: "The present data indicate that global ratings and global clinical impressions are more likely to be useful to the clinician than specific individual markers" (p. 34). Despite this, a new assessment in the beginning stages of development, the Bird's Nest Drawing also attempting to assess attachment, was originally oriented toward single indicators (Kaiser & Deaver, 2009). And art therapists—especially students—who use art-based assessments often get enamored of individual signs, perhaps because we do not at this point have reliable ways of totaling the scores for clusters of drawing features so we can arrive at degrees of clinical pathology reflected in the drawings.

The latter problem mentioned above is a general problem with all art therapy assessments of this nature. For example, Kessler (1994) reports that controls and a combined sample of eating disorder patients (including women with bulimia, anorexia, and eating disorder NOS) show a considerable difference in the use of knotholes in their tree drawings. With controls only using knotholes 20 percent of the time and the combined eating disorder patients using them 55 percent of the time, a conclusion of statistical significance is reasonable. However, consider the fact that making a diagnosis based on these figures would involve a large percentage of error: 45 percent of the time a diagnosis of eating disorder would be missed and 20 percent of the time a person without an eating disorder would be so labeled. A person would certainly not want his or her personal physician to be fallible to such a degree.

In all fairness, Kessler (1994) points out that there are other sources of error in this data; the participants with anorexia and eating disorder NOS drew relatively few knotholes (17.6% and 33.3%, respectively). It was the participants with bulimia (70.8%) who made the difference. Nonetheless, this example points out what frequently happens in art therapy research when the researcher is less careful about reporting the limitations of the data: Statistical significance is highlighted and clinical significance is ignored.

Conclusion

Scientifically-based art therapy assessments have a way to go to become more global in their scoring procedures. In addition, more attention needs to be paid to clinical versus statistical significance. And, although these two features may be improved with further studies, I am not so sanguine about the perfecting of differential diagnosis when it comes to lesser degrees of pathology. To be sure, the history of art therapy research indicates that from their drawings, the troubled can be separated from the well-functioning with a certain degree of accuracy; this can be immensely helpful when dealing with a large number of children or adults about whom one has little information. It can provide the first signal that certain individuals might need special attention. But there are too many variables in, say, a substance-use disordered population, to be definitively detected in a single drawing or even a stack of drawings. In addition, many symptoms overlap when it comes to personality and behavioral disorders and psychiatric syndromes, and many individuals with psychological and psychiatric problems have multiple problems. Still, the researchers who have been responsible for developing and continuing to refine the assessments reviewed in this chapter are a committed and highly creative lot. Perhaps they will ultimately prove me wrong.

Important Dates and Events

1926–Psychologist Florence Goodenough designs the *Draw a Man Test*, an intelligence test for children.

1947–*The House-Tree-Person Test* is designed by psychologist John Buck.

1949–Psychologist Karen Machover's *Personality Projection in the Drawing of the Human Figure* is published. Although psychological tests do not stand up well to scientific scrutiny, many art therapists continue to use them.

1950s, '60s and '70s–Art therapy clinicians such as Kwiakowska, Kramer and Landgarten use specific drawing tasks to assess clients. This is called "clinical interpretation."

1980s–Barry Cohen and colleagues develop The Diagnostic Drawing Series.

The Formal Elements Art Therapy Scale (FEATS) is developed by Linda Gantt and Carmello Tabone. It is based on the work of Elinor Ulman and Bernard Levy.

Silver's tests of Draw a Story (DAS) are first published. She will later develop a Drawing Test of Cognition and Emotion (SDT).

1998–Francis Kaplan's *Art, Science and Art Therapy: Repainting the Picture* is published making a convincing case for the place of science in art therapy.

2009–*The Levick Emotional and Cognitive Art Therapy Assessment (LECA-TA)* is published.

Study Questions

1. Define "validity" and "reliability" in research.
2. Discuss the validity of psychological projective tests.
3. Discuss clinical assessment and interpretation in art therapy. Differentiate it from statistical significance.
4. Describe three important diagnostic art therapy assessments.
5. Discuss advantages and disadvantages of using these assessments.
6. What is your opinion of the state of assessment research in art therapy today?

MULTICULTURALISM

The Context of Multiculturalism

The two words "multiculturalism" and "diversity" are used almost interchangeably these days. A dictionary definition of "multicultural" is "relating to or including several cultures."[3] Definitions of "diversity" are "the fact or quality of being diverse; different"[4] and "the inclusion of diverse people (as people of different races or cultures in a group or

---

3. Retrieved September 15, 2009 from www.thefreedictionary.com/multicultural.
4. Retrieved September 15, 2009 from www.thefreedictionary.com/diversity.

organization."[5] For the purposes of this chapter the term "multicultur-al" will be used. The word "cultures" are now understood to charac-terize differences of all kinds and for a long time the multicultural thrust of art therapy as a profession has been toward *cultural competen-cy,* meaning an understanding that there are differences and how they can best be managed clinically.

Although many art therapists are well intentioned and go a long way personally and individually toward establishing a nondiscriminatory community and practice, art therapy today remains a predominantly white and female profession.[6] Whereas a few professional organ-izations have taken a public social justice stance against various forms of discrimination, to date the American Art Therapy Associa-tion never has.

In the 1970s, anti-racism and ethnic nondiscrimination came to the forefront and became an established focus for people of good will including the art therapy community and the American Art Therapy Association. Although most art therapists were Caucasian, by this time many of the clients they were seeing in their internship experiences were other than white. People of color like Cliff Joseph (1973, 2006) attempted to move AATA towards a more inclusive approach. Notions of cultural awareness and inclusivity were embraced. But the underly-ing assumptions and issues are difficult to get at and, as we all know, deep and long-held cultural attitudes are not easy to move or change. Many people of color who had worked long and hard at social change within the art therapy community eventually grew impatient and frus-trated and even sometimes left the profession. White allies, sometimes frustrated, went on to other issues.

Multicultural Committee is Formed

In 1978, the American Art Therapy Association formed an "Ad Hoc Committee to Investigate Encouraging Minority Groups to Enter and Study in the Field of Art Therapy."[7] Lucille Venture and Georgette

---

5. Retrieved September 15, 2009 from www. Merriam-webster.com/dictionary/diversity.
6. For a more extensive discussion of these issues, see Chapters 9 and 10 in Junge (2008) *Mourning, Memory and Life Itself, Essays by an Art Therapist* and Kaplan's (2007) *Art Therapy and Social Action.*
7. This information is from Cheryl Doby-Copeland's report in the American Art Therapy Association *Newsletter,* Spring 1998. Doby-Copeland was the Chair of AATA's Multicultural Committee in 1998.

Powell were Co-Chairpersons. This group was focused on increasing the multicultural nature of AATA's membership. At the 10th American Art Therapy Association Conference, in about 1979, the "Special Committee on Recruitment of Third World Groups (Asian, Black and Hispanic), Diaspora and Native Americans to Study and Practice Art Therapy" was formed. This committee accomplished a comprehesive cross-cultural bibliography, assembled a list of financial aid, grants and scholarships, did fundraising and presented a panel "Cultural Awareness and the Creative Process."

In 1990, a group of American Art Therapy Association art therapists formed the "Mosaic Committee." The Mosaic Committee came about because of concerns about the lack of education and awareness in the clinical practice of art therapists who often worked with culturally or racially different clients: "The Ad Hoc Committee endeavored to raise the consciousness of the predominately Caucasian art therapy assocation" (Doby-Copeland, 2006, p. 83). In 1995, the Mosaic Committee's name was changed to the "Multicultural Committee." Again, the Committee's mission was to increase "the sensitivity, awareness, and insight of art therapists working with clients who are culturally different from themselves" and to "assist AATA to move in the direction of organizational cultural competence . . . it will be more common than not to find each of us working cross-culturally" (Doby-Copeland, 1998, n.p.). One of the Committee's accomplishments was to assemble a "Roster of Mentors." Reactions both within the committee and the art therapy community to the need for cultural competence were mixed. Doby-Copeland wrote: "Twenty-eight years later, it is frustrating how long it has taken for AATA to embrace the need for organizational cultural competence" (2006, p. 83). It should be noted that mental health organizations have usually not been in the forefront of achieving true multiculturalism and anti-racism and have often adopted a clinical philosophy of helping the client adapt to the social climate instead of changing it.

The International Expressive Arts Therapy Association and Multiculturalism

In 1994, the International Expressive Arts Therapy Association (IETA) was established. Defining the Association as a "global community," the founders of this organization regard it as a "model for inclusiveness which represents social action. We believe the language of the arts spans across cultures and bridges cultural gaps" (N. Koethner in M. Gonzalez-Blue, personal communication, 2009). The IETA vision was to establish an organization which would internationally support the expressive arts without regard to group, class or ethnicity: [As an organization] "IETA was formed with a deep and conscious commitment to being truly democratic and inclusive. . . . Besides the efforts to create a diverse membership, our mission is also to make the arts accessible to all" (A. Utigaard, in M. Gonzalez-Blue, personal communication, 2009). The International Expressive Arts Therapy Association has a multicultural executive board that is also multigenerational.

It should be noted that the move toward global multiculturalism tends to move the focus outward and away from enhancing American multiculturalism and anti-racism. Even in the age of Obama, many people of color in the United States believe this to be an avoidance of American cultural realities.

Changing Definitions of Multiculturalism

Before racism and ethnic discrimination could be adequately addressed (1960s-1990s), cultural mores in the United States moved to a broader definition of multiculturalism to include all marginalized and discriminated-against minority groups such as disabled people, gay and lesbian people, people with AIDS, women and immigrants. While this was unquestionably a good-hearted move toward a more inclusive social justice perspective in the United States, functionally it caused a dilution of efforts toward any resolution of racism and ethnic discrimination. Rather than groups cohering to battle discrimination in all its forms, many people of color felt abandoned as the focus moved to others who then often fought each other for the spotlight.

Multicultural Education is Mandated
Within Art Therapy Training Programs

By the 1990s, multicultural education was mandated as approved curriculum by the American Art Therapy Association. This meant that a graduate art therapy training program, following AATA's educational standards and hoping to gain "Approval" from the organization, needed to include a certain number of units of multicultural education within its curriculum. The ongoing argument of the time between "ghettoizing" multicultural education in one class versus attempting to include multiculturalism in the whole curriculum was resolved by the American Art Therapy Association at least, by its mandate of one multicultural class. Some programs and some faculty still focus on inclusion in the whole curriculum and some faculty and art therapy graduate programs do it better than others.

It should be noted that the more expansive definition today of what is "multiculturalism" can cause a dissonance within the minority groups included. While there has been certain forward movement, oppressed and marginalized groups have very different internal specificities and needs. Fighting against discrimination itself these days tends to be a rather abstract and elevated concept before the functional problems endemic to a particular group have been resolved.

Mentors of Color

Multicultural art therapy graduate students were sometimes lucky to have role models who were faculty members in their programs and actively took on mentoring responsibilities. Phoebe Farris (2006) states: "When I reflect on my career paths as an art therapist, professor, artist, and author, I know it would have been impossible without the support, love and guidance from my 'mentors of diversity' (p. 87). Among others, she mentions Georgia Mills-Jessup, Georgette Powell, Cliff Joseph and Gwen Short. Joseph founded a support group for people of color at the Pratt Institute in New York City. Unquestionably, many white art therapists have also fulfilled this role: Doby-Copeland, 1998 mentions becoming an AATA board member and being mentored there by Deborah Good and Marcia Rosal. A major theme of the People of Color life stories in *Art Therapy, Journal of the American Art Therapy Association* was that mentors to students of color were largely themselves people of color and many were introduced to other art therapists through mentors. Mentor's support and encouragement often influenced the choice of art therapy as a professional career. Those authors who did not "find mentors of color . . . noted feeling they were not understood" (Hoshino & Junge, 2006, p. 141). As the art therapy profession progresses, it is essential to have multicultural people who act as mentors and role models in educational and clinical settings and in professional organizations and on boards.

Invisibility of People of Color in Art Therapy

Thus far, there is little written history of multiculturalism as it has influenced and integrated with the development of the art therapy profession. Like most early art therapists and many since, a number of multicultural people typically started as artists and came to understand for themselves the power of art to delve profoundly into the human psyche and to express it. Yet virtually no documentation from multicultural people appears in the AATA archives.[8] My 1994 art therapy history relied heavily on those archives[9] and mentioned only one person of color, Georgette Powell (Junge, 1994). This "invisibility" of people of color has been critiqued by Jordon Potash (2005) in his article "Rekindling the Multicultural History of the American Art Therapy Association."

In 2004, Janice Hoschino–a bicultural Seattle art therapist–and I proposed a series of life stories of people of color to the *Art Therapy* journal. I guest edited the memoirs. Those life stories of nine art therapy people of color appeared in the four journal editions in 2006. My further hope for the series was that it would become a monograph of the American Art Therapy Association available to members and others. So far, this has not occurred.

I had many experiences over the years on academic search committees and elsewhere where American-born people of color were overlooked in favor of international people of color and people with various disabilities or differences. It began to seem that anyone from this "pot" would do. I viewed this as a "skipping over" which increased invisibility of our own and I chose for the series a focus on "American born or raised." I was convinced that minority group narratives while all probably exhibiting tragic and difficult discrimination, would be different group to group and especially different from those raised in America with our tragic past of slavery. I wanted to highlight those stories first as I considered them especially American stories.

As it turned out, my definition was more controversial within the art therapy community than I had supposed it would be. Many people of color who fit my definition were supportive and encouraging. Many

---

8. The Archives of the American Art Therapy Association, known as the Robert Ault Archives are housed at Emporia State University in Emporia, Kansas. Ault founded the art therapy training program at Emporia. More on him can be found in Chapter 12.
9. Then housed at the Menninger Foundation in Topeka, Kansas.

from other minority groups, who favored the more expansive definition were not. I was called "privileged . . . [and] imperialistic" and accused of promoting another form of oppression and exclusion. Many art therapy pioneers and others wrote letters to the journal supporting the series and saying "It's about time."

The final essay of the *Art Therapy* collection described and discussed the major themes of the life stories (Junge & Hoshino, in Junge, 2008). Feelings of *difference* were ubiquitous. In addition, racism in educational settings, clinical institutions and the American Art Therapy Association was experienced by the memoirists and frankly outlined in their life stories. These themes were underlined in the concluding article "Themes and Reflections from the People of Color in Art Therapy Series." I learned again how complex and sensitive these feelings are, how endemic racism is in the United States, that the wounds are deep and no one with any sensitivity, conscience or consciousness gets out unscathed—and perhaps shouldn't.

Still today many art therapy clients and patients are people of color and most art therapists are white. Many art therapists have presented and published case studies where the patient or family is multicultural (e.g., Malchiodi, 2003). Sometimes, the particular qualities of the multicultural client are not even acknowledged as an important part of the assessment and plan by the therapist. That these issues are essential parts of the client or family's *zeitgeist* and systemic oppression and may be part of their suffering, in my opinion is an awareness that all too few therapists carry. AATA's Multicultural Committee would call this the beginning of cultural competency. In my experience, white is still the norm. There are just two published books that I know of on the subject of multiculturalism in art therapy. These are Hiscox and Calish (Eds.), *Tapestry of Cultural Issues in Art Therapy* (1998), and Kaplan (Ed.), *Art Therapy and Social Action* (2007.)

Important Dates and Events

Late 1960s and 1970s—Racism and ethnic discrimination form the definition of multiculturalism. Institutional racism as systemic discrimination is recognized. The Women's Liberation Movement comes into being and focuses on gender discrimination. The Stonewall riot, named for a bar in Greenwich Village, New York, in which gays resisted police for the first time is the beginning of the Gay

Liberation Movement.

1973–Cliff Joseph attempts to move the American Art Therapy Association to recognize and act against inherent institutional racism, to be more inclusive and to reach out to art therapists and art therapy students who are people of color.

1970s through 1980s–People of color such as Georgette Powell, Lucille Venture and Cliff Joseph, mostly informally, act as mentors to novice art therapists. Many white people in the profession are also mentors.

1990–The Federal Americans with Disabilities Act is passed prohibiting discrimination against the disabled and a broader definition of multiculturalism comes into being.

1990–The Mosaic Committee of the American Art Therapy Association is established.

1994–*A History of Art Therapy in the United States* is published by the American Art Therapy Association. Only one person of color, Georgette Powell, is mentioned. (Only one person of color, Georgette Powell, appears in the Archives of the American Art Therapy Association.)

1994–The International Expressive Arts Therapy Association is founded.

1995–The name of AATA's Mosaic Committee is changed to the Multicultural Committee. The name change is controversial.

1998–Hiscox and Calish's (Eds.), *Tapestry of Cultural Issues in Art Therapy,* is published.

2006–"People of Color in Art Therapy" series is published in *Art Therapy, Journal of the American Art Therapy Association.* Co-Edited by Maxine Borowsky Junge and Janice Hoshino, it causes some controversy because of its definition of "American born or raised."

2007–*Kaplan's Art Therapy and Social Action* is published.

Study Questions

1. Compare the advantages and disadvantages of focusing on "differences" rather than similarities.
2. Compare differences in the two definitions of multiculturalism.
3. Describe your own approach to multiculturalism in art therapy–include a discussion of both client multiculturalism and therapist multiculturalism.

CENTRALITY OF THE ART IN ART THERAPY

Art Psychotherapy Versus Art as Therapy

The question of the centrality of art in art therapy has been argued over since art therapy's inception. The two main theorists in the profession, Margaret Naumburg and Edith Kramer, although both working from a Freudian theory base, proposed very different ideas about the varieties of art product and process. Speaking for the art in psychotherapy position, Naumburg sees art as a *form of communication* between client and therapist. She does not advocate for a focus on the artwork as an aesthetic product in psychotherapy at all. To Naumburg, with art as communication, the client's sometimes unfinished, quick and even surface renderings are acceptable and useful. It is the art *within* the total psychotherapeutic process that can be helpful and healing and is usually expanded through verbal means. Within this perspective, the therapist holds an important role and is a psychotherapist who uses art in psychotherapy.

On the other hand, Kramer views the completed art product as a visible and visual indicator of successful *sublimation* (originally defined by Freud as a defense mechanism[10]) by the client and states that it is the client's involvement in the *creative process itself that is healing.* To Naumburg, the psychotherapeutic process as a whole is focused on; with Kramer the emphasis on the therapy process switches to a focus on the creative experience, the depth, profundity and value of which are manifested in the art product. Thus to Kramer, *the more fully realized and aesthetic the art product is, the more successful the art therapy.* For Kramer, the process of sublimation through the art process is the centerpiece of her theory. While neither Naumburg nor Kramer traditionally teach art skills and techniques, Kramer's view is close to psychologically informed art education and she stated that the art therapist is not a psychotherapist.[11]

During the earlier days of the art therapy profession and as Masters-level training programs were founded in the late 1960s and 1970s,

---

10. Although Freud himself changed his definition of sublimation as a defense mechanism and the ego psychologists and Anna Freud believed sublimation to be a *normal* process of the ego, Kramer's theory retains Freud's original concept of sublimation as a defense.

11. A description of this old, still existing argument and a plea for integration is in my chapter "Reconsidering the Wars Between Art and Therapy" which can be found in *Mourning, Memory and Life Itself, Essays by an Art Therapist* (Junge, 2008).

many saw as their mission the training of psychotherapists first, who used art in therapy. But some worried about the erosion, even loss of the art in art therapy. Wadeson remembers:

> In 1983, Judy Rubin set up a "Great Debate" at the American Art Therapy Association conference to settle the controversy once and for all between "art as therapy" and "art psychotherapy." She asked Edith Kramer, who had published a book with "art as therapy" in its title, to debate with Harriet Wadeson, who had recently published *Art Psychotherapy*. Wadeson spoke about the need to include "both and," rather than "either/or." Kramer spoke about what poor artists some art therapists are and criticized AATA's logo and the image used for the cover of the conference brochure. Obviously, nothing was settled. (Personal communication, 2010)

Although she separates art therapy and art psychotherapy, even Kramer eschews the "historical rift" which started as art therapy began to organize as a discipline and continues in the field to this day. She writes of the difference as the assumed necessity to use *words* for exploration in Naumburg's art psychotherapy and her version of art as therapy as nonverbal. Kramer attributes this historical argument to the fact that she worked with nonverbal children, and Naumburg's theory, she says, evolved from her work with middle-class adults within a classical psychoanalytic framework. All in all, according to Kramer, there are fewer differences between them than people say.

After almost 40 years of practicing art therapy, it is my belief that the therapist must thoughtfully and differentially assess the client's needs and current state and adjust the art process and media in order to further specific and unique therapeutic goals. It is not about theoretical orientation—Freud, Jung or anyone else. Art in therapy processes will enhance the work with some clients, whereas art psychotherapy ideas and methods will work best for others. Sometimes, both are used with a single client and sometimes the therapist switches approaches along the way. But teaching a student to be a psychotherapist who is comfortable using art in therapy is more complicated than teaching one or the other. Unfortunately and for a variety of reasons, including the demands of standardization, accreditation and licensing, as I see it, today many training programs are more comfortable with a primary focus on the *art in therapy method*. This philosophy has typically become the current perspective with the stated rationale of a greater focus on art making. The necessary and important process of understanding the existential world of a client and making a differential plan, unfortunately in my opinion, is not as ubiquitous as it once was. As my father used to say: "Artists can think."

Open Studio Art Therapy

In the early 1990s, the opening panel at the annual art therapy conference of the American Art Therapy Association was titled "Death of Art Therapy." The main thrust of the panel members' presentation was that art therapists in their drive to acquire licensing were becoming too much like other mental health professionals and were in danger of literally *losing the art making* in their practice. The dual identity (some said "split") of the artist and the therapist proved to be a continuing puzzle and require an immensely challenging integration.

Then in 1992, Patricia Allen published a journal article titled "Artist in Residence: An Alternative to Clinification for Art Therapists." Calling the art psychotherapy perspective "clinification," Allen stated that any reasonably trained clinician could do it and proposed instead that clients should come into the art environment of the art therapist's studio in the community and paint alongside the art therapist. In this way, art could regain its necessary central position in practice, Allen asserted; the use of words as in psychotherapy would not be necessary. It is interesting that when Vick and Sexton-Radek (2008) studied therapeutic art-based studios in Europe and compared them to those in the United States, most in Europe insisted they were not doing art therapy, despite the fact that many of their goals and methods were no different than those in the United States. The Studio Art perspective became a method to enable some art therapists to solve the artist/therapist dilemma.

The Studio Art approach is a community art studio in which the art therapist as artist acts as a *facilitator* of art media and processes, rather than as a *doctor* of a patient with a mental illness or dysfunction. Materials are not used to further therapeutic goals. Rather a variety of artist-quality materials are provided and clients are given enough knowledge about their potentialities to enable their own choices. Sometimes projects go on over time. While continuing their own work, the "artist in residence" can provide a steady hand and a supportive environment for the client offering a free painting opportunity with encouragement, but with very little guidance or direction from the facilitator. The intention of the art studio perspective is toward normalization with an underlying philosophy based on assumptions that through art, the person can find meaning, wholeness and health. When the client finishes artwork, the facilitator asks a series of probing questions to further the exploration. Ault's (1989) discussion of the "unidentified patient" who came to his Ault's Academy of Art predates Allen's influential "clinification" article and the founding of the first art therapy open studio and speaks to art therapy within the studio approach. Some argue that an open studio philosophy leaves ethical boundaries such as confidentiality and dual relationships too fluid.

The Studio Art approach relies on the notion that all human beings can benefit from finding the creativity within and, as Allen says "Art is a way of knowing" (1995). The Open Studio Project began in Chicago in 1991 and is now in Evanston, Illinois. Co-founders were Pat Allen, Dayna Block and Deborah Gadiel. The mission of the Open Studio was to make art and "be of service to others" (Malchiodi, 2007, p. 213). "Obviously these services," according to Allen, "are not usually called 'therapy' as neither the artist nor the 'client' sees them as deriving from any illness or deficiency" (P. Allen, personal communication, 2009).

How can the art therapist with an open studio make a living as a professional art therapist? According to Allen, fees are charged for workshops, contracts are made with agencies that may want services for a particular population and social service and arts grants may be earned by working collaboratively with community institutions. Some studios sell artwork through exhibitions or contain a store selling arts and crafts. According to Allen: "A living can be made as a studio art therapist presuming that one has some common sense and rudimentary business skills and isn't hung up on the trappings of therapy" (P. Allen, personal communication, 2009).

The studio arts form of community services has existed for years and in many parts of the country, usually as an example of the integration of artists and the arts with needy populations. But it did not flourish as a *form of art therapy* until Allen's questioning of "clinification" and her proposal of the art studio as a different approach to art therapy—one that moved more toward *the art therapist as artist and the client as art student.* Like, Edith Kramer's ideas, the centrality of art as essential to the human being and its innate qualities as healing are core values of this philosophy.

An additional driving force of the Studio Arts movement was the renewed focus on the *art* in art therapy by Mildred Chapin and her Art Committee of the American Art Therapy Association. Chapin states:

> At the beginning of AATA we were all artists, of course. But our professional identity and efforts were, for the most part, in the direction of our clinical expertise–medical at first and then spreading out in many additional directions. Now, in many ways [with the establishment of AATA's Art Committee], the artist part of us has achieved almost equal status. (M. Chapin, personal communication, 2009).

Personal Artwork of the Art Therapist

Kramer talked long ago and consistently over the years of the essential need for the art therapist to practice their own personal art. She was not the only one. Yet, paradoxically as students undertook the demands of graduate studies and entered into clinical practice, their personal art often became a source of guilt rather than of expressive pleasure in that they felt they had little time or energy for it. I remember a graduate student who said "I felt I abandoned my art." Personal artwork as a source of conflict and even envy of the art therapy client who is encouraged to engage in creating art continues for art therapists even into retirement. In a survey of retired art therapists conducted by Wadeson and myself in 2004-05, many stated that they "should have been making more art."

In the 1980s, art therapists expressed the urgent need for a place to discuss and focus on *their own art as a part of professional identity* within the art therapy field and their professional organization–the American Art Therapy Association. Beginning as a discussion between two people at the annual AATA conference, they were convinced that the continuation of an art therapist's personal art making was crucial to helping clients. Spurred on by Mildred Lachman Chapin, an early art therapist and painter (see Chapter 22), there is a presentation at the beginning of each annual AATA conference of the personal artwork by art therapy members. In addition, proposed by Chapin, an Art Committee was formed by the American Art Therapy Association, to promote art making by art therapists and to enhance art in therapy (M. Chapin, personal communication, 2009).

Community Arts and Social Change

In the history of art, there are many artists who have used their art-work for social justice and social change: Goya, Daumier, Kathe Kollwitz and Ben Shahn come to mind. A more recent example is Los Angeles artist Judy Baca's bringing together of ethnically and racially diverse groups to make murals. She was the Director of the City Wide Mural Project, founded in 1976 and funded by the Los Angeles City Council to create community murals. She co-founded Social and Public Arts Resources, a non-profit agency to support social change. In 1976, Baca worked with high school students from the juvenile justice program and other disadvantaged youth to paint "The Great Wall of Los Angeles" a mural on a wall of the L.A. river, depicting Los Angeles' multicultural and pluralistic history (Junge, 1998). Like Baca, there are many contemporary illustrations of artists bringing together disparate groups of people to create art together.

The therapy side of the community art therapy equation is a some-what more checkered proposition. While there have been plenty of therapists of all mental health disciplines who have pushed for a more just society, in my opinion, psychotherapy has also had the history of a decided thrust of helping "sick" people *adjust and adapt* to the socie-ty at hand. The question of whether the society to be adapted to is equitable and fair was typically not in the forefront until the 1970s when the Women's Movement began to ask probing queries about the nature and assumptions of the culture itself. Feminist Therapy asserts that western culture, based in white male privilege, impacts women in powerful and sometimes unacknowledged ways. The therapist using feminist principles, for example, will help the female client understand that some of her difficulties are due to outside inescapable cultural pressures and will encourage her to change the oppressive culture to a more fair one, as she changes herself.

Social justice in contemporary art therapy practice has often been complicit in maintaining the status quo. There is no way the profession of art therapy, which is part and product of its culture, can escape the strong underlying biases and assumptions which give form to it. Kaplan (2007) wonders whether art, social action and therapy are "seemingly incompatible"(p. 13). Hocoy (2005) describes the difficul-ties of integrating art therapy which aims toward *healing,* and social action which intends *political change.* He writes: "One way in which social action and art therapy are linked is through the versatility and power of the image" (p. 7). Art therapy, Hocoy says, may have to take place "outside the consulting room and outside the traditional therapeutic frame and engage according to community norms" (p. 12). He proposes that the art therapist's awareness of individual and collective suffering can provide the linkage. Kaplan (2007) argues that social action art therapy is a way of *thinking,* not a place of practice. She writes:

> The solution is both complicated and simple–that is, it is complicated in practice yet ultimately simple in concept: we cannot separate the people we treat from the cultural settings in which they live and by which they have been influenced. None of us exists in a social vacuum: each of us comprises a unique amalgam of genetic endowment, family upbringing, environmental influences and collective history . . . the inescapable conclusion is that whether we take art therapy into the streets or we remain secluded in our treatment settings, we would do well to "think" social action. (pp. 13 & 14)

Community Arts Therapy essentially means taking art into the streets–to neighborhoods, inner cities and communities and with marginalized populations. It is an arts focus, not a therapy one. Years ago, in the 1960s I was the Director of "Operation Adventure" an alternative education program in the East Los Angeles Latino barrio. Every week we would load art supplies and staff into a van which we drove to the local housing project. We unloaded the art supplies and invited children and their parents to make art. I view this as a form of community art.

Within the community arts perspective, the art therapist can utilize the arts as a tool for reflection, expression and personal growth and toward the goal of a more just and socially responsible society. Some populations art therapists have worked with are immigrants and political victims and refugees (Junge, Alvarez, Kellogg & Volker, 1993), homeless people (Timm-Bottos, 1995, 1997; Allen in Kaplan, 2007), Hurricane Katrina victims and people enduring other natural disasters (Asawa in Pitt, 2006), people suffering from Post Traumatic Stress Syndrome and trauma (such as returning war veterans) (Gantt, 1979, Klorer, 1999), victims of domestic violence and in battered women's shelters (Clothespin Project), people who are incarcerated and street gangs (Wadeson, 2000), and AIDS and HIV infected adults and children (Junge, 2007). Art therapists sometimes focus on the aim of community building itself (Timm-Bottos, 1995). They also aim to help resolve geographic and/or political conflict such as that of middle eastern Israeli-Palestinian conflict (Byers, 1996, 1998, 2007).

Study Questions

1. Discuss the importance of the arts in Naumburg's version of art psychotherapy and in studio and community arts.
2. Describe the studio arts movement within the historical context of art therapy. What do you think are advantages and disadvantages of this approach for the professional art therapist?
3. What is the importance of community arts for the art therapist? How can it be similar to or different from an artist's goals.
4. Write a short essay about the importance of your personal art making to your clinical practice as an art therapist.

REGISTRATION, CERTIFICATION, LICENSING AND THE DIFFERENCES

Both Art Therapy Registration (ATR) and art therapy Board Certification (BC) are presently managed by the Art Therapy Credentials Board, a national organization which is separate from the American Art Therapy Association but standards mandated by the American Art Therapy Association.

While these are traditional certifications for art therapists, it should be noted that they are different forms and levels of credentialing and *have nothing to do with state licensing.* Both these credentials may be applied for *after* Masters art therapy education and, in addition, after a specified number of supervised hours of clinical practice. The International Expressive Arts Therapy Association, a separate organization from AATA offers two forms of Registration, which are described below.

Registration (ATR) By the American Art Therapy Association

At the first annual conference of the American Art Therapy Association in 1970, it was decided to certify art therapists and Registration was planned.[12] This move followed the tradition of many national professional organizations which certified their practitioners. For example, social workers, with no available licensing in many states, had long awarded *a national certification of competency* by examination–the ACSW (Academy of Certified Social Workers).

Registration was a tremendously important move which jump-started the art therapy profession because *required standards of practice* were established for the new field. There were so few art therapists nationwide at the time, a series of different options were established for achieving the ATR such as self-education, apprenticeships, in-service hospital training and university programs. Sandra Kagin (Graves-Alcorn) invented the system which, after much debate, was finally agreed on and which awarded Professional Quality Points for certain accomplishments. Sixty-one long-time art therapists were invited to be grandparented in.[13] In the first *AATA Newsletter,* President Myra Levick wrote:

> The American Art Therapy Association took a giant step forward at its very first meeting in Warrenton, Virginia. The decision to certify art therapists under the Grandfather's [sic] Clause, who have been working in psychiatric settings for five years, was passed and the first registry will be published this year.
>
> An organization is recognized by the professional standards it maintains and aspires to. The decision to establish certification lays the groundwork for the development of these professional standards. . . . It is important . . . that the organization identify itself with specific goals. (Levick, 1970b, p. 1)

As professions and professional organizations develop, credentialing requirements become more stringent. The ATR, based on education and experiences is one of the lower levels of professional credentials for art therapists. "Board Certification" discussed in the following section is an ATR who passes a written exam which requires a level of competency.

---

12. For more information on this important move forward in art therapy, see Chapter 11 "Myra Levick and the Establishment of the American Art Therapy Association."
13. At first, Edith Kramer wrote to say she did not want registration. Arthur Robbins was another art therapist who initially rejected registration. Both later accepted.

Board Certification (BC) by the American Art Therapy Association

The ATR was originally established by the American Art Therapy Association and the evaluation of art therapists for the ATR was done by AATA for 20 years. However, in 1991, an organization separate from AATA–the Art Therapy Credentials Board–was developed to coordinate both the ATR and the BC credentials. Located in North Carolina, it assesses qualifications for ATR and BC designations and awards the credentials. (Persons seeking these credentials are encouraged to search the ATCB's internet website for specific requirements for Registration and Board Certification.)

A "Board Certified" art therapist is one who has met all the requirements for ATR and, in addition, has successfully passed a written examination covering the scope of practice and ethics of the art therapy profession. The exam was first developed by art therapy educators who submitted questions and evaluated the test. The BC is generally accepted as a higher level assessment of standards and requirements for the professional art therapist. There was no general grandparenting for the BC when it began and an art therapist seeking this designation needed to take the test. However, the American Art Therapy Association awarded the BC to some Honorary Life Members, but not all. Its decision to do this was chronological and not based on qualifications or experience. At a certain point, it stopped combining the two.

Registration as an Expressive Arts Therapist (REAT and REACE)

The International Expressive Arts Therapies Association offers two forms of Registration. Registered Expressive Arts Therapist (REAT) is for clinicians and Registered Expressive Arts Therapist-Consultant/ Educator (REACE) is for those educating and consulting in the training of expressive arts therapists. Like the requirements of the American Art Therapy Association and its credentialing board, the certified expressive arts therapist must meet standards of education and experience, and agree to abide by the ethical codes of IETA.

What Does It Mean When an Education Program is "Approved" by the American Art Therapy Association?

In 1973, the American Art Therapy Association established guidelines for art therapy education and training and it designated a required curriculum. These guidelines were written by Gladys Agell (see Chapter 13). Most art therapy educational programs were designed to include these requirements. In 1975, through its Education and Training Board (ETB, now EPAB–Education Program Approval Board), the American Art Therapy Association began to assess programs as to their compliance with the established curricular standards. If the program documented that it adequately met standards, AATA granted "Approval." Essentially, an "Approved" educational program *as a whole* is endorsed by the American Art Therapy Association as having fully met its standards. For the graduate of an "Approved" program, this status means that when they apply for ATR they do not have to document each requirement, but automatically receive a certain number of *Professional Quality Points* for their education. Although graduates from non-approved programs can still apply for and receive certification, coming from an AATA endorsed program is a tremendous advantage in time and effort.

Licensing

A license for clinical practice is granted *by the state* and is a separate certification than those offered by the Arts Therapies Associations. States are quite different in their standards for licensing, but often will require a certain number of post-masters practice experience and supervised hours by a supervisor with appropriate credentials. Then the applicant must pass a written exam and sometimes an oral exam as well. There are only three states where art therapists are currently licensed as "art therapists." These are New Mexico[14]–the first to pass art therapy licensing in 1993–Mississippi and Kentucky. In New York art therapists can be licensed under a "Creative Arts Therapies" umbrella. There are a few states where art therapists can attain a license as a "Licensed Mental Health Counselor."[15]

---

14. When the New Mexico bill was finally adopted, it was called the "Counselors and Therapists Practice Act." Nevertheless, Deborah Good calls it "the first state licensure for art therapists" (Good, 1993).
15. California has adopted this license.

To create a license is a lengthy and intense political process. It is unlikely that art therapy practitioners will be able to achieve specific named licensing in the future, because there are simply not enough of them to make the necessary large political base. One answer for the future will be collaboration.

State licensing is intended as a *legal method of protection for the consumer* because to gain a license, the applicant must have achieved certain specific requirements set out by the state and pass the required exams; thereby they have achieved certain standards of practice. A license usually mandates the legal practice of psychotherapy, enables the practitioner to engage in private practice and often means that the recipient can accept client health insurance payments. Without a license the art therapist cannot do these things. For example, in California, only a *licensed* person with specific stated licenses can *legally* practice psychotherapy. However, some art therapists maintain they do not do psychotherapy and therefore do not need a license. Under an "equivalent curriculum" clause, in 1979, Californian Bobbi Stoll, along with one other, was the first art therapist to receive a Marriage and Family Therapy License in the United States. Art therapists who attain a mental health license are sometimes seen as "abandoning their art." This is a wrong assumption: A license is necessary for many for legality and for employment.

In order to attain a license, many art therapy Master's programs align or integrate with a mental health discipline that is licensable in the particular state and has the required degree title, such as counseling or marriage and family therapy; a very few may even have an integrated curriculum. A student graduating from such a program will be able to meet licensing requirements as well as basic requirements for the ATR and BC awarded by the American Art Therapy Association. *State rules and regulations are listed on the internet.* There is little state reciprocity and some states do not have any licensing for mental health workers at all. However, requirements are becoming more stringent and, in my opinion, will continue to tighten.

The applicant for state licensing and art therapy Registration and Board Certification by the American Art Therapy Association or Registration by the International Expressive Therapy Association must satisfy the specific *post-masters requirements* of each. While some can be accomplished at the same time, typically the requirements are different from each other. *Graduate art therapy programs usually help stu-*

dents understand these differences and their requirements.

New art therapy graduates often work under the umbrella of an agency or institution. With the proper clinical supervision, their hours may be counted for licensing. It is not expected that the graduate art therapist will be an unpaid "volunteer" but should, hopefully, acquire a paid position. Often, the same hours may be counted for licensing and for art therapy credentialing. *It is highly recommended that anyone planning an art therapy career or currently engaged in an art therapy Masters program find out licensing requirements in the state in which they intend to work.*

Following is a story of licensing in New York State by Ellen Greene Stewart, a Registered and Board Certified art therapist who lives in rural upstate New York. She has published two books *Kaleidoscope* (2006) about art therapy with people who have dementia, and *Superheroes Unmasked* with Steven R. Hitt (2009), a book to help children empower themselves and grow in self-esteem. Steward graduated with a Masters Degree in Psychology and Counseling from Goddard College, which is not an AATA approved program and is a breast cancer survivor. It should be noted that although Ellen Greene Stewart experienced plenty of bureaucratic frustration along her licensing journey, she *did* eventually earn the license. *Necessary persistence* is one of the morals of this story. Along with her license and credentials from the American Art Therapy Association, Stewart is a certified school counselor.

JOURNEY TO AN ART THERAPY
LICENSE IN NEW YORK STATE

Ellen Greene Stewart, M.A., ATR-BC, LCAT

In 2004, the New York State Task Force on Occupational Regulation announced a long awaited licensing opportunity for art therapists. Under the New York State Education Department, Office of the Professions, Title VIII, Article 163, Section 8404, four categories of mental health licensing options were announced. These were Psychoanalysis, Marriage and Family Therapy, Mental Health Counselor, and Creative Arts Therapist.

Licensed Creative Arts Therapist (LCAT) is a credential used only by New York State. Those eligible for inclusion in this licensing category include dance, music, drama, and art therapists. The good news was that there was now an opportunity for licensing in the state which houses the largest number of art therapists on the east coast. The bad news was that art therapists were being lumped into a category of expressive arts therapies. Applications were accepted beginning January 1, 2005.

Thousands of New York art, music, movement and drama therapists awaited the list of requirements and the application form to become available. When they finally were, the State Education Department was inundated with over 5,000 applications. A grandparenting deadline for experienced people had been set for January 2006, but had to be rolled back a year in order to allow the state to catch up with the numerous applications. According to the State Education website, as of 1/1/08, there were 1195 active creative arts licenses, leaving 4,000 applicants to battle it out.

My battle was unique in many ways. When I decided to return to school to obtain my MA in Art Therapy, no school offered it within a two-hour drive from my rural upstate New York home. I was 40, had a one-year-old daughter, a husband, a house, job, and all the trimmings. There was no way I could relocate to attend school. After more research, I learned that Goddard College in Vermont offered a degree within their Psychology and Counseling Department in which I could specialize in Art Therapy and work with a credentialed art therapist on the faculty.

Those familiar with Goddard will remember it as the original "school without walls," and "that old hippie school." There are no grades at Goddard; rather, there are extensive written evaluations. The good news [for the student] about that was Goddard's transcripts contained more specific information and lots of it. The bad news was that the New York State Department of Education was unprepared for cases which didn't have traditional letter grades.

I applied for an LCAT license through the individual evaluation pathway, Goddard is a fully accredited school and I fulfilled their requirements for their MA in Counseling program, including the standard internship. These requirements were almost identical to those of any other such program in this country. Naively, I thought it would be an easy process.

The State Education Department had other ideas. Through a year and a half of correspondence back and forth, I had to explain that although some classes might not be called by the same name as a College within New York, it was indeed the same class. Letters would arrive after what I felt were unreasonably long periods of time, and would state: The good news is that we are accepting 15 of your 60 credits, they wrote. The bad news was they did not tell me which classes were accepted, which were not and why. Another series of letters travelled back and forth until one of the first warm spring days in 2006, when I walked to the mailbox shocked to find my LCAT, complete with calligraphy, in a neatly put-together package. I framed it immediately.

I think it only fair to say that I had simultaneously applied to the Art Therapy Credentials Board for my ATR and BC credentials, and the process was only slightly less daunting. At least they were available for phone calls. At that time, one could gain the BC credential with grandparenting if one was exempt from taking the state licensing exam. Fortunately, New York State went along with the national agencies. So I got the BC.

What's it worth? I hung my LCAT license proudly on the wall of my office and felt relieved. I looked at it frequently and with a big smile. As time went by, however, I began to realize that the battle wasn't over. The good news was that I was able to practice legally and freely now that I had a New York State LCAT license. The bad news was that my license doesn't entitle me to Third Party Insurance Reimbursement [insurance payments] nor to a great many of the available jobs at mental health clinics, schools, hospitals, and other institutions who hire art therapists. A large percentage of these jobs are only able to be filled by LCSW [licensed] social workers or higher.[16]

So, what indeed is the good news here? Good is that art therapists are recognized within a licensing category by the State of New York. But we have a long way to go to become a true and equal part of the mental health system in this state. Ultimately, we must be able to help those who need our services but cannot afford to pay for them out of pocket.

Licensing was created for the protection of consumers. Licensing may be protecting the public from those who would call themselves art therapists with none of the proper training. I am confident that the

---

16. A warning: Remember these requirements differ state to state and Stewart's licensing experience in New York is not necessarily the same in other states.

licensing, job qualifications and insurance issues, eventually, will catch up with each other. But I am equally confident that these will not happen any time soon.

Why Should an Art Therapist Attain Registration and Board Certification?

Given by the Art Therapy Credentialing Board, these are the *only* art therapy credentials in the United States (except those of the International Expressive Arts Therapy Association, which are relatively new). While the general public and even many mental health professionals, do not understand what these credentials are, these initials after a person's name indicate a certain level of education and training. They are a "code" in a way that the person has achieved this level and is a professional art/expressive arts therapist. In the same way that a Board Certified Physician is known to be a higher level of practitioner than an M.D., for art therapists the ATR in particular is increasingly recognized by other mental health professionals as important acknowledgment of the art therapist's experience and level of practice.

Why Should an Art Therapist Attain a State License?

The art therapist's attainment of a state license enables the clinician *to legally practice in the state.* Someone who practices without a license is open to action by the state and by clients. Except for the three states mentioned (New Mexico, Mississippi, and Kentucky) currently there are no states in America where the art therapist can gain a license as an art therapist. (As outlined in Stewart's story, New Year State awards a "Creative Arts Therapies" License.) This means that the art therapist who seeks a state license must be a "hybrid" and fulfill the requirements of another mental health discipline such as mental health counseling or marriage and family therapy.

Arguments persist in art therapy over whether this undermines an art therapist's *identity* and even may incline an art therapist to abandon art therapy and *become* the kind of mental health professional that they are licensed as. I am one of these "hybrids." I have had a clinical social work license in California since 1973. This license enables me to legally practice psychotherapy in California. Without it, I do not believe I can ethically do art psychotherapy practice. I am a "Registered

Counselor" in Washington State where I now live. This is *not* a license, but a credential. I am an ATR-BC which is the art therapy part of my credentialing. I am not one nor the other: *I am an integrated "both."* And I am and always have been an *art psychotherapist.* Remember Shakespeare's "a rose by any other name. . . ."

Study Questions

1. Describe the history and intentions of art therapy registration.
2. What is the art therapy B.C. and how is it different from the ATR?
3. What is state licensing as a mental health professional?
4. Why should an art therapist seek both national art therapy credentialing and state licensing?

THE RESEARCH CONUNDRUM

Conflicts about art therapy research reside in the interdisciplinary nature of the field. Art therapy is an integration of both art and psychology. The conflict then appears to be about art versus science.

The argument that in order to "prove itself" as valuable and to help the discipline further develop in today's competitive mental health climate, art therapy must produce rigorous empirical outcome research, has been around for a long time (Malchiodi, 1995.) It comes from the psychology "side" or science side of the profession. This argument begins with the necessity to "prove" that art therapy is worthwhile through quantitative research. It says, probably rightly, that qualitative research, which typically has more of a natural affinity with art therapy (the *art* in art therapy), even at its best and most rigorous cannot really provide evidence that art therapy "helps," nor can it be generalized to larger populations. There are many contemporary art therapists who believe that through research—particularly outcome research—art therapy can show its value and that this will make the field more acceptable to other mental health professionals and to the public leading to a broader credibility for the profession. Gantt, who with Carmello Tabone, developed the art therapy assessment the Formal Elements Art Therapy Scale (FEATS) feels that FEATS is a milestone for art therapy in that it provides a powerful statistical quantitative measurement (L. Gantt, personal communication, 2009).

In my opinion, the notion that art therapy should prove itself comes from a simplistic and partial understanding of the political nature of the mental health system and disciplines. Rubin writes: "I believe strongly in the healing power of making art, and while I expect that we will be able to prove it scientifically some day, I have also become convinced that one Grandma Layton is as good as several outcome studies for convincing others" (Rubin in Junge & Wadeson, 2006, p. 121). Grandma Layton is Elizabeth Layton of Kansas, discovered by Robert Ault and others, who after a long history of depression seems to have cured herself of her dysfunction through her own drawing and art making. Rubin's statement is what Rosal (1998) calls an "anti-research argument." Echoing this argument, Robert Wolf (1995), a New York art therapist, teacher and sculptor, wrote that research may "contribute to the diminution of our credibility" (p. 259). On the other hand, Silver believes that movement in brain research today shows the value of art through right hemisphere thinking (R. Silver, personal communication, 2009).

As is true of most psychotherapy and counseling practice until behaviorism—the results of which can be "counted"—art therapy for the most part has existed and flourished within a common, accepted wisdom about its efficacy. For example, although we may not be able to truly plum the mysteries of art and the creative process, we know that art "works" and that art involvement seems to have healing properties. We have never known and we don't really know now, how or why or, for that matter, what makes good or great art. We do know that it is a notoriously difficult proposition to truly "prove" that any form of psychotherapy—even behaviorism—"helps" because human beings are immensely complicated and difficult to quantitatively research. The many "variables" in human life are virtually impossible for researchers to adequately control in order for results to have any broad generalizable meaning.

Rosal (1989, 1998) in the Masters art therapy program at Florida State University directed a number of students who undertook *single-case research*. This form of quasi-experimental inquiry assesses the effect of an intervention or treatment like art therapy on a single person or group by measuring before and after the intervention. No matter, how tightly controlled the variables, it is difficult to be convinced by this research because a human life outside the consulting/research room is complicated. One cannot be sure that there are not many tacit influences on the research data. Other forays into quantitative research using art tasks are the various assessment instruments developed by art therapists Cohen, Silver, Gantt and Tabone and Levick. Please see the beginning section of this chapter (Chapter 24) for Kaplan's description and critique of these assessments.

Research in art therapy has been around for a long time. Gantt who did early work in trauma started by publishing case studies. She remembers how this work developed:

> I discussed a case of a child who was stabbed by his psychotic mother. I worked with him to tell his story and it was really an early example of what Lou[17] and I now call the "graphic narrative." I had read a paper by Bernard Stone, an art therapist from Ohio, who wrote about a technique he called the "sequential graphic Gestalt" technique which involved a series of drawn images to complete a nightmare.
>
> Our development was (1) to use the Instinctual Trauma Response to organize the story and (2) to do a "re-presentation" of the story. We pin the pictures on the wall and tell the story back to the artist . . . people tell us they feel that they have really been heard and that the event is truly over. We have at least two witnesses and we videotape the re-presentation . . . we make a digital copy of the representation. (L. Gantt, personal communication, 2009)

There are many reasons why research in art therapy has been problematic: First, the history of the fledgling profession so far has primarily been one of clinicians struggling to use the arts and therapy and then writing about their case histories. Examples of these are Gantt's trauma work above and Landgarten's *Clinical Art Therapy: A Comprehensive Guide* (1981) and *Family Art Psychotherapy: A Clinical Guide and Casebook* (1987). Sometimes this literature has expanded to the author's very useful–but "unprovable"–ideas and philosophies about the nature of art therapy practice and imagery, but historically, what is presented is usually anecdotal.

To date, most art therapists have not been trained nor are much interested in research philosophies, approaches and methods. Many art therapists are naturally disinclined to pursue research at all because they view it as "scientific and not creative"–white coat stuff–which is

---

17. Psychiatrist Lou Tinnin.

generally unacceptable to an artist. Here, we see the art versus science conflict manifested. Gender issues may be at play here as well in that many still consider the sciences primarily man's domain.

Deaver (2002) asks the essential question: "What is researchable in art therapy?" Her answer is: The therapeutic relationship, art therapy assessment, intervention, and dimensions of art therapy as a profession. But she concludes: "We [art therapists] lack the practical, theory-building and instrumental research foundations that would enhance our clinical acumen, clarify and build the theoretical underpinnings of the work we do and bolster our identity as a profession" (Deaver, 2002, p. 26). According to Deaver ". . . most art therapists are reluctant to engage in research" (2002, p. 23).

Entry level for art therapy practice is mandated as the Masters degree. Currently, in the United States most master's programs of the various mental health disciplines do not teach research at all–this is left to Ph.D programs. (A Doctor of Philosophy–Ph.D–degree is defined as a *research* degree.) Many faculty for art therapy masters programs are master's-level practitioners who may not have any careful training for, experience in, or liking for research. Nationwide, however, universities and colleges which house art therapy graduate programs, increasingly require that to hire a tenure track faculty member they must be at the doctoral level, thus there are more Ph.Ds in art therapy today. But most of these have, by necessity, earned their doctorates in other kinds of programs–such as psychology–and may not have had experience researching art therapy questions at all. Some art therapists have earned expressive arts or interdisciplinary art and psychology doctorates from Union Graduate University. A distance learning institution, Union had the advantage that the degree earned could be called "art therapy."[18] Today, there are two Ph.D. programs for the art therapist: Lesley University awards a Ph.D. in Expressive Arts: Beginning in 2001, Lesley graduated its first two students in 2006; one was an art therapist. Florida State University grants a doctorate in Art Education with a specialization in art therapy.[19] Drexel University in

---

18. I believe Union Graduate University is still an option for an expressive arts or interdisciplinary doctorate.

19. For many years there was a doctorate at New York University–a Doctorate of Arts (DA). I believe the degree was in the Art Education Department. It no longer exists.

Philadelphia (formerly Hahnemann Medical College and University) expects to open a doctoral program in Fall 2010.

In 1992, the American Art Therapy Association published *A Guide to Conducting Art Therapy Research* (Wadeson, Ed.). Well-known art therapist/researchers contributed chapters to the *Guide* describing, in particular, methodological issues in art therapy research. Also in 1992, Linesch surveyed the teaching of research in art therapy Masters programs and found at that level *clinical training* was a priority; there was little agreement about appropriate research philosophies and even whether to have research at all within a Masters art therapy program. In a journal article, Kaplan (2000) proposed that the assumed objectivity of science and the subjectivity of art do not necessarily divide the two disciplines in art therapy and make research impossible. She proposed that objectivity and subjectivity exist in both quantitative and qualitative research and that they are a matter of the *viewpoint* of the researcher, rather than a necessary science versus art conflict (Kaplan, 1998, 2000). In 1993, Junge and Linesch in "Our Own Voices: New Paradigms for Art Therapy Research," suggested that art therapists conduct research from their own natural proclivities for creativity in both quantitative and qualitative research.

By 1998, Gantt (1998,) Malchiodi (1995,) and Rosal (1998), among others, had all called for research as a priority in the art therapy profession and a special issue of the journal *Art Therapy, Journal of the American Art Therapy Association* was devoted to research. McNiff's book *Art- Based Research* appeared in 1998. In it he defines art-based research as a method of inquiry focusing on the broad creative arts experience and including the art expressions of the researcher to comprehend the meaning and importance of art therapy practice. McNiff states:

> I like to think that my books, especially *Art as Medicine* . . . and *Art-Based Research* . . . have contributed to the more pervasive understanding of artistic knowing and the realization that art-based inquiry and epistemology can be fully integrated with more verbally oriented psychological approaches. (S. McNiff, personal communication, 2009)

McNiff's books utilizing all the arts are broadly used in the expressive arts therapies and art therapy communities.

In 1999, the American Art Therapy Association created an initiative intended to place a focus on research which would encourage art therapists to do more and better research.[20] In 2002, a special section appeared in the *Art Therapy* journal: This contained an excellent article by Deaver called "What Constitutes Art Therapy Research?" (p. 13).

Forty-five years ago, in 1964, Thomas Kuhn published *Structure of Scientific Revolutions*. He proposed that science does not progress in a linear fashion producing new knowledge, but rather a drastic paradigm shift may come along to change the way we see things. He convincingly argued that science was not wholly objective in that it depended on the interests of the particular researcher who chose what was to be studied. That is, what the researcher decides to focus on is subjective. Kuhn's tremendously influential book, in fact, changed the way science is viewed in many quarters.

Despite Kuhn's "paradigm shift" and a flurry of research activity within the art therapy field, including support for more and better art therapy research, the questions about the potential conflict between science and art remain prevalent today. The art therapy profession is primarily a master's level endeavor and with education for art therapists being focused almost exclusively on the training of clinicians, research is likely to remain problematic. As more doctoral programs begin to emerge to train art therapists in leadership, scholarship and research inquiry, it is possible that important and convincing art therapy research will be forthcoming.

It is commonly acknowledged that artwork has meaning and art therapy clinicians who have looked at drawings for many years claim certain conclusions about those meanings; these interpretations relay important clinical knowledge. Unfortunately, in my opinion, there is little scientific evidence to support clinical claims and much believed to be true as common wisdom may not be. For example, although there was great emphasis on psychological projective tests and on the psychoanalytic interpretation of drawing as diagnostic tools during past decades, flagrantly biased and inadequately researched methods for diagnosing are, in my opinion, more the rule than the exception. As an example, I remember the argument as I prepared to publish my 1994 volume, *A History of Art Therapy in the United States,* and wanted a red cover. I was told by a prominent art therapist that red was not an appropriate color because it indicated child abuse. I had been told by

---

20. The current AATA website has a whole section on research, including how to do it and prizes for it.

a publisher that books with red covers attract more readers. Probably neither was convincingly "proven" nor "true." There is increasing clarity today that our cultural biases influence the way we see, draw and make artwork and that there may not exist imagery that is universal, timeless and even cross-cultural as had been previously supposed.

Study Questions

1. Describe the research conflict between art and science.
2. Discuss how this art/science conflict plays out in art therapy.
3. Discuss the proposed importance of quantitative research for art therapy.
4. Write an essay about your opinion of the value of quantitative and qualitative research in art therapy.
5. Describe a small art therapy research project. What is the question it asks?

INTERNATIONAL ART THERAPY[21]

In a time and culture in which the world has come to be known as the "global village" and with more permeable national boundaries because of computers and new communication systems such as the internet, the support of art therapy and arts therapies in other countries becomes an especially important concern and practice for American art therapy today. Communication media have brought international art therapy to the forefront. The essential idea of the integration of arts and therapy has gained important footholds in many countries as mental health experts have discovered for themselves the value and potentials of the arts in therapy. Stoll (2009) states:

> Thirty-three countries have art therapy or arts therapies associations established or in formation . . . [but] amazingly, the same obstacles to furthering the profession are encountered by country after country: Upstart art therapists are, by necessity, pioneers at heart and seem to persevere against all odds as governments, competitors, regulatory bod-

---

21. Much of the information for this section comes from Bobbi Stoll, past President of the American Art Therapy Association, who almost single-handedly since its inception in 1989 managed "The International Networking Group." ING was formed to support and expand the arts therapies in other countries. She gives credit to Gerry Hurlbut who has been key in this work.

ies, healthcare systems, payers and employers demand definition, professional standards, ethics and research validating successful outcomes. (B. Stoll, personal communication, 2009)

In 1994, the International Association of Expressive Arts Therapy was formed. American-based, it promotes the expressive arts in many countries and recently held a conference called "Expressive Arts in Social Action: Peace-ing Our World Together" in Cambridge, MA. The International Society for the Psychopathology of Expression and Art Therapy continues on with its 14th conference in Lisbon, Portugal.

Because it is so new, standards of practice and education opportunities for expressive therapists are not well developed.[22] But expressive arts may be a major part of the art therapy profession in the future. Surely, the global walls of art therapy are expanding much past the limits of the American Art Therapy Association which once was one and the same as United States art therapy. This is no longer the case. In my opinion, American art therapists must open their boundaries to the spread of global knowledge, to help our international colleagues. Otherwise, the results will be short-sighted and unfortunately isolationist for art therapy in the United States. For the "cross-pollinization" process in world art therapy to succeed, it will need a philosophy of inclusion and encouragement.

United States art therapists who, with the British, are considered to be the most advanced, have taught abroad and helped their international colleagues. For example, I gave invited presentations and workshops in Japan and Korea. In Korea, I took Harriet Wadeson and Robert Ault along with me. There, a painter, Dr. Kim, Dong-Yeun had established an art therapy graduate training program in the Rehabilitation Department at Taegu University and founded the Korean Art Therapy Association.[23] He had read articles in American art therapy journals, later became a member of the American Art Therapy Association and earned an ATR. Some other art therapists who have taught art therapy internationally are Mala Gitlin Betensky, Julia Byers and others from Lesley University, Michael Campanelli, Nancy Slater and Harriet Wadeson who has returned each summer for many years to teach in Sweden.

---

22. It is my understanding that IETA designates "Approved" clinics around the world for internship experience.
23. After me, many art therapists presented work in Korea.

According to Stoll, the developmental process of the profession is similar in most countries and similar to the developmental processes of art therapy in the United States: First, there must be definition, then education, research, credentialing and regulation and monitoring. Obviously, promotion and public relations are essential. Serious national occurrences and disasters such as the tragedy at Chernobyl have focused on the uses of art with victims and survivors.

Some Countries With Art Therapy

Art therapy has been practiced in the Netherlands longer than in any other place (B. Stoll, personal communication, 2009). It evolved and developed as an adjunctive therapy only, in psychiatric hospitals. It remains solely an adjunctive practice today (Schweizer, 1990). Quite possibly, art therapy in the Netherlands was fashioned after Adamson in England who established artists in psychiatric hospitals. Edward Adamson, an artist himself, was hired at Netherne Psychiatric Hospital in 1946[24] (Junge, 1994).

In 1968, the Japan Society for Psychopathology of Expression and Arts Therapy was founded. The Society consists mostly of psychiatrists and psychologists who use art as a diagnostic instrument. It should be remembered that many cultures have different philosophies of mental illness and treatment procedures than does the United States, and it is difficult for art therapists who are not psychiatrists to find adequate employment in Japan.

Israel's art therapies association was started by Mala Betensky in 1990. A major focus for Israel's art therapists is the school system (Steinhardt, 1986). Lesley University in Cambridge, as part of its international mission, has training programs in Israel. Lesley's Julia Byers (1996) has worked with Palestinian and Israeli children of the West Bank.

Even before the Berlin Wall fell in 1989, art therapy had been burgeoning in Russia and the former Soviet Union. Since then, Arrington and Yorgin (2001) practiced art therapy with homeless and orphaned children in Kiev, Kopytin (1999) wrote "Russian art therapy–Problems and perspectives" and Stoll (2001) published "The Art Reach project in

---

24. For a more extensive description of art therapy in Great Britain and Adamson's work, see Chapter 9 in this book.

Bosnia-Herzegovena." She reports that on a visit 17 years ago, she started an art therapy association for all of Russia. Despite this, she says, the only real training for art therapists is in St. Petersburg. As the guiding force of the International Networking Group, Stoll has given presentations at conferences and published papers on global art therapy since 1985. A selection is listed in the Reference section of this book (Stoll, 1985, 1989, 1990-2009, 2004). Contemporary American art therapist Jordan Potash is pursuing his doctorate in art therapy and social change at Hong Kong University in the Department of Social Work and Social Administration. He helped host the "Asian Art Therapy Symposium" which had 120 participants from five different Asian Countries.

Another avenue for the support and development of international art therapy is in the education of international people in America who return to their country after graduation. Currently and historically, there are many international students in art therapy Masters programs and I predict there will be more in the future. An example is in Riyadh, Saudi Arabia where Awad Al-Yami established an art therapy unit at KFMC Rehabilitation Hospital and became licensed by the Saudi Health Minister as the first art therapist. He is also Assistant Professor of Art Education at King Saud University. Dr. Awad Al-Yami trained in art therapy in the United States and received a doctorate from Pennsylvania State University in 1995.

American and British Art Therapists Internationally

America and Great Britain are generally considered to be the most professionally developed in art therapy. Other countries invite Americans and British to present at their conferences and to describe the progression of art therapy in their country which can then be used as a model for the development of art therapy in another country.[25] American art therapists have taught and trained in over 20 countries across the world. A number of American art therapy educators pioneered training programs in Australia (Campanelli & Kaplan, 1996 & Slater, 2001). British art therapists have tended to pioneer the development of art therapy in Europe (Dokter, 1998; Waller, 1998; della Cagnoletta, 1990).

---

25. For example, when I presented a keynote address at a first art therapy conference in Korea, I was asked to speak on the formation of art therapy in the United States.

International Education and Training of Art Therapists

Without consistent and systematic educational experiences for the training of art therapists, the profession has a difficult time developing globally. Without education, there can be little replenishing of professionals. Thus far, because of financial constraints and a variety of other reasons, unfortunately, art therapy training internationally is in its infancy at best and nonexistent in many countries. Increasing numbers of international students come to be trained in the United States carrying the hope of returning to their home country and promoting art therapy there. They come with a passion for art and healing, but United States graduate programs do not necessarily train for the kind of pioneering necessary to establish a profession in another country. In fact, usually international students are expected not only to learn English, but also to assimilate as much as possible into the American culture and psychotherapy "style." Perhaps it would be wise if American graduate programs would institute a program of special information and ongoing support for its foreign students to enhance the spread of art therapy across the globe.

A new and potentially very important internet art therapy organization, founded in 2009 by Cathy Malchiodi is the International Art Therapy Organization (IATO). Membership is free and to date 2000 members across the world are claimed. This is the first viable organization to be established for global and United States art therapists after the American Art Therapy Association. The intention of this new global community is to bring together "art therapists, related professionals and students involved in art therapy, therapeutic art making and art for health and social transformation" (C. Malchiodi, personal communication, 2009). Currently, IATO is working with medical doctors and public health people to set up an art therapy program in Africa for women and children who have endured gender-based violence. Malchiodi is an art therapy educator and author[26] of long standing. She writes a blog for *Psychology Today* and, for many years, was a public relations person for the American Art Therapy Association. She earned AATA's Honorary Life Membership in 2002.

---

26. See References for some of Malchiodi's books.

Important Dates and Events

1946–Edward Adamson is hired at Netherne Psychiatric Hospital in England. He becomes a prominent art therapist and his model of artists in hospitals is used in many countries. Art therapy in America and Great Britain are considered to be the most professionally developed. Other countries model themselves after them.

1968–Japanese Society for Psychopathology of Expression and Arts Therapies is established. Consisting mainly of psychiatrists and psychologists, the Society focuses on art as a diagnostic tool.

1985–Bobbi Stoll founds the International Networking Group of the American Art Therapy Association. She is the editor of its *Newsletter* to the present.

1990–Israel's arts therapies association is founded by Mala Gitlin Betensky.

1992–Stoll founds the National Art Therapy association in Russia.

2009–Stoll states: Thirty-three countries have art therapy or arts therapies association established or in formation.

2009–The American Art Therapy Association initiates an international membership category.

2009–The International Art Therapy Organization (IATO) is founded by Malchiodi. Membership in this global internet art therapy community is free.

Study Questions

1. Describe the advantages and disadvantages for American art therapists of extending and supporting art therapy globally.
2. What kinds of problems might arise for an international art therapist attempting to establish the profession in their country?

Chapter 25

THE PROFESSION OF ART THERAPY: MILESTONES

EXPANSION AND AWARENESS

When I first began to teach art therapy in the early 1970s, that it existed as a developing and legitimate mental health discipline which could contribute to a client's health and healing was largely unknown. This is no longer the case. There has been a ground-swell in general knowledge about art therapy everywhere. For example, recently, on a "60 Minutes" segment, art therapy was provided to Iraqui prisoners and when Tara, of *The United States of Tara* on Showtime TV, struggling with Multiple Personality Disorder,[1] enters a psychiatric hospital, one of the treatments she undergoes is art therapy. Frances Anderson writes: "This past decade has seen enormous growth in our field. It also is experiencing the effects of our economical down turn" (personal communication, 2009).

This awareness of art therapy in popular culture is indicative of its tremendous strides in becoming known as a profession. Many art therapists found employment and through clinical practice illustrated to colleagues and clients the value of art therapy. With consciousness of the field, has come tremendous expansion. In 35 years in the profession, I have noticed that when I identify myself as an art therapist, whomever I am talking with is fascinated and wants to know more. The same level of interest never happens if I don't mention art. Judith Rubin says: "We have been very successful in making the term 'art therapy' known to the general public . . . [it] was a great idea to begin

---

1. In the *DSM-IV*, multiple personality disorder is renamed to "Dissociative Identity Disorder."

with . . . wherever it occurs it has been effective" (personal communication, 2009).

Yet, Don Jones, a pioneer art therapist, calls art therapy a "field" and asserts that it has not yet become a "profession." Jones believes that classically the only three professions are clergy, medicine and law. He says: "The truth is we really do have unique tools in our imagery, "psychic ultra-sound probes" and "anything worth doing takes more than one lifetime" (D. Jones, personal communication, 2009). Jones states:

> I anticipate that the future will bring a true, independent identity to our field of art therapy. (We are not yet a profession.) Academic-clinical respectability is coming through the expanded recognition and acceptance by other mental health disciplines. National legal licensing will follow with the confirmation of our treatment modalities which *contribute a new model* to be added to medicinal techniques, psychology, and the language, word-narrative forms of analysis and counseling. (D. Jones, personal communication, 2009)

WHAT *IS* AN ART THERAPIST?

With more recognition of art therapy, has come public confusion about the nature of art therapy and its training; indeed what *is* an art therapist? Rubin told me she decided to update her 1998 book, *Art Therapy: An Introduction,* because she feels "there is a difference between approaches that needs to be explained." Her definition of art therapy follows:

> Art therapy is a unique profession, in that it combines a deep understanding of art and the creative process with an equally sophisticated comprehension of psychology and psychotherapy. It seemed therefore imperative at this historical juncture to clarify the differences between artists or teachers who provide "therapeutic" art activities, psychologists or social workers who request drawings in their work, and those who are trained as art therapists to do a kind of work which is similar, but qualitatively different. As I worked on this second edition, that need for clarification seemed at least as important as the need to update the content. (J. Rubin, personal communication, Statement from the 2nd edition of *Introduction to Art Therapy: Sources & Resources,* 2009)

Although some think of art therapy as a modality, technique and/or series of "recipes," which can be easily learned and applied to any theory or approach, it is far more than that. A well-trained art therapist is quite different from someone who uses art as a sometime intervention in educational or clinical settings. An art therapist is someone who has learned both disciplines of art and psychology and, on top of that, seamlessly integrates them in an effort to help and heal.

While it is true that most pioneer art therapists were dedicated artists first–they deeply understood that art making is a human behavior that has meaning–they also learned about the psychological vicissitudes of the clients and patients they worked with. In the early days, before education specifically tailored to training art therapists existed, they were mostly self taught, or sought out the kinds of training they needed. An artist who works in a mental health setting is quite different from an art therapist. Sorting out this confusion may well be a major challenge for art therapists in the years to come.

MILESTONES

Preparing to end this history, I asked many pioneer art therapists to comment on what they thought were the most important milestones of art therapy in the last years. Many of their thoughts are included in the different sections of this chapter and the last, but some answers to the question about milestones follow:

Frances Anderson: "This past decade has seen enormous growth in our field. It also is experiencing the effects of our economical down turn. We have moved to accept all kinds of research, including 'hard data' research. Gantt's [& Tabone's] Formal Elements Art Therapy Scale [FEATS] is a marvelous example. We have recognized our need to 'speak the language' of others who are outside of our discipline (while not compromising our own language). . . . I have seen our journal become a recognized scholarly publication that is now part of the psychological databases [*Art Therapy: Journal of the American Art Therapy Association*]. . . . I have seen the demographics of AATA shift to a younger group. It is these bright, dedicated energetic art therapists who will lead the field through the decades to come."

Judith Rubin: "[The] field as a separate discipline IS unique because of the combination [of art and psychology.] It is a unique synthesis, a synergy. I believe our field will go on and expand . . . it grows like mad. . . . I think we should be going more in the direction of *collaboration* . . . [art therapy has] gotten much too rigid in standards and training programs. Professionalization has led to too many rules and regulations."

Cathy Malchiodi: "Entering the twentieth-first century, art therapy has moved into the culture in leaps and bounds. It has grown exponentially and is part of popular culture, blogging and on-line print material. But the profession of art therapy is at its most threatened point at this time because of health care reform . . . [there is the] need to be adaptable or we may end up watching the parade go by."

Helen Landgarten: "Much more is known everywhere about art therapy. The first art therapy clinic in an academic setting to serve the community in the United States has been founded at Loyola Marymount University."

Don Jones: "We are not yet a profession. . . . I do believe that in the future we will have a true, independent professional status. Time!!"

"Who are we? We are artist-clinicians, shamans, healers, not always fully realizing or completely understanding the power of this imagery in healing and affirming of life itself . . . we are . . . containers of the pain. We are the brushes, the colors, musical instruments, meter in poetry and gesture in the dance. It is a sacred obligation to be creative while treading the holy ground of art therapy."

Shaun McNiff: "The more complete integration of the artistic process into art therapy is the most significant advance in art therapy over the past two decades."

Rawley Silver: "I think the most important [milestones] were changes in the relationship between "art as therapy" and [art] psychotherapy . . . in the early days, the American Art Therapy Association included members who preferred 'Art as Therapy' led by Elinor Ulman, who described it as two overlapping circles: one titled 'Art,' the other 'Psychiatry,' and where they overlapped, 'Art Therapy.' AATA also included members who preferred 'Art Psychotherapy,' led by Myra Levick whose views subsequently prevailed."[2]

Linda Gantt: ". . . hiring a public policy person who is full-time in Washington . . . in the past we have not devoted this much in the way of support and resources to what we should have been doing 30 years ago (playing with the big guys on Capitol Hill and demonstrating that

2. For a time.

we are a profession in every sense of the word)."

Bernard Stone: "AATA [American Art Therapy Association] membership has gained but this is due to university education positions while available clinical opportunities are not increasing. . . . AATA has failed to expand its clinical base by making it difficult for licensed professionals from related psychosocial fields to gain ATR [Registration] status. . . . I would give AATA a C- grade since 1990 and would maintain [art therapy] has stayed the same. Until AATA takes a more honest and realistic direction, I doubt its influence will improve. New concepts demand a new approach especially in these difficult times of financial crisis for our nation's healthcare delivery system."

Sandra Kagin (Graves-Alcorn): "I just left the 40th anniversary conference [of the American Art Therapy Association] and am awed by what we have all accomplished–and it was not easy. Art therapists are very creative and very opinionated . . . the first boards used to meet very late and [we] changed into our pajamas to be more comfortable. . . . I think it is very important that I was involved in a case that went all the way to the Supreme Court of Kentucky that has established case law that allows art therapists to be expert witnesses. . . . [After many appeals] the Supreme Court stated: ['art therapy] may be the language by which these injured children can finally be heard.'"

Myra Levick: "Your question about what I thought happened in the 1980s and '90s prompted me to look at the most recent list of approved[3] graduate art therapy programs. . . . It was enlightening and distressing. . . . We lost eight programs! . . . that we have increased [only] seven graduate programs in three decades is devastating . . . [there are] 27 undergraduate programs–an outrageous number[4] . . . where is the commitment to educate professionals in our field?"

Vija Lusebrink: "The most important change for art therapy as a profession is Board Certification and increased numbers of licensed art therapists. . . . Both of these changes have increased the professional status of art therapists."

Harriet Wadeson: "International expansion is a positive. [On the negative side], AATA's fiasco in firing the old management firm and replacing it with questionable management to which the membership

---

3. "Approval" is like accreditation. It signifies that the graduate program has the curriculum required by the American Art Therapy Association and has undergone a rigorous review process.
4. The American Art Therapy Association mandates that entry level into the profession is at the Masters' degree level. It does not encourage undergraduate art therapy programs.

had little access. And secondly eliminating Option C from ATR routes–requiring a Masters in art therapy for everybody, thus eliminating related therapists from counseling and social work who have been interested in contributing to our profession."

Arthur Robbins: "The profession of art therapy has become increasingly institutionalized. Our definitions and criteria have been formalized and there are licenses in various states that recognize the existence and discipline of art therapy. This process has many merits and is an inevitable outcome of a young profession seeking recognition. I offer you one lament: As we increasingly define ourselves, the excitement and chaos of something new and original becomes less possible. We are now in a role and hopefully we will find the courage to break out of it."

EXPANSION OF ART THERAPY LITERATURE

When I began teaching art therapy in 1974, there was very little art therapy literature at all. But as the profession developed, art therapy literature began to be written and published. By 1994 when I wrote *A History of Art Therapy in the United States,* there was enough to include a section called "The Art Therapy Literature." This section had originated as a paper written by my graduate students researching their "art therapy ancestors." The chapter on literature in the 1994 art therapy history highlighted the major literature to that date and included journals and bibliographies. As to be expected, the emerging art therapy literature reflects the developing interests and perspectives of the evolving field and has served to provide credibility and an education base within mental health disciplines.

Much of the early literature written by art therapists–as it should be in a developing profession–contained ancedotal case studies which explained the particular author/ therapist's philosophy and approaches to clinical practice, provided a bedrock foundation for the field and manifested its value. Typical of art therapy, there was a wide variety of beliefs and definitions of the profession and the practice. Although sometimes art therapists from opposing ideological viewpoints attempted to stamp each other out in the eternal argument about "truth," I believe that it is this very diversity that has kept art therapy alive and exciting. Some examples of a descriptive case focus are in the published work of Huntoon, Naumburg, Kramer, Wadeson, McNiff, Landgarten, Levick and Kwiatkowska. The focus on art within therapy and specific case studies provide credibility for the field.

In 1974, Gantt and Schmal compiled an annotated bibliography of art therapy literature from 1940 to 1973. In 1981, Moore updated this. These bibliographies were both published by the National Institute of Mental Health and were the first examples of the federal government's awareness of the evolving field. They were also immensely helpful to art therapists and students.

Ulman's journal the *Bulletin of Art Therapy* (later changed to *The American Journal of Art Therapy*) was the first journal for the field (see Chapter 7). Along with Ulman's original journal, founded in 1961, there came others. In 1973, a psychiatrist Ernest Harms founded *Art Psychotherapy*. Before he died, Harms appointed as Editors in Chief, art therapists Myra Levick and Edith Wallace along with Hahnemann psychiatrist Paul Fink. These editors made the decision to include the creative arts, changed the name of the journal to *The Arts in Psychotherapy* and created a new cover. In addition, a section on student theses was added.

After more than 20 years of independent existence, in 1983 an attempt to have the American Art Therapy Association take ownership of the *American Journal of Art Therapy* failed. Subsequently, the American Art Therapy Association created its own journal, *Art Therapy, Journal of the American Art Therapy Association,* and the *American Journal of Art Therapy* moved to Norwich University in Vermont. After Ulman's retirement, Gladys Agell became Executive Editor. Unfortunately, this journal ceased publication in 2001. Editors of *Art Therapy, Journal of the American Art Therapy Association,* have been Linda Gantt, Mildred Lachman Chapin, Gary Barlow, Cathy Malchiodi, Frances Anderson and Lynn Kapitan. Gary Barlow[5] of Ohio was the first editor and, without any stipend but thousands of volunteer hours, designed this journal and got it up and running. Currently, there are two journals for art therapists, *Art Therapy* and the *Arts in Psychotherapy;* the latter has been edited by a drama therapist and a movement therapist, among others and contains articles pertinent to all the arts in

---

5. Barlow, with Lew Shupe ATR, also established an art therapy graduate program at Wright State University in Dayton, Ohio. The program, which specialized in educating the physically disabled to be art therapists is unfortunately no longer in existence.

therapy.

The burgeoning art therapy literature is both necessary and expected for a developing profession. Case studies continue to proliferate. They are typically more sophisticated than the earlier work and often focus on specific populations and their needs. Among these are viewpoints about child abuse (Malchiodi, 1997), adolescents (Linesch, 1988; Riley, 1999), the artist as therapist (Robbins, 1987; Moon, 1995), domestic abuse (Wadeson, 2000; Malchiodi, 2008), spirituality (Horowitz-Darby, 1996; McNiff, 2004; Allen, 2005; Farelly-Hansen, 2009), and family art therapy (Landgarten, 1987; Riley & Malchiodi, 1994; Kerr & Hoshino, 2008). There are the more general books explaining art therapy (Rubin, 1984, 1998, 1999, 2005; McNiff, 1988, 2009; Malchiodi, 2003, 2007) and Rubin's 2001's *Approaches to Art Therapy* in which, as editor, Rubin collected essays by art therapists who wrote about a broad variety of theoretical underpinnings and approaches within their clinical practice. In an advertisement in the current *Art Therapy* journal, one publisher lists 13 art and arts therapies books, with books soon to come on chemical dependencies (Brooke, 2009), the autism spectrum (Brooke, 2009), assessment and the developmentally disabled (Snow & D'Amico, 2009), and at risk students (Stepney, 2010).

In 2006, *Architects of Art Therapy, Memoirs and Life Stories* was published. This book can be considered a companion piece to this volume of art therapy history in that it contains material never printed before and sometimes not known, in the life stories of many of art therapy's pioneers (Junge & Wadeson, 2006).

A few books worthy of mention and of very different kinds are Lusebrink's (1990) *Imagery and Visual Expression in Therapy* which describes a wide range of psychophysiological theories and aspects of imagery, Kaplan's (2007) *Art Therapy and Social Action,* and my 2008 volume *Mourning, Memory and Life Itself, Essays by an Art Therapist.*

EXPANSION OF RESEARCH

Art therapy research has come to be understood as an important endeavor which can help to show mental health professionals and the public how art therapy works and that it *does* work. Nevertheless, in its history thus far, art therapy has been primarily a profession of clinicians. As doctoral programs increase in the future and there are more opportunities for research and for the training of researchers, I believe that art therapy research will be an important and necessary element of the field. Malchiodi says "There is no tradition for research [but] clinical skills are related to research" (C. Malchiodi, Personal communication, 2009). Rubin states: "Training films are needed" (J. Rubin, personal communication, 2009). The reader is directed to Chapter 24 "The Research Conundrum" for a full description of the complex and intriguing research issues in the field today.

The various art therapy assessments attempt to connect science with art imagery. The older ones have suffered questions about their validity. Please see Chapter 24 "The Question of Art Therapy Assessment and Assessment Procedures" for a discussion of assessments and their credibility. Gantt and Tabone's assessment, Formal Elements Art Therapy Scale (FEATS), which measures psychological states through form is a research advance. Gantt says:

> I feel it is a milestone in art therapy research because it provides a [more powerful] method for quantitative measurement. . . . We have had inquiries about the use of the FEATS . . . from . . . England, Italy, Mexico, Japan, South Korea and Australia as well as [from] students and researchers in the U.S. (L. Gantt, personal communication, 2009)

The most recent art therapy assessment is the Levick Emotional and Cognitive Art Therapy Assessment (LECATA) designed by Myra Levick (2009a). The theory base for the emotional section of the LECATA assessment is Anna Freud's defense mechanisms of the ego and for the cognitive section, Jean Piagets concepts.

In 1992, Wadeson edited *A Guide to Art Therapy Research* which formally began the focus on qualitative and quantitative research by art therapists. McNiff's book *Art Based Research* (1998a) has had a major influence on art therapy and expressive arts research and in 2000, Kaplan's *Art, Science and Art Therapy: Repainting the Picture* made a convincing case that the art and science of art therapy were not so different and could be effectively integrated in research. Kapitan's *An Introduction to Art Therapy Research* is due to be published spring of 2010.

ADVANCES IN NEUROSCIENCE

The mind/body connection has long been of interest in psychology and art therapy. With the dissatisfaction in mental health of traditional western medicine, there is an expansion in mind/body medicine—sometimes called "alternative" medicine. Some refer to this as "pseudoscience" and, in reality, there is little empirical scientific evidence which proves the mind/body connection, nor do we know convincingly how or if the brain can be made to interact in a positive fashion with the body. Nonetheless, the concept that making artwork can influence the body in such areas as stress and trauma, is a generally accepted idea. An example is the use of art making in many cancer support groups.

Right brain/left brain notions[6] postulated a split brain theory in which the two distinct hemispheres of the brain govern different functions. The left hemisphere is analytical, verbal and sequential, while the right hemisphere is holistic, visual and intuitive: it is this part of the brain which creates imagery and story. The concept was developed by American neuroscientist Roger W. Sperry[7] in the late 1960s. The term "right brain/left brain" made its way into mental health parlance and popular culture, despite there being very little scientific evidence for it. In 1980, Betty Edwards published *Drawing On the Right Side of the Brain* which applied right/left brain thinking to drawing. She postulated that learning to access right brain processes could dramatically improve drawing ability. Her book was influential in art therapy in that it focused on the artistic potential of creativity as connected to the right brain. Right brain/left brain notions were a simple, useful way of talking about brain functions, but the story is not as scientifically convincing as it once seemed to many and is obviously much more complex.

In the early days of art therapy, there were a number of studies to investigate artwork created by patients undergoing different drug treatments and electroconvulsive shock (ECT) interventions. It was hoped that, through visual expression of internal processes, it could be established that drugs or ECT therapies (electroconvulsive shock therapy) changed the brain and rendered a positive effect. These studies

---

6. Much right brain/left brain information in this book is from en.wikipedia.org/wiki/laterization-al_of_brain
7. Roger Sperry received the Nobel Prize for this work in 1981.

hypothesized that art work could reflect brain changes.

For some art therapists, the focus on a mind/body interaction moved them into the area of spirituality. For others, from a scientific perspective, recent advances in body imaging technology and resulting investigations into brain research provide evidence for the value of art therapy and show how it works neurologically. According to Malchiodi:

> Neuroscience has pretty much proven that art therapy works the way art therapists thought it worked . . . we knew art stimulated the brain, but we didn't know why. . . . Now we know it's a whole brain endeavor. Your whole brain is tapped, stimulating creativity . . . creative activity [starts] to reform neural pathways because of meaningful sensory experiences and processes. (C. Malchiodi, personal communication, 2009)

Jones calls art therapy "neuroaesthetics." Silver states:

> I have found that mental health professionals with studio art experience tend to be more aware of the subtle meanings in response drawings than mental health professionals without studio art experiences. I believe the differences are caused by preferences as well as experience in right hemisphere thinking which perceives emotional content and communicates through images. (R. Silver, personal communication, 2009)

Hass-Cohen and Carr's (2008) book *Art Therapy and Clinical Neuroscience* is an example of this genre.

Although there is little scientific evidence thus far to support these perhaps useful hypotheses, it is clear that art therapists passionately believe that art imagery helps the human psyche grow, develop and heal. Historically and currently, they are fascinated with *how* it works and struggle to answer this seminal question. What makes art great is a question not satisfactorily answered by scholars and philosophers down through the ages; it remains fascinating and mysterious. How the art in art therapy heals may remain largely unknown, but it is a question worth grappling with and will continue to be.

EDUCATION, LICENSING AND EMPLOYMENT

Beginning in the late 1960s, art therapy masters degree programs were initiated across the country and many art therapy pioneers saw it as their mission to train future generations. The original educational programs for art therapists tended to have the definite stamp of the philosophy of its founder in its beliefs and curriculum. That is, a particular variety of art therapy was taught in each program and graduates of a certain program often carried that tradition into their future careers. This is one manner in which the arguments over "which is best" continued and persisted.

In the early days like other mental health students, as part of their education art therapy students undertook essential practical training with internships in community agencies and clinics. Like other mental health students, they received regular and close supervision of their clinical work; within this system, they learned and grew. One supervisor was often a mental health professional in the clinic or agency. The art therapy supervisor was often not a staff member in the agency, but was provided by the educational program. An important side effect of this *supervisory dyad* for art therapy was often that a mental health professional within the clinic or agency learned the value of art therapy and art therapists by seeing it over time in action. But requirements for hours of internship and supervision varied widely from program to program. Excellent training, resulting in excellent art therapy professionals opened up job opportunities and increased visibility and credibility of the profession. Landgarten said: "The best way to further the profession is to train terrific art therapists. Our graduates show how good our profession is" (H. Landgarten, personal communication, 1974). But those were the halcyon days of innovation and financial expansiveness.

As art therapy developed and educational standards were established, there came into art therapy a great many curricular requirements—particularly for those programs seeking "Approval" from the American Art Therapy Association. Robbins refers to this increasing regulation as the natural progression of a fledgling profession. There were so few art therapists in the beginning years, that a number of different avenues for becoming an art therapist were established by the American Art Therapy Association. Currently, standards for becoming an art therapist are stringent and getting tighter. (For example, in the future, an art therapist seeking Registration must have a named art therapy degree.) This limitation is positive in that it produces a more professional art therapist, but it is negative in that it has a way of stamping out creative freedom and the student must be able to fit into an already established "box" of requirements. This high-wire-act balance of creative freedom versus professional credibility is precarious at best and takes a great deal of sensitivity and thought from program directors to avoid getting "locked in" by required rules and regulations. In a very real sense this paradox can arbitrate against the innate tenets of the profession.

The problem of state licensing for the art therapist, beginning in the 1980s and spreading across the United States, added another layer of requirements and difficulty for art therapy education. State licensing enhanced employment opportunities and many art therapy programs today are integrated with another discipline in which the art therapist can become licensed. Licensing has become a necessity, because without it, particularly in today's difficult economic climate, the art therapist may not be able to find employment.

In 1993, the first art therapy licensure bill was adopted in New Mexico (Good, 1993, a followup article is Good & Sly-Linton, 1995). The Licensed Professional Art Therapist (LPAT) was created with only five art therapists in the state of New Mexico[8] (D. Good, personal communication, 2009). It was expected and hoped that other states would follow. Unfortunately, this was not to be. In my opinion, the small number of art therapists in the United States will always preclude widespread licensing as art therapists, because there are simply not enough people to volunteer their time and energy to launch a political battle and that is what legislative state licensing is. Usually, collaboration with other creative arts therapies organizations is the only answer. At this time, art therapy licensing exists only in New Mexico and Mississippi, and in 2009 Kentucky passed legislation to grant licensing to art therapists. In New York, art therapists can be licensed under a "Creative Arts Therapies" bill but they cannot receive reimbursement from insurance. (See Chapter 24, "Registration, Certification, Licensing and the Differences.") Increasingly, art therapists are licensed, but they are licensed as something "other"–psychologists, social workers, counselors.

---

8. The bill went through various legislative changes and when Governor Bruce King signed it and it went into law, it was called the "Counselors and Therapist Practice Act."

When an art therapist is licensed as "other" theoretically, it may play havoc with identity and a relatively new profession is rightfully concerned. For example, for almost 30 years the art therapy program which I directed at Loyola Marymount University provided an integrated curriculum which enabled students to also meet the requirements for the Marriage and Family Therapy License in the state of California, because we felt it essential for art therapist's post-graduate employment. Many within the art therapy community accused us of "abandoning the art." This statement was ridiculous, insulting and downright wrong. Facts, notwithstanding, this accusation persisted and, in some quarters persists today. Imagine the identity difficulties for a student who is "accused" of being in an art therapy program that does not revere art! I believe that the concept of "art therapist *identity*" is a major challenge that should be continuously addressed throughout art therapy education and throughout the profession.

Another prevalent notion today is that if an art therapist has earned a license of another mental health discipline, they are likely to stop being an art therapist and become the "other." This belief has been consistently challenged, most recently by Levick (2009b). She states:

> Over the years I have been reminded (nicely and sometimes not so nicely) that I acquired a license in psychology. . . . I also recall that while trying to organize the first meeting that established the AATA, Elinor Ulman referred to me as 'that young, red-headed upstart in Philadelphia.' Well, with a little help, I am still a redhead, no longer a young upstart, but nevertheless determined . . . to see that art therapy, the passion of my professional life, may obtain the recognition this incredible, unique profession deserves. And I invite all the red, black, brown and blond-headed art therapists to stand with me. (p. 139)

I was an art therapist before I knew its name and in my thirties, when I finally found the profession, knew I had found my career that I had been practicing all along and could now name. An art therapist with a strong identity does not become the "other." It can be lonely because we are small in numbers, but we don't ordinarily yearn to be one of "the crowd." Levick's views reflect my own and, I suspect, those of many art therapists.

We are left with a systems problem: With specific curriculum requirements for an art therapist, with the mandates of state licensing

boards, and sometimes even other accreditation requirements, in a
time-limited Masters program, the art therapy educator has little room
for spontaneity and innovation. With shrinking state budgets, it is likely that licensing specifically for art therapists will not be evident in the
profession's future for a long time. It will be necessary to recognize the
realities of the professional mental health world, to focus on enhancing the identity of art therapists everywhere, to pay particular attention
to students in educational programs and to support and encourage our
art therapy colleagues nationally and globally as they struggle and succeed.

COMPUTERS AND ART THERAPY

Despite the old joke about ex-Vice President of the United States Al
Gore inventing the internet, it is no surprise that the tremendous
growth in the personal use of computers has begun to exert a major
influence on the art therapy profession. Such computer applications as
imagery creation, distance therapy, organizational, social and individual websites and e-mail are all current practices and undoubtedly will
increase. Sometimes new ideas take a long time to become integrated
into formal art therapy and generally, computer-driven practices and
technological advances are of this variety. Art therapists tend to veer
to the art side of the profession and many do not think they are technological experts. For example, the American Art Therapy Association recently has a new website for members and those interested in
the field–it will take awhile to work out the electronic kinks for the
website and for its users. But as computers become more simple and
more ubiquitous–as they have and will continue to do–I predict that
art therapy as a profession will explore many avenues for their use. It
seems a natural.

There is a small but increasing number of art therapists who focus
on computers and art therapy. This group includes, Cathy Malchiodi,
Barbara Parker-Bell, Gretchen Miller, Carol Lark[9], Gussie Klorer,
David Gussak and Paige Asawa. More than 15 years ago, in what was
perhaps the first writing about art therapy and computers in book
form, Canter contributed a chapter to *Advances in Art Therapy* called

9. Carol Lark died in 2009.

"Art Therapy and Computers" (Wadeson, Durkin & Perach, 1989). Ten years later, *Art Therapy, Journal of the American Art Therapy Association* was devoted to computers and art therapy (McLeod, 1999; Gussak & Nyce, 1999; Parker-Bell, 1999). As mentioned before, the American Art Therapy Association has an internet website as does the International Expressive Arts Therapy Association (IEATA). The International Art Therapy Organization (IATO) is entirely web-based.

When she was a student, Gretchen Miller founded the Art Therapy Student Networking Forum on the web in 1997, for students and others interested in art therapy to ask questions, network and find resources. Still active, this forum moved to Yahoo Groups in 2005. Carol Lark founded and maintained an electronic forum for art therapists—the Art-Tx Dialogue E-Group (http://groups.yahoo.com/group/ art-tx) for art therapists and art therapy educators. Since Lark's death, Miller moderates this electronic site. Another on-line group established by Miller is the Art Therapy Alliance (www.arttherapyalliance.org). Using networking sites, this group "embraces social media and connection on-line to promote art therapy, the work of art therapists, and build community" (G. Miller, personal communication, 2009). It is related to the globalization of art therapy.

Malchiodi writes a regular blog for the popular magazine *Psychology Today* covering the arts in therapy and in 2009 established the International Art Therapy Organization (IATO) which is an internet global community. To join is *free*. She writes:

> [The internet] creates a virtual global community of art therapists through electronic mail, online discussion groups and real-time cyber chats. It has made possible an international network of interchange between people who might otherwise not been in communication with each other. (2000)

The goal of the International Art Therapy Organization is:

> To establish a community rather than a hierarchical organization. This is a socially conscious organization, using free or low-cost means to bring art therapists and others interested in the field together as a network. . . . My ultimate goal is to create a group that honors contributions to art therapy-practice, research, writing and intelligent thought . . . . art therapy is an idea that is widespread and inclusive. (C. Malchiodi, personal communication, 2009)

In 2009, Malchiodi and Miller established an electronic magazine called FUSION, an e-zine for the Art Therapy Alliance and International Art Therapy Organization (IATO) as a voice for the worldwide art therapy community.

CONCLUSIONS

I have met frustrated and angry art therapists who would like better acceptance in the mental health community and better employment, but I have never met a *bored* art therapist: Created imagery is too fascinating and too powerful for boredom. Within art and therapy, there are many roads for growth, healing and change. For the continued development of the profession, I believe art therapists must move forward as respectful colleagues who may often hold vastly different beliefs, but who, nevertheless, can be cooperative collaborators because we all see art therapy as "a calling" of depth, fascination and importance.

In its short history on the mental health stage, art therapy has come a long way. The American Art Therapy Association, a national professional organization was formed and provided a place for art therapists and their ideas to congregate. It created standards for clinical practice, education and ethics. It offered Registration (ATR) which qualified art therapists; later the Art Therapy Credentialing Board was formed which took over Registration processes and offered Board Certification for art therapists at a higher level than Registration. A second web-based art therapy organization, the International Art Therapy Organization, has come into being.

Although there are many who believe that the American Art Therapy Association and art therapy education programs may be experiencing a kind of stasis responding to financial difficulties and other matters, all agree about art therapy's tremendous thrust forward in the last 20 years. Vija Lusebrink, art therapy educator, writes: "As a discipline, the field of art therapy has expanded in scope and depth" (personal communication, 2009). Masters level education has been established across America, doctoral-level education is beginning, and Masters graduates achieve a higher level of professionalism. But professionalism has its problems and this paradox between moving forward with rules and regulations versus the value of innate, unbridled creativity is perhaps the major issue for art therapy today–and may always be. Arthur Robbins description of art therapy's status and his concerns for its future are worth repeating:

> The profession of art therapy has become increasingly institutionalized. Our definitions and criteria have been formalized and there are licenses in various states that recognize the existence and discipline of art therapy. This process has many merits and is an inevitable outcome of a young profession seeking recognition. I offer you one lament: As we increasingly define ourselves, the excitement and chaos of something new and original becomes less possible. We are now in a role and hopefully we will find the courage to break out of it. (A. Robbins, personal communication, 2009)

Robbins wrote: "Our challenge will be one of utilizing these concepts from psychiatry and psychoanalysis while maintaining the visions and perceptions we have as artists" (Robbins, 1987a, p. 74).

I have looked at the dictionary definition of "profession": It is "a calling requiring specialized knowledge and often long and intensive academic preparation." And a "professional" is "characterized by or conforming to the technical or ethical standards of a profession."[10] The simple answer to the question "Is art therapy a profession?" is YES.

THE LAST STUDY QUESTION

1. Review the "Important Dates and Events" sections at the end of most chapters and create your own *comprehensive chronology*. For your chronology, include what you consider are the most important dates to the current time in the history of art therapy in the United States.

---

10. Definitions are from *Webster's Ninth New Collegiate Dictionary,* Springfield, MA: Merriam-Webster Inc., p. 939.

REFERENCES

Adamson, E. (1984). *Art as healing.* York Beach, ME: Nicholas-Hays.

Allen, P. (1992). Artist in residence. An alternative to "clinification" for art therapists. *Art Therapy, Journal of the American Art Therapy Association, 9,* 22-29.

Allen, P. (1995). *Art is a way of knowing.* Boston, MA: Shambhala.

Allen, P. (2005). *Art is a spiritual path.* Boston, MA: Shambhala.

Allen, P. (2006). Facing homelessness: A community mask making project. In F. Kaplan (Ed.), *Art therapy and social action.* London, England & Philadelphia, PA: Jessica Kingsley.

Allen, P. (2006). Wielding the shield: The art therapist as conscious witness in the realm of social action. In F. Kaplan (Ed.), *Art therapy and social action.* London, England & Philadelphia, PA; Jessica Kingsley.

American Art Therapy Association. (1969). Roster: Members in good standing. Archives of the American Art Therapy Association. Emporia State University, Emporia, KS.

American Art Therapy Association. (retrieved March 30, 2009.) AATA website. http: www.art therapy.org/awardshonors.htm

American Art Therapy Association Pamphlet. (1977). Mundelein, IL: American Art Therapy Association.

Anastasi, A., & Foley, J. (1940). A survey of the literature on artistic behavior in the abnormal: III. Spontaneous productions. *Psychological monographs, 52,* 1-71.

Anastasi, A., & Foley, J. (1941a). A survey of the literature on artistic behavior in the abnormal: I. Historical and theoretical background. *Journal of General Psychology, 25,* 111-142.

Anastasi, A., & Foley, J. (1941b). A survey of the literature on artistic behavior in the abnormal: IV. Experimental investigations. . 187-237.

Anderson, F. (1973). Survey on the use of art therapy in the Midwest. Conference of the American Art Therapy Association, Columbus, Ohio, November.

Anderson, F. (1978). *Art for all the children: A sourcebook for impaired children.* (2nd edition, 1992). Springfield, IL: Charles C Thomas.

Anderson, F. (1994). *Art-centered education for children with disabilities.* Springfield, IL: Charles C Thomas.

Anderson, F., & Landgarten, H. (1974). Survey on the status of art therapy. *American Journal of Art Therapy, 13,* 40-50.

Anderson, F., & Landgarten, H. (1975). Art therapy in the mental health field. *Studies in Art Education, 15,* 45-56. (Revision of Anderson & Landgarten, 1974.)

Arnheim, R. (1969). *Visual thinking.* Berkeley & Los Angeles, CA: University of California Press.

Arnheim, R. (1984). For Margaret Naumburg. *The Arts in Psychotherapy, 11,* 3-5.

Arrington, D., & Yorgin, P. (2001). Art therapy as a cross-cultural means to assess psychosocial health in homeless and orphaned children in Kiev. *Art Therapy, Journal of the American Art Therapy Association, 18,* 80-88.

Ault, R. (1975). An oral history: Art therapy pioneers [audiotape]. Louisville, KY: Department of History, University of Louisville.

Ault, R. (1977). Are you an artist or therapist?–A professional dilemma of art therapists. In R. Shoemaker & Gonick-Barris (Eds.), *Creativity and the art therapist's identity*. Proceedings of the 7th Annual AATA Conference. Baltimore: MD: American Art Therapy Association.

Ault, R. (1986). Draw on new lines of communication. Costa Mesa, CA: *Personnel Journal,* September.

Ault, R. (1989). Art therapy with the unidentified patient. In H. Wadeson, J. Durkin, & D. Perach (Eds.), *Advances in art therapy* (2nd ed.). New York, NY: John Wiley.

Ault, R. (2001). "Commentary." In J. Rubin (Ed.) (2nd ed.), *Approaches to art therapy*. New York, NY: Brunner-Routledge.

Ault, R. (2006). In M. Junge & H. Wadeson (Eds.), *Architects of art therapy, memoirs and life stories*. Springfield, IL: Charles C Thomas.

Barch, L. (2003). Art therapy in Canada: Origins and explorations. *Canadian Art Therapy Association Journal, 16,* 2–8.

Baynes, H. (1940). *Mythology of the soul*. London, England: Routledge.

Betensky, M. (1973). *Self-discovery through self-expression*. Springfield, IL: Charles C Thomas.

Betensky, M. (1987). Phenomenology of therapeutic art expression and art therapy. In J. Rubin (Ed.), *Approaches to art therapy*. New York, NY: Brunner/Mazel. Second edition, Rubin, J. (Ed.) 2001. Phenomenological art therapy, New York, NY: Brunner/Routledge.

Betensky, M. (1995). *What do you see? Phenomenology of therapeutic art experience*. London, England & Philadelphia, PA: Jessica Kingsley.

B. F. Skinner. (2008, October 3). In *Wikipedia, The free encyclopedia*. Retrieved October 4, 2008 from http://en.wikipedia.org/w/index.php?title=B.F.Skinner&oldid=242633974

Boston, C., & Short, G. (2006). Notes: Georgette Seabrook Powell. *Art Therapy, Journal of the American Art Therapy Association, 23,* 89–90.

Brekke, J., & Ireland, M. (1980). The mandala in group psychotherapy, personal identity and intimacy. *The Arts in Psychotherapy, 7,* 217–231.

Brooke, S. (2009). *The use of the creative therapies with chemical dependency issues*. Springfield, IL: Charles C Thomas.

Brooke, S. (2009). *The use of creative therapies with autism spectrum disorders*. Springfield, IL: Charles C Thomas.

Buck, J. (1948). The House, Tree, Person technique: A quantitative and qualitative scoring manual. *Clinical Psychology Monograph, 5,* 1–20.

Buck, J. (1970). *The House Tree Person technique* (Rev. Ed.). Los Angeles, CA: Western Psychological Services.

Byers, J. (1996). Children of the stones. Art therapy interventions in the West Bank. *Art Therapy, Journal of the American Art Therapy Association, 1,* 238–243.

Byers, J. (1998). Hidden borders, open borders: A therapist's journey in a foreign land. In A. Calisch & A. Hiscox (Eds.), *Tapestry of cultural issues in art therapy*. London, England & Philadelphia, PA: Jessica Kingsley.

Byers, J., & Gere, S. (2007). Expression in the service of humanity: Trauma and temporality. *Journal of Humanistic Psychology, 47,* 384–391.

Campanelli, M., & Kaplan, F. (1996). Art therapy in Oz: Report from Australia. *The Arts in Psychotherapy, 23,* 61–67.

Cane, F. (1929). Art and the child's essential nature. *Creative Art, 4,* 120–126.

Cane, F. (1951/1983). *The artist in each of us*. Craftsbury Common, VT: Art Therapy Publications. [Originally published by Pantheon, New York.]

Canter, D. (1989). Art therapy and computers. In H. Wadeson, J. Durkin, & D. Perach (Eds.),

Advances in art therapy. New York, NY: John Wiley.

Carey, B., Cave, D., & Alvarez, L. (November 8, 2009). A military therapist's world: Long hours, filled with pain. New York, NY: *The New York Times,* 1 & 27.

Carl Rogers. (2008, September 30). In *Wikipedia, The free encyclopedia.* Retrieved 30 Sept. 2008, 23:28 UTC. Oct 4, 2008 from http://en.whkipedia.org/w/index.php?title=Carl_Rogers& oldid=242110601

Cocteau, J., Schmidt, G., Steck, H., & Bader, H. (1961). *Insania pingens* [If this be madness.] Basel: Ciba.

Cohen, B. (Ed.) (1983). *The Diagnostic Drawing Series handbook.* Alexandria, VA: Barry M. Cohen, P. O. Box 9853.

Cohen, B. (Ed.) (1986). *The Diagnostic Drawing Series rating guide.* Alexandria, VA: Barry M. Cohen, P. O. Box 9853.

Cohen, F. (April 16, 1969). Unpublished letter to Miss Elinor Ulman. Robert Ault Archives of the American Art Therapy Association. Emporia State University, Emporia, KS.

Cohen, F. (1970). Letter. *American Art Therapy Association Newsletter, l,* 2.

Cohen, F. (1975a). An oral history: Art therapy pioneers [audiotape]. Louisville, KY: Department of History, University of Louisville.

Cohen, F. (1975b). Introducing art therapy into a school system: Some problems. *Art Psychotherapy, 2,* 121-135.

Cohen, F. (1976). Art psychotherapy: The treatment of choice for a six-year-old boy with a transsexual syndrome. *Art Psychotherapy, 3,* 55-67.

Cohen, F., & Phelps, R. (1985). Incest markers in children's art work. *The Arts in Psychotherapy, 12,* 265-283.

Corrons, P. (1967). Psychotherapy through art. *Proceedings of International Society for Psychopathology of Expression* (Jakab, I., Ed.). New York, NY & Basel: S. Karger.

Cox, C. (2002). The MARI card test. In C. Malchiodi (Ed.), *Handbook of art therapy.* New York, NY: Guilford Press.

Deaver, S. (2002). What constitutes art therapy research? *Art Therapy, Journal of the American Art Therapy Association, 19,* 23-27.

della Cagnoletta, M. (1990). Art therapy in Italy. *Inscape: Journal of the British Association of Art Therapists.* Summer, 23-25.

Detre, K., Frank, T., Kniazzeh, C., Robinson, M., Rubin, J., & Ulman, E. (1983). Roots of art therapy: Margaret Naumburg (1890-1983) and Florence Cane (1882-1952)–A family portrait. *American Journal of Art Therapy, 22,* 111-123.

Dewey, J. (1958). *Art as experience.* London, England: Putnam.

Doby-Copeland, C. (1998). Report on multiculturalism. *AATA Newsletter.* Spring, 14.

Doby-Copeland, C. (2006). Things come to me. *Art Therapy, Journal of the American Art Therapy Association, 23,* 81-85.

Dokter, E. (Ed.) 1998). *Art therapists, refugees and migrants: Reaching across borders.* London, England & Philadelphia, PA: Jessica Kingsley.

Edwards, B. (1980). *Drawing on the right side of the brain.* Los Angeles, CA: Tarcher.

Edwards, M. (1987). In J. Rubin (Ed.) (1987a), *Approaches to art therapy.* New York, NY: Brunner/Mazel. Second edition: Rubin, J. (2001). *Approaches to art therapy.* New York, NY: Brunner/Routledge.

Efland, A. (n.d.). "Viktor Lowenfeld," retrieved September 28, 2008 from Education Encyclopedia Web site: http://www.answers.com/topic/viktor-lowenfeld

Erikson, E. (1951). *Childhood and society* (1950). New York, NY: W.W. Norton & Co., Inc.

Encyclopedia Britannica. (1980). VIII.

Exner, J. (2002). *The Rorschach: Basic foundations and principles of interpretation, Volume I.*

Hoboken, NJ: John Wiley.

Farrelly-Hansen, M. (2009). *Spirituality and art therapy: Living the connection.* London, England & Philadelphia, PA: Jessica Kingsley.

Farris, P. (2006). Mentors of diversity: A tribute. *Art Therapy, Journal of the American Art Therapy Association. 23,* 86–88.

Feder, B., & Feder, E. (1998). *The art and science of evaluation in the arts therapies: How do you know what's working?* Springfield, IL: Charles C Thomas.

Feen, H., (2008). Service learning in a homeless shelter. *The Arts in Psychotherapy, 35,* 20–33.

Fink, P., Goldman, M., & Levick, M. (1967). Art therapy, a new discipline. *Pennsylvania Medicine, 70,* 60–66.

Freire, P. (2000). *Pedagogy of the oppressed* (20th anniversary ed.) (Trans M. Ramos). New York, NY: Continuum International.

Francis, N., & Kritsonis, W. (2006). A brief analysis of Abraham Mazlow's original writing of self-actualizing people: A study of psychological health. *Doctoral Forum, National Journal of Publishing and Mentoring Student Research, 3,* 1–7.

Freud, S. (1963). Dreams. In J. Strachey (Ed. & Trans.), *New introductory lectures on psychoanalysis, Vol. XV, Part II.* London, England: Hogarth Press.

Friedman, L. (1990). *Menninger: The family and the clinic.* New York, NY: Alfred A. Knopf.

Gantt, L., & Schmal, M. (1974). *Art therapy: A bibliography. January 1940–June 1973.* Rockville, MD: National Institute of Mental Health, DHEW Publication No. (ADM) 74–51.

Gantt, L. (1979). Art therapy. In P. Valletutti & Christoplos (Eds.), *Preventing physical and mental disabilities: Multidisciplinary approaches.* Baltimore, MD: University Park Press.

Gantt, L. (1990). *A validity study of the Formal Elements Art Therapy Scale (FEATS) for diagnostic information in patients' drawings.* Unpublished doctoral dissertation. Pittsburgh, PA: University of Pittsburgh.

Gantt, L. (1998). A discussion of art therapy as a science. *Art Therapy, Journal of the American Art Therapy Association, 15,* 3–12.

Gantt, L. (2001). The Formal Elements Art Therapy Scale: A measurement system for global variables in art. *Art Therapy, Journal of the American Art Therapy Association, 18,* 50–55.

Gantt, L., & Tabone, C. (1998). *The Formal Elements Art Therapy scale: The rating manual.* Morgantown, WV: Gargoyle Press.

Gantt, L., & Tabone, C. (2003). The Formal Elements Art Therapy Scale (FEATS). In C. Malchiodi (Ed.), *Handbook of art therapy.* New York, NY: Guilford Publications.

Garai, J. (1971). *The humanistic approach to art therapy and creativity development.* Paper presented at the Second annual conference of the American Art Therapy Association, Milwaukee, WI.

Garai, J. (1985). Meet the ole timers: Perspectives on the American Art Therapy Association. Panel discussion, 16th Annual Conference of the American Art Therapy Association, New Orleans, LA.

Gebser, J. (1985). *The ever-present origin.* Noel Barstad (Trans.). Athens, Ohio: University of Ohio Press. (Originally published in German 1949–53.)

Geogheghan, T. (February 24, 1969). By any other name. Brass tacks. *Harvard Crimson,* Cambridge, MA.

Gilroy, A. (2006). *Art therapy, research and evidence-based practice.* Thousand Oaks, CA: Sage.

Good, D. (1993). The history of art therapy licensure in New Mexico. *Art Therapy, Journal of the American Art Therapy Association, 10,* 136–140.

Good, D., & Sly-Linton, K. (1995). Art therapy licensure update. *Art Therapy, Journal of the American Art Therapy Association, 12,* 100–103.

Goodenough, F. (1926). *Measurement of intelligence by drawings.* New York, NY: Harcourt, Brace

& World.

Groth-Marnat, G. (1997). *Handbook of psychological assessment* (2nd ed.). New York, NY: John Wiley-Interscience.

Gussak, D., & Nyce, J. (1999). To bridge art therapy and computer technology, the visual toolbox. *Art Therapy, Journal of the American Art Therapy Association, 16,* 194–196.

Hagaman, S. (1986). Mary Huntoon: Pioneering art therapist. *American Journal of Art Therapy, 24,* 92–96.

Harris, D. (1963). *Children's drawings as measures of intellectual maturity.* New York, NY: Harcourt, Brace & World.

Harris, J., & Joseph, C. (1973). *Murals of the mind.* New York, NY: International Universities Press.

Hass-Cohen, N., & Carr, R. (Eds.). (2008). *Art therapy and clinical neuroscience.* London, England & Philadelphia, PA: Jessica Kingsley.

Hill, A. (1948). *Art versus illness: A story of art therapy.* London, England: Allen & Unwin.

Hill, A. (1951). *Painting out illness.* London, England: Williams & Norgate.

Hillman, J. (1975). *Revisioning psychology.* New York, NY: Harper.

Hillman, J. (2004). *Archetypal psychology. Uniform edition, Vol. 1.* Putnam, CT: Spring Publications.

Himelstein, J. (1970). How to tell if your child is a potential hippie. *Parent Teacher Association Pamphlet.*

Hiscox, A., & Calisch, A. (Eds.). (1998). *Tapestry of cultural issues in art therapy.* London, England & Philadelphia, PA: Jessica Kingsley.

Hocoy, D. (2005). Art therapy and social action: A transpersonal framework. *Art Therapy, Journal of the American Art Therapy Association, 22,* 7–16.

Hogan, S. (2001). *Healing arts, the history of art therapy.* London, England & Philadelphia, PA: Jessica Kingsley.

Holden, W. (1965). Ars Gratia Hominis: The world of Tarmo Pasto. *California Mental Health Progress,* 5–9.

Holt, R. (1989). *Freud reappraised: A fresh look at psychoanalytic theory.* New York, NY: Guilford Press.

Horowitz-Darby, E. (1996). *Spiritual art therapy: An alternative path.* Springfield, IL: Charles C Thomas.

Hoshino, J., & Junge, M. (2006). Themes and reflections on the stories of art therapists of color. *Art Therapy, Journal of the American Art Therapy Association, 23,* 139–143.

Huntoon, M. (1948). Creative art therapy showing clinical classifications of art used as treatment. Unpublished manuscript. Lawrence, KS: University of Kansas, Huntoon Archives.

Huntoon, M. (1949). The creative arts as therapy. *Bulletin of the Menninger Clinic, 13,* 198–203.

Huntoon, M. (1953). Art therapy for patients in the acute section of Winter VA Hospital. Washington, D.C.: *VA* [Veteran's Administration] *Department of Medicine & Surgery Information Bulletin, 10,* 29–33.

Huntoon, M. (1959). Art for therapy's sake. *Mental Hospital,* January, 20.

Huntoon, M. (1961). Introducing Mary Huntoon. *Bulletin of Art Therapy, 1,* 5–6.

Husserl, E. (1976). *Ideas.* New Jersey: Humanities Press. (Original work published 1913.)

Irwin, E., & Rubin J. (2008). *The Green Creature Within: Art and Drama in Group Psychotherapy with Adolescents.* (2nd ed.). Pittsburgh, PA: Expressive Media, Inc.

Jakab, I. (Ed.) (Vol. I.1968). *Psychiatry and art.* Proceedings of the IVth International Colloquium of Psychopathology of Expression, Washington, D.C., New York, NY and Basel: S. Karger.

Jakab, I. (Ed.). (Vol. II. 1969). *Art interpretation and art therapy.* Proccedings of the Vth

International Colloquium of Psychopathology of Expression, Los Angeles, CA. New York, NY and Basel: S. Karger.

Jakab, I. (Ed.). (Vol. III. 1971). *Psychiatry and art.* Proceedings of the American Society for Psychopathology of Expression. New York, NY and Basel: S. Karger.

Jakab, I. (Ed.). (Vol. IV. 1975). *Psychiatry and art.* Proceedings of the American Society for Psychopathology of Expression. New York, NY and Basel: S. Karger.

Johnson, J., Dupuis, H., & Johansen, V. (1973). *Introduction to the foundations of American education.* Boston, MA: Allyn & Bacon.

Jones, D. (1946). *PRN in a mental hospital.* Washington, D.C.: Civilian Public Service Unit.

Jones, D. (1947). *Tunnel.* Unpublished Manuscript.

Jones, D. (1962). Art and the troubled mind. *Menninger Quarterly, 16,* 12–19.

Jones, D. (1975). An oral history: Art therapy pioneers [audio tape]. Louisville, KY: Department of History, University of Louisville.

Jones, D. (1983). An art therapist's personal record. *Art Therapy, Journal of the American Art Therapy Association, 1,* 22–25.

Jordan, H. (1988). An interview with Elinor Ulman. *American Journal of Art Therapy, 26,* 107–112.

Joseph, C. (1973). *Art therapy and the third world.* Panel discussion presented at the 5th Annual Conference of the American Art Therapy Association, New York City.

Joseph, C. (2006). Creative alliance: The healing power of art therapy. *Art Therapy, Journal of the American Art Therapy Association, 23,* 30–33.

Jung, C. (1916). *Psychology of the unconscious* (Hinkle, Trans). London. [Published in 1956 as *Symbols of transformation in the Collected works, Vol. 5,* Bollingen Series XX. Princeton, NJ: Princeton University Press.]

Jung, C. (1954). *The aims of psychotherapy. The practice of psychotherapy,* Bollingen Series XX. New York, NY: Pantheon.

Junge, M. (1987a). *Art therapist: Model job description.* Mundelein, IL: American Art Therapy Association.

Junge, M. (1987b). Research notes on Mary Huntoon from Huntoon collection archives. Lawrence, KS: University of Kansas.

Junge, M. (with Asawa, P.) (1994). *A history of art therapy in the United States.* Mundelein, IL: American Art Therapy Association.

Junge, M. (1998). *Creative realities, the search for meanings.* Lanham, MD & Oxford, England: University Press of America.

Junge, M. (2007). The art therapist as social activist: Reflections on a life. In F. Kaplan (Ed.), *Art therapy and social action.* London, England & Philadelphia, PA: Jessica Kingsley.

Junge, M. (2008). *Mourning, memory and life itself, essays by an art therapist.* Springfield, IL: Charles C Thomas.

Junge, M., Alvarez, J., Kellogg, A., & Volker, C. (1993). The art therapist as social activist: Reflections and visions. *Art therapy, Journal of the American Art Therapy Association, 10,* 148–155.

Junge, M., & Linesch, D. (1993). Our own voices: New paradigms for art therapy research. *The Arts in Psychotherapy, 20,* 61–67.

Junge, M., & Wadeson, H. (2006). *Architects of art therapy, memoirs and life stories.* Springfield, IL: Charles C Thomas.

Kagin, S. (Graves-Alcorn). (1969). *The effects of structure on the painting of retarded youth.* Unpublished master's thesis, University of Tulsa, Oklahoma.

Kagin, S., & Lusebrink, V. (1978). The expressive therapies continuum. *Art Psychotherapy, 5,* 171–179.

Kahill, S. (1984). Human figure drawing in adults: An update of the empirical evidence, 1967-1982. *Canadian Psychology, 2,* 269-292.

Kaiser, D., & Deaver, S. (2009). Assessing attachment with the Bird's Nest Drawing: A review of the research. *Art Therapy, Journal of the American Art Therapy Association. 26,* 26-33.

Kapitan, L. (2008). Not art therapy: Revisiting the therapeutic studio in the narrative of the profession (Editorial.) *Art Therapy, Journal of the American Art Therapy Association, 25,* 2-3.

Kapitan, L. (In press). *An introduction to art therapy research.* Florence, KY: Routledge.

Kaplan, F. (1998). Scientific art therapy: An integrative and research-based approach. *Art Therapy, Journal of the American Art Therapy Association, 15,* 93-98.

Kaplan, F. (2000). *Art, science and art therapy: Repainting the picture.* London, England & Philadelphia, PA: Jessica Kingsley.

Kaplan, F. (2003). Art-based assessments. In C. Malchiodi (Ed.), *Handbook of art therapy.* New York, NY: Guilford Press.

Kaplan, F. (Ed.) (2007). *Art therapy and social action.* London, England & Philadelphia, PA: Jessica Kingsley.

Kauffman, A. (1996). Art in boxes: An exploration of meanings. *The Arts in Psychotherapy, 23,* 1-11.

Kellogg, J., MacRae, M., Bonny, H., & DiLeo, F. (1977). The use of the mandala in psychological evaluation and treatment. *American Journal of Art Therapy, 16,* 4.

Kerr, C., & Hoshino, J. (2008). *Family art therapy.* New York, NY: Taylor & Francis Group, Routledge.

Kessler, K. (1994). A study of the Diagnostic Drawing Series with eating disordered patients. *Art Therapy, Journal of the American Art Therapy Association, 11,* 116-118.

Keyes, M. (1974). *The inward journey: Art as psychotherapy for you.* Millbrae, CA: Celestial Arts Press. [Republished, 1983, in a revised edition with the title *Inward journey: Art as therapy.* LaSalle, IL: Open Court.]

Kiell, N. (1965). *Psychiatry and psychology in the visual arts and aesthetics: A bibliography.* Madison, WI: University of Wisconsin Press.

Kinsolver, B. (2009). *The Lacuna.* New York, NY: Harper Collins.

Klorer, G. (1999). *Expressive art therapy with troubled children.* New York, NY: Jason Aronson.

Kniazzeh, C., Kramer, E, Kwiatkowska, H., Naumburg, M., & Ulman, E. (May 6, 1969). Letter "To whom it may concern." Archives of the American Art Therapy Association. Emporia State University, Emporia, KS.

Kopytin, A. (1999). Russian art therapy–Problems and perspectives. In L. Kossolapow (Ed.), *Abstract book of the 5th European arts therapies conference.* LIT Verlag: Berlin-Hamburg-Munster.

Kramer, E. (1958). *Art therapy in a children's community.* New York, NY: Charles C Thomas.

Kramer, E. (1961). Art and emptiness: New problems in art education and art therapy. *Bulletin of Art Therapy, 1,* 7-16.

Kramer, E. (1962). Art education and emptiness. *Bulletin of Art Therapy, 1,* 20-24.

Kramer, E. (1963). The problem of quality in art. *Bulletin of Art Therapy, 3,* 3-19.

Kramer, E. (1965). Art therapy and the severely disturbed gifted child. *Bulletin of Art Therapy, 5,* 3-20.

Kramer, E. (1966). Art and craft. *Bulletin of Art Therapy, 5,* 149-152.

Kramer, E. (1967). The problem of quality in art II: Stereotypes. *Bulletin of Art Therapy, 6,* 151-171.

Kramer, E. (1970). Letter. *American Art Therapy Association Newsletter, 1,* 4.

Kramer, E. (1971a). *Art as therapy with children.* New York, NY: Schocken.

Kramer, E. (1971b). Letter to Felice Cohen, February 25. Robert Ault Archives of the

American Art Therapy Association. Emporia State University. Emporia, KS.

Kramer, E. (1979). *Childhood and art therapy.* New York, NY: Schocken.

Kramer, E. (1992). Reflections on the evolution of human perception: Implications for the understanding of the visual arts and of the visual products of art therapy. *American Journal of Art Therapy, 30,* 126–142.

Kramer, E. (2000). *Art as therapy: Collected papers.* London, England & Philadelphia, PA: Jessica Kingsley.

Kramer, E. in Junge, M. & Wadeson, H. (Eds.) (2006). *Architects of art therapy, memoirs and life stories.* Springfield, IL: Charles C Thomas.

Kramer, E., & Garity, L. (Ed.) (2000). *Art as therapy: Collected Papers.* London and Philadelphia, PA: Jessica Kingsley.

Kramer, E., & Scher, J. (1983). An art therapy evaluation session for children. *American Journal of Art Therapy, 23,* 3–12.

Kramer, E. (1992). Tributes. *American Journal of Art Therapy, 30,* 67–68.

Kuhn, T. (1964). *Structure of scientific revolutions.* Chicago, IL: University of Chicago Press.

Kwiatkowska, H. (1962). Family art therapy: Experiments with a new technique. *Bulletin of Art Therapy, 1,* 3–15.

Kwiatkowska, H. (1967). The use of families' art productions for psychiatric evaluation. *Bulletin of Art Therapy, 6,* 52–69.

Kwiatkowska, H. (1978). *Family therapy and evaluation through art.* Springfield, IL: Charles C Thomas.

Kwiatkowska, H., Day, J., & Wynne, L. (1962). *The schizophrenic patient, his parents, and siblings: Observations through family art therapy.* Catalogue of exhibit presented at the annual meeting of the American Psychiatric Association. Washington, D.C.: U.S. Department of Health, Education & Welfare, Public Health Service.

Kwiatkowska, H., & Perlin, S. (1959). *A schizophrenic patient's response in art therapy to changes in the life of the psychotherapist.* DHEW Publication No. NIH-33807. Bethesda, MD: U.S. Public Health Service.

Landgarten, H. (1975a). An oral history: Art therapy pioneers [audiotape.] Louisville, KY: Department of History, University of Louisville.

Landgarten, H. (1975b). Group art therapy for mothers and their daughters. *American Journal of Art Therapy, 14,* 2.

Landgarten, H. (1976). Changing status of art therapy in Los Angeles. *American Journal of Art Therapy, 15,* 4.

Landgarten, H. (1978). Status of art therapy in Greater Los Angeles, 1974: Two-year followup study. *The Arts in Psychotherapy, 5,* 4.

Landgarten, H. (1981). *Clinical art therapy: A comprehensive guide.* New York, NY: Brunner/Mazel.

Landgarten, H. (1987). *Family art psychotherapy, a clinical guide and casebook.* New York, NY: Brunner/Mazel.

Landgarten, H. (1987). *Magazine photo collage: A multicultural assessment and treatment technique.* New York, NY: Brunner/Mazel.

Landgarten, H., & Lubbers, D. (Eds.). (1991). *Adult art psychotherapy: Issues and applications.* New York, NY: Brunner/Mazel.

Landgarten, H., Tasem, M., Junge, M., & Watson, M. (1978). Art therapy as a modality for crisis intervention. *Journal of Clinical Social Work, 6,* 221–229.

Levick, M. (1970a). Unpublished letter to Elinor Ulman, December 3. Robert Ault Archives of the American Art Therapy Association, Emporia State University, Emporia, KS.

Levick, M. (1970b). President's message. *American Art Therapy Association Newsletter, 1,* 4.

Levick, M. (1971). Letter to Edith Kramer, November 9. Robert Ault Archives of the American Art Therapy Association, Emporia State University, Emporia, KS.

Levick, M. (1975). An oral history: Art therapy pioneers [audiotape]. Louisville, KY: Department of History, University of Louisville.

Levick, M. (1981). Art therapy: An overview. In R. Corsini (Ed.), *Handbook of innovative psychotherapies.* New York, NY: John Wiley.

Levick, M. (1983). *They could not talk and so they drew: Children's styles of coping and thinking.* Springfield, IL: Charles C Thomas.

Levick, M. (1986). *Mommy, daddy. Look what I'm saying: What children are telling you through their art.* New York, NY: M. Evans & Co.

Levick, M. (1998, 2nd ed. 2003). *See what I'm saying: What children tell us through their art.* Dubuque, IW: Islewest Publishing.

Levick, M. (2006). In Junge, M. & Wadeson, H., *Architects of art therapy, memoirs and life stories.* Springfield, IL: Charles C Thomas.

Levick, M. (2009a). *Levick Emotional and Cognitive Art Therapy Assessment: A normative study.* Bloomington, IN: AuthorHouse.

Levick, M. (2009b). Commentary. *Art Therapy, Journal of the American Art Therapy Association, 26,* 139.

Linesch, D. (1988). *Adolescent art therapy.* New York, NY: Brunner/Mazel.

Linesch, D. (1992). Research approaches within Master's level art therapy training programs. *Art Therapy, Journal of the American Art Therapy Association, 9,* 129-134.

Lowenfeld, V. (1964). *Creative and mental growth* (5th ed.). New York, NY: MacMillan.

Lowenfeld, V. (1987). Therapeutic aspects of art education. *American Journal of Art Therapy, 5,* 4.

Lusebrink, V. (1990). *Imagery and visual expression in therapy.* New York, NY: Plenum Press.

Lyle, J., & Shaw, R. (1937). Encouraging fantasy expression in children. *Bulletin of the Menninger Clinic, 1,* 78-86.

Machover, K. (1949). *Personality projection in the drawing of the human figure.* Springfield, IL: Charles C Thomas.

Madigan, S., Ladd, M., & Goldberg, S. (2003). A picture is worth a thousand words: Children's representations of family as indicators of early attachment. *Attachment & Human Development, 5,* 19-37.

MacGregor, J. (1989). *The discovery of the art of the insane.* Lawrenceville, NJ: Princeton University Press.

Mahler, M., Pine, F., & Bergman, A. (1975). *The psychological birth of the human infant.* New York, NY: Basic.

Malchiodi, C. (1990). *Breaking the silence: Art therapy with children from violent homes.* New York, NY: Brunner/Mazel.

Malchiodi, C. (1995). Does a lack of art therapy research hold us back? *Art Therapy: Journal of the American Art Therapy Association, 12,* 261-265.

Malchiodi, C. (2000). *Art therapy and computer technology, a virtual studio of possibilities.* London, England & Philadelphia, PA: Jessica Kingsley.

Malchiodi, C. (2003). *Handbook of art therapy.* New York & London, England: The Guilford Press. McGraw-Hill.

Malchiodi, C. (2007). *The art therapy sourcebook* (2nd ed.). New York, NY:

Malchiodi, C. (2008). Telling without talking: Breaking the silence of domestic violence. *Psychology Today blog,* September 28, 2008.

Malchiodi, C., & Riley, S. (1996). *Supervision and related issues: A handbook for professionals.* Chicago, IL: Magnolia Street.

McMahan, J. (1989). An interview with Edith Kramer. *American Journal of Art Therapy, 27,* 107-114.

Mary Huntoon Archives. (n.d.). Collection of Spencer Library, University of Kansas, Lawrence, KS.

McLeod, C. (1999). Empowering creativity with computer-assisted art therapy: An introduction to available programs and techniques. *Art Therapy, Journal of the American Art Therapy Association, 16,* 201-205.

McNiff, S. (1973). A new perspective in group art therapy. *Art Psychotherapy, 1,* 3-4.

McNiff, S. (1974). *Art therapy at Danvers. Addison Gallery of American Art.* Phillips Academy, Andover, MA.

McNiff, S. (1981). *The arts in psychotherapy.* Springfield, IL: Charles C Thomas.

McNiff, S. (1985). Meet the ole timers: Perspectives on the American Art Therapy Association. Panel discussion, 16th Annual Conference of the American Art Therapy Association, New Orleans, LA.

McNiff, S. (1986). *Educating the creative arts therapist: A profile of the profession.* Springfield, IL: Charles C Thomas.

McNiff, S. (1988). *Fundamentals of art therapy.* Springfield, IL: Charles C Thomas.

McNiff, S. (1989). *Depth psychology of art.* Springfield, IL: Charles C Thomas.

McNiff, S. (1992). *Art as medicine.* Boston, MA: Shambhala.

McNiff, S. (1995). *Earth angels.* Boston, MA: Shambhala.

McNiff, S. (1998a). *Art-based research.* London, England & Philadelphia, PA: Jessica Kingsley.

McNiff, S. (1998b). *Trust the process: An artist's guide to letting go.* Boston, MA: Shambhala.

McNiff, S. (2003). *Creating with others, the practice of imagination in life, art and the work place.* Boston, MA: Shambhala.

McNiff, S. (2004). *Art heals: How creativity cures the soul.* Boston, MA: Shambhala.

McNiff, S. (2009). *Integrating the arts in therapy: History, theory and practice.* Springfield, IL: Charles C Thomas.

Mills, A. (2003). The Diagnostic Drawing Series. In C. Malchiodi (Ed.), *Handbook of art therapy.* New York, NY: Guilford Press.

Mills, A., Cohen, B., & Meneses, J. (1993). Reliability and validity tests of the Diagnostic Drawing Series. *The Arts in Psychotherapy, 20,* 83-88.

Minutes for Art Therapy Meeting held in Philadelphia. December 5, 1968. Robert Ault Archives of the American Art Therapy Association. Emporia State University, Emporia, KS.

More, R. (1981). *Art therapy in mental health* (Literature survey series No. 3). DHHS Publication No. (ADM) 81-1162. Rockville, MD: National Institute of Mental Health.

Morris, M. (1995). The Diagnostic Drawing Series and the Tree Rating Scale: An isomorphic representation of multiple personality disorder, major depression, and schizophrenia populations. *Art Therapy, Journal of the American Art Therapy Association, 12,* 118-128.

Muller, E. (1968). Family group art therapy: Treatment of choice for a specific case. In *Psychiatry and art.* Proceedings of the IV International Colloquium of Psychopathology of Expression, I. Jakab (Ed.) Washington, D.C., New York, NY & Basel: S. Karger.

Naumburg, M. (1928). *The child and the world.* New York, NY: Harcourt Brace.

Naumburg, M. (1943). Children's art expression and war. *The Nervous Child, 2,* 360-373.

Naumburg, M. (1944). The drawings of an adolescent girl suffering from conversion hysteria with amnesia. *Psychiatric Quarterly, 18,* 197-224.

Naumburg, M. (1944). A study of the art expression of a behavior problem boy as an aid in diagnosis and therapy. *The Nervous Child, 3,* 277-319.

Naumburg, M. (1945a). A study of the psychodynamics of the art work of a nine-year-old behavior problem boy. *Journal of Nervous and Mental Disease, 101,* 28-64.

Naumburg, M. (1945b). Phantasy and reality in the art expression of behavior problem children. In N. Lewis & B. Pacella (Eds.), *Modern trends in child psychiatry.* New York, NY: International Universities Press.

Naumburg, M. (1946). A study of the art work of a behavior problem boy as it relates to ego development and sexual enlightenment. *Psychiatric Quarterly, 20,* 74-112.

Naumburg, M. (1947). Studies of the "free art expression of behavior problem children and adolescents as a means of diagnosis and therapy. *Nervous and Mental Disease Monographs, No. 71.* New York, NY: Coolidge Foundation. [Revised edition printed in 1973; see Naumburg, 1973.]

Naumburg, M. (1950). *Schizophrenic art: Its meaning in psychotherapy.* New York, NY: Grune & Stratton.

Naumburg, M. (1953). *Psychoneurotic art: Its function in psychotherapy.* New York, NY: Grune & Stratton.

Naumburg, M. (1958a). Art therapy: Its scope and function. In E. Hammer (Ed.), *The clinical application of projective drawings.* Springfield, IL: Charles C Thomas.

Naumburg, M. (1958b). Art therapy with a seventeen-year-old schizophrenic girl. In E. Hammer (Ed.), *The clinical application of projective drawings.* Springfield, IL: Charles C Thomas.

Naumburg, M. (1966). *Dynamically oriented art therapy: Its principles and practice.* New York, NY: Grune & Stratton. [Reprinted in 1987, Chicago, IL: Magnolia Street.]

Naumburg, M. (1973). *An introduction to art therapy: Studies of the "free" art expression of behavior problem children and adolescents as a means of diagnosis and therapy.* New York, NY & London, England: Teachers College Press, Columbia University.

O'Kane, A. (December 5, 1968). Minutes for art therapy meeting held in Philadelphia. Robert Ault Archives of the American Art Therapy Association. Emporia State University, Emporia, KS.

Parker-Bell, B. (1999). Embracing a future with computers and art therapy. *Art Therapy, Journal of the American Art Therapy Association, 16,* 180-185.

Pasto, T. (1962). Meaning in art therapy. *Bulletin of Art Therapy, 2,* 73–76.

Pitt, M. (2006). Using the arts to tame Katrina's emotional force. www.connect for kids.org/node/4273. Retrieved August 2, 2009.

Potash, J. (2005). Rekindling the multicultural history of the American Art Therapy Association. *Art Therapy, Journal of the American Art Therapy Association, 22,* 184-188.

Prinzhorn, H. (1972). *Artistry of the mentally ill.* (E. von Brockdorff, Trans.) New York: Springer-Verlag. [Originally published in 1922 as *Bildnerei der geisteskranken,* Berlin: Verlag Julius Springer.]

Remnick, D. (February 2, 2009). Comment: The President's Hero. *New Yorker,* 21-23.

Rhyne, J. (1973). *The Gestalt art experience.* Monterey, CA: Brooks/Cole. [Reprinted in 1984, Chicago, IL: Magnolia Street.]

Rhyne, J. (1975). An oral history: Art Therapy pioneers [audiotape] Louisville, KY: Department of History, University of Louisville.

Riley, S. (1999). *Contemporary art therapy with adolescents.* New York, NY: Routledge.

Riley, S. (2000). *Group process made visible.* London, England & Philadelphia, PA: Jessica Kingsley.

Riley, S., & Malchiodi, C. (1996). *Integrative approaches to family art therapy.* Chicago, IL: Magnolia Street.

Robbins, A. (1980). *Expressive therapy: A creative arts approach to depth-oriented treatment.* New York, NY: Human Sciences Press.

Robbins, A. (1987a). *The artist as therapist.* New York, NY: Human Sciences Press.

Robbins, A. (1987b). Object relations art therapy. In J. Rubin (Ed.) (1987), *Approaches to art therapy.* New York, NY: Brunner/Mazel.

Robbins, A. (1989). *The psychoaesthetic experience.* New York, NY: Human Sciences Press.

Robbins, A. (1994). *A multi-modal approach to art therapy.* London, England & Philadelphia, PA: Jessica Kingsley.

Robbins, A. (Ed.) (1998). *Therapeutic presence: Bridging expression and form.* London, England & Philadelphia, PA: Jessica Kingsley.

Robbins, A. (2000). *Between therapists: The processing of transference/countertransference.* London, England & Philadelphia, PA: Jessica Kingsley.

Robbins, A. (2001, 2nd ed. Originally published 1987). Object relations and art therapy. In J. Rubin (Ed.), *Approaches to art therapy.* New York: NY: Brunner/Mazel.

Robbins, A. (2006). Moving in and out of the sandbox. In M. Junge & H. Wadeson (Eds.), *Architects of art therapy, memoirs and life stories.* Springfield, IL: Charles C Thomas.

Robbins, A., & Sibley, L. (1976). *Creative art therapy.* New York, NY: Brunner/Mazel.

Robinson, M. (1983). Foreword. In F. Cane, *The artist in each of us.* Craftsbury Common, VT: Art Therapy Publications.

Rockwell, P., & Dunham, M. (2006). The utility of the Formal Elements Art Therapy Scale in assessment for substance use disorder. *Art Therapy, Journal of the . . . .American Art Therapy Association, 23,* 104–111.

Rogers, N. (1980). *Emerging woman, a decade of midlife transitions.* Copyright: Natalie Rogers.

Rogers, N. (1993). *The creative connection: Expressive art as healing.* Palo Alto, CA: Science and Behavior Books.

Rogers, N. Website (n.d.). Retrieved July 13, 2009. www.nrogers.com

Rosal, M. (1989). CoPerspective: Master's papers in art therapy: Narrative or research case studies. *The Arts in Psychotherapy, 16,* 71–75.

Rosal, M. (1998). Research thoughts: Learning from the literature and from experience. *Art Therapy, Journal of the American Art Therapy Association, 15,* 47–50.

Rubin, J. (1973). A diagnostic interview. *Art Psychotherapy, 1,* 31–44. John Wiley.

Rubin, J. (1984) *The art of art therapy.* New York, NY: Brunner/Mazel.

Rubin, J. (1985). Meet the ole timers: Perspectives on the American Art Therapy Association. Panel discussion, 16th Annual Conference of the American Art Therapy Association. New Orleans, LA.

Rubin, J. (Ed.) (1987a). *Approaches to art therapy.* New York, NY: Brunner/Mazel Second edition: 2001. New York, NY: Brunner/Routledge.

Rubin, J. (1987b). Freudian psychoanalytic theory: Emphasis on uncovering and insight. In J. Rubin (Ed.), *Approaches to art therapy.* New York, NY: Brunner/Mazel.

Rubin, J. (1998). *Art therapy: An introduction.* New York, NY: Brunner/Routledge.

Rubin, J. (1999). *Art therapy.* New York, NY: Brunner/Routledge.

Rubin, J. (Ed.). (2001). *Approaches to art therapy* (2nd ed.). New York, NY: Brunner/Routledge.

Rubin, J. (2002). *My mom & dad don't live together anymore.* Washington, D.C.: Magination Press.

Rubin, J. (2005a). *Artful therapy.* New York, NY: John Wiley.

Rubin, J. (2005b). *Child art therapy: Third anniversary edition.* New York, NY: John Wiley.

Rubin, J. (2006). In M. Junge & H. Wadeson (2006), *Architects of art therapy, memoirs and life stories.* Springfield, IL: Charles C Thomas.

Rubin, J. (2008a). "Art Therapy Has Many Faces." DVD. Pittsburgh, PA: Expressive Media, Inc.

Rubin, J. (2008b). "Art Therapy With Older Adults." DVD. Pittsburgh, PA: Expressive Media, Inc.

Rubin, J. (2008c). "The Arts as Therapy With Children." DVD. Pittsburgh, PA: Expressive Media, Inc.

Rubin, J. (2008d). "Art Therapy With Blind Children." DVD. Pittsburgh, PA: Expressive Media, Inc.

Sacks, O. (2009). The lost virtues of the asylum. *New York Review of Books, LVI, 14,* 50–52.

Sand, M. (2008). Investigating the limits of the Formal Elements Art Therapy Scale: Assessing substance use disorder. Unpublished Masters study. Marylhurst University, Marylhurst, OR.

Saybrook Graduate Institute. www.Saybrook.edu. Retrieved July 13, 2009.

Schweizer, C. (1990). Art therapy in Holland: Defining a position in a hierarchical structure. *American Journal of Art Therapy, 28,* 66–67.

Shamdasani, S. (Ed.). (2009). *The red book, C.G. Jung.* New York, NY: W.W. Norton.

Silver, R. (1999). *Studies in art therapy 1962-1968.* Sarasota, FL: Ablin Press.

Silver, R. (2001). *Art as language: Access to thoughts and feelings through stimulus drawings.* Philadelphia, PA: Brunner/Routledge.

Silver, R. (2002). *Three art assessments: Silver Drawing Test of cognition and emotion, Draw a Story, screening for depression and stimulus drawings and techniques.* New York, NY: Brunner/Routledge.

Silver, R. (2003). The Silver Drawing Test of Cognition and Emotion. In C. Malchiodi (Ed.), *Handbook of art therapy.* New York: Guilford Press.

Silver, R. (2007). *The Silver Drawing Test and Draw a Story: Assessing depression, aggression and cognitive skills.* New York, NY: Routledge.

Silver, R. (2006). In M. Junge & H. Wadeson, *Architects of art therapy, memoirs and life stories.* Springfield, IL: Charles C Thomas.

Slater, N. (2001). Letter from Australia: Teaching art therapy abroad 1998-2000. *American Art Therapy Association Newsletter, 26,* 208–303 & 34, 1–2.

Slegelis, M. (1987). A study of Jung's mandala and its relationship to art psychotherapy. *The Arts in Psychotherapy, 14,* 301–311.

Smith, D., & Dumont, F. (1995). A cautionary study: Unwarranted interpretations of the Draw-A-Person Test. *Professional Psychology: Research and Practice, 23,* 298–303.

Smith, D., & Stone, B. (1984). The harlequin complex indicated by graphic expressions of sex-death fantasies among acute psychiatric inpatients. In *The Role of the Imagination in the Healing Process,* Proceedings International Congress of Psychopathology of Expression (Jakab, I. Ed.). New York & Basel: S. Karger.

Snow, S., & D'Amico, M. (2009). *Assessment in the creative arts therapies.* Springfield, IL: Charles C Thomas.

Steinhardt, L. (1986). Art therapy in Israel. *Art Therapy, Journal of the American Art Therapy Association, 3,* 115–121.

Stepney, S. (2010). *Art therapy with students at risk* (2nd ed.). Springfield, IL: Charles C Thomas.

Stewart, E. (2006). *Kaleidoscope, color and form illuminate darkness: An exploration of art therapy and exercises for patients with dementia.* Chicago, IL: Magnolia Street.

Stewart, E., & Hitt, S. (2009). *Superheroes unmasked.* Chapin, SC: Youth Light.

Stoll, B. (1985). A survey of art therapy around the world. Paper presented at the 11th Triennial Congress of the International Society for the Study of Art and Psychopathology. London, England.

Stoll, B. (1989). Art therapy and art therapists in global perspective. Keynote address at conference of the Australian National Art Therapy Association. Brisbane, Australia.

Stoll, B. (2001). The ArtReach project in Bosnia-Herzegovena: How can you say it's "good fortune" to spend three weeks in a war-torn country? *ING Newsletter, Newsletter of the*

International Networking Group of Art Therapists, 13, 1–8. Mundelin, IL: American Art Therapy Association.

Stoll, B. (Ed.) (1990–2009). *ING Newsletter, Newsletter of the International Networking Group of Art Therapists.* Mundelein, IL: American Art Therapy Association.

Stoll, B. (2004). Growing pains: The international development of art therapy. *The Arts in Psychotherapy, 32,* 171–191.

Stoll, B. (2009). Notes for a chapter on international art therapy. Unpublished manuscript.

Stone, B. (1971). Escape into space, the graphic expression of anaclitic anxiety. .In *Conscious and Unconscious Expressive Art, Volume* 3 (Jakab, Ed). New York, NY & Basel: S. Karger.

Stone, B. (1983). The graphic expression of blackbirds as an omen of suicide. Presentation at the conference of the American Art Therapy Association, Chicago, IL.

Swensen, C. (1968). Empirical evaluation of human figure drawings: 1957–1968. *Psychological Bulletin, 70,* 20–44.

Tan, A. (2003). *The opposite of fate.* New York, NY: Penquin Group.

Timm-Bottos, J. (n.d.). In Joan Flynn Fee interviews Janis Timm-Bottos. Salt.claretianpubs. org/issues/homeless/bottos.html. Retrieved August 2, 2009.

Timm-Bottos, J & Kahn, L. (1995). Finding home . . . Joining community through art. Paper at the conference of the American Art Therapy Association Conference, San Diego, CA.

Tuchman, M., & Eliel, C. (1992). *Parallel visions.* Los Angeles, CA. & Princeton, NJ: Los Angeles County Museum of Art and Princeton University Press.

Tyler, L. (1999). Introduction of the pill and its impact. *Contraception, 59,* 115–165.

Ulman, E. (1975). An oral history: Art therapy pioneers [audiotape]. Louisville, KY: Department of History, University of Louisville.

Ulman, E., & Dachinger, P. (Eds.). (1975b). *Art therapy in theory an practice.* New York, NY: Schocken.

Ulman, E., Kramer, E., & Kwiatkowska H. (1978). *Art therapy in the United States.* Craftsbury Commons, VT: Art Therapy Publications.

Ulman, E., & Levy, B. (1975). An experimental approach to the judgment of psychopathology from paintings. In E. Ulman & P. Dachinger (Eds.), *Art therapy: In theory and practice.* New York, NY: Schocken.

Ulman, E., & Levy, C. (Eds.) (1980). *Art therapy viewpoints.* New York, NY: Schocken.

Ulman, E. in Jordan, H. (1988). An interview with Elinor Ulman. *American Journal of Art Therapy, 26,* 107–112.

Venture, L. (1977). *The Black beat in art therapy experiences.* Unpublished doctoral dissertation, Union Institute and University (formerly Union Graduate School), Cincinnati, Ohio.

Vick, R., & Sexton-Radek, K. (2008). Community-based art studios in Europe and the United States: A comparative study. *Art Therapy, Journal of the American Art Therapy Association, 25,* 4–11.

Viola, W. (1936). *Child art and Franz Cizek.* New York, NY: Reyual and Hitchcock.

Volavkova, H. (Ed.) (1994). *I never saw another butterfly, children's drawings and poems from Terezin Concentration Camp, 1942–1944.* New York, NY: Schocken; revised edition. (Originally published in 1964.)

Wadeson, H. (Sinrod) (1964). Communication through paintings in a therapy group. *Bulletin of Art Therapy, 3,* 133–147.

Wadeson, H. (1980). *Art psychotherapy.* New York, NY: John Wiley. 2nd edition, 2010.

Wadeson, H. (1987a). *The dynamics of art psychotherapy.* New York, NY: John Wiley.

Wadeson, H. (1987b). An eclectic approach to art therapy. In J. Rubin (Ed.), *Approaches to art therapy.* New York, NY: Brunner/Mazel.

Wadeson, H. (Ed.) (1992). *A guide to art therapy research.* Mundelein, IL: American Art Therapy

Association.

Wadeson, H. (2000). *Art therapy practices: Innovative approaches with diverse populations.* New York, NY: John Wiley.

Wadeson, H. (2006). In M. Junge & H. Wadeson (Eds.), *Architects of art therapy, memoirs and life stories.* Springfield, IL: Charles C. Thomas.

Wadeson, H., Durkin, J., & Perach, D. (Eds.). (1989). *Advances in art therapy.* NY: Brunner/Mazel.

Wallace, E. (1975). Creativity and Jungian thought. *The Arts in Psychotherapy, 2,* 181-187.

Wallace, E. (1987). Healing through the visual arts–A Jungian approach. In J. Rubin (Ed.), *Approaches to art therapy.* New York, NY: Brunner/Mazel.

Wallace, E. (1990). *A queen's quest.* Velarde, NM: Moon Bear Press.

Waller, D. (1991). *Becoming a profession.* London, England: Routledge.

Waller, D. (1992a). The development of art therapy in Italy: Some problems of definition and context in professional training and practice. *Inscape, Journal of the British Association of Art Therapists,* Winter: 9-17.

Waller, D. (1992b). Different things to different people: Art therapy in Britain–A brief survey of its history and current development. *The Arts in Psychotherapy, 19,* 87-92.

Waller, D. (1998). *Towards a European art therapy: Creating a profession.* Buckingham, England: Open University Press.

Wanderer, Z. (1997). Validity of clinical judgments based on human figure drawings. In E. Hammer (with contributors), *Advances in projective drawing interpretation.* Springfield, IL: Charles C Thomas.

White, C., Wallace, J., & Huffman, L. (2004). Use of drawings to identify through impairment among students with emotional and behavioral disorders: An exploratory study. *Art Therapy, Journal of the American Art Therapy Association, 21,* 210-218.

Williams, K. (2006). In M. Junge & H. Wadeson (Eds.), *Architects of art therapy, memoirs and life stories.* Springfield, IL: Charles C Thomas.

Winkle, M. (2009). Interview with Kay Collis, founding President of the British Columbia Art Therapy Association. Unpublished manuscript.

Winnecott, D. (1971). *Playing and reality.* New York, NY: Basic.

Wolf, R. (1995). Invited response. *Art Therapy, Journal of the American Art Therapy Association, 12,* 259.

Yalom, I. (1985). *The theory and practice of group psychotherapy.* New York, NY: Basic Books.

Zubin, J., Eron, L., & Shumer, F. (1965). *An experimental approach to projective techniques.* New York, NY: John Wiley.

NAME INDEX

A

Adamson, Edward, 80, 83, 280, 283
Agell, Gladys, 153–154, 184, 188, 266, 290
Aldrin, Buzz, 92
Allen, Patricia, 171, 258, 259, 262, 291
Alper, Thelma, 15, 162
Alpert, Richard, 87
Alvarez, J., 262
Al-Yami, Awad, 281
Amatniek, Kathie, 91
Anastasi, A., 11
Anderson, Frances, 151–152, 284, 286, 290
Arnheim, Rudolph, 37, 209, 242
Arrington, D., 280
Asawa, Paige, 71–72, 262, 298
Ault, Robert, 1–7, 8, 15, 54, 62, 65, 66, 82, 83, 98, 103, 104, 105, 106, 110, 113, 114, 119–124, 157n1, 160, 162, 259, 273, 279

B

Baca, Judy, 170
Bader, H., 12
Barch, Lois Woolf, 81, 83
Barlow, Gary, 290
Baynes, H.G., 218
Bender, Loretta, 109
Berger, Lynn Flexner, 97
Bernard, Viola, 15, 20, 45
Betensky, Mala Gitlin, 172, 201–204, 238, 279, 280, 283
Biden, Joe, 236
Block, Dayna, 259
Boenhiem, Curt, 8, 15, 162

Bonheim, Curt, 64
Boszormeny-Nagy, Ivan, 117
Bowen, Murray, 75, 162
Bridgeman, George, 56
Brierer, Joshua, 79, 83
Brill, A. A., 25
Bronfenbrenner, Urie, 126
Brooke, S., 291
Brown, Saul, 15, 134, 160, 162
Buck, John, 16, 20, 237, 247
Bush, George H. W., 179
Bush, George W., 233, 236
Byers, Julia, 210, 263, 279, 280

C

Calish, A., 254, 255
Campanelli, Michael, 279
Cane, Florence, 9, 18, 20, 31–33, 35, 43, 44, 76, 145, 148, 218
Canter, D., 299
Capote, Truman, 87
Carr, R, 294
Carson, Rachel, 87
Carter, Jimmy, 179
Champernowne, Gilbert, 80, 83
Champernowne, Irene, 80, 83, 218, 223
Chapin, Mildred Lachman, 225–226, 260, 290
Chodorow, Nancy, 91
Cizek, Franz, 18, 20
Clinton, Bill, 233
Cocteau, Jean, 12
Cohen, Barry, 239, 240, 248, 274
Cohen, Felice, 8, 14, 15, 103, 106, 108–110, 113–114, 115, 162, 168

319

SUBJECT INDEX

Photo by Benjamin Junge.

ABOUT THE AUTHOR

Maxine Borowsky Junge, PhD, LCSW, ATR-BC, HLM, began formally in the art therapy profession in 1973. She is Professor Emerita at Loyola Marymount University, Los Angeles where she taught for 21 years and was Chair of the Department of Marital and Family Therapy (Clinical Art Therapy). She has also been a professor at Immaculate Heart College, Hollywood, CA, Goddard College in Vermont and Antioch University, Seattle, WA.

The Modern History of Art Therapy in the United States is her fifth book and is the only history in book form of the innovative and fascinating mental health profession of art therapy. Her other books are *Mourning, Memory and Life Itself, Essays of an Art Therapist, Architects of Art Therapy, Memoirs and Life Stories,* which she edited with Dr. Harriet Wadeson, *Creative Realities, the Search for Meanings* and *A History of Art Therapy* which was her first take at the history of art therapy.

Dr. Junge has presented her work nationally and internationally. She has published widely and her favorites appear as essays in *Mourning, Memory and Life Itself.* Her phenomenological study of visual artists and writers, which resulted in *Creative Realities,* establishes an important alternative theory of creativity to the usual unitary ones and hypothesizes that creativity is born out of differing personality world views and is manifested and illuminated in artwork.

Dr. Junge's clinical work has included agencies, consulting and private practice. She previously had an organizational development practice. She continues with clinical work and consultation.

Since childhood, her main passions have been art and psychology. Currently, she lives on Whidbey Island, north of Seattle with her Golden Retriever and her folk art collection where she paints, draws and writes. She dedicates this book "to all art therapists everywhere who have struggled to make art therapy a profession."

343